Second Gr
Thinking Skills and Key Concepts

Thinking Skills and Key Concepts products available in print or eBook form.

• Kindergarten • First Grade • Second Grade

Written by

Sandra Parks
Howard Black

Edited by
Patricia Gray

Graphic Design by
Howard Black

THE CRITICAL THINKING CO.™
www.CriticalThinking.com
Phone: 800-458-4849 • Fax: 541-756-1758
1991 Sherman Ave., Suite 200 • North Bend • OR 97459
ISBN 978-1-60144-844-6

Printed in the United States of America by Sonic Media Solutions, Medford, NY (Mar. 2016)

Table of Contents

How to Use This Book

GOALS

The *Thinking Skills and Key Concepts* program has three goals:

1. Provide instruction in the thinking skills required for clear understanding of important concepts in the primary grades (describe, compare/contrast, sequence, and classify)
2. Develop the academic vocabulary necessary to describe the characteristics of key concepts in mathematics, social studies, and science
3. Promote clear conceptualization of key concepts introduced in the primary grades and made more complex in subsequent grades

Lessons provide carefully sequenced instruction that clarifies the steps in each thinking process and provides discussion of key curriculum concepts, describing them in greater detail than found in common textbooks.

INSTRUCTIONAL METHODS

- **Teaching Thinking Skills Explicitly**
  Clarifying the thinking skill and reinforcing it by asking the student to repeat the steps in the thinking process. To explain the subtle steps in each thinking process, consult the teachers manual.
- **Using Different Learning Styles to Teach Concepts**
  The student book is one part of a three-step process: careful examination of detailed photographs in the student book and in related picture books, completing exercises in the student book, and discussion of each item to express the thinking process and the content meaningfully. The intended benefit of this program will not be realized if children use the student book as a workbook without discussing each item.
- **Responding in Whole Sentences**
  Young children are just learning to use words like "classifying" and "sequencing," as well as adjectives and verbs that convey their thinking. As they speak whole sentences, they must be taught to use the terms associated with the thinking skill and the concept.
- **Applying the Concept in a New Form**
  Supplement exercises with drawing activities, story telling, simple writing, and related picture books.

TEACHING SUGGESTIONS

- Lessons should not be given as homework assignments or as independent activities. The lessons are designed to enhance cognitive development through discussion and observation. Exercises in the student book should never be used without discussion.
- Conduct short exercises. Each lesson could take 20-30 minutes. Be sure to discuss the steps in the thinking process and find examples of when students will use that thinking skill. Discuss a few exercises with ample time for students to explain their thinking, rather than conducting additional lessons.
- Conduct these lessons before or after your social studies or science activities. Supplement these lessons with picture book discussion or other social studies or science materials.
- Use correct terms for the thinking skill to transfer it to other lessons. Apply these thinking skills and mental models to other concepts in mathematics, science, and social studies. An explanation of each mental model is provided on the next page.

MENTAL MODELS OF CONCEPTS

A mental model is a framework for understanding a concept. It helps a student:

- find and remember what he or she needs to know to understand a new topic.
- remember the characteristics of concepts.
- state clear definitions or write adequate descriptions.
- explain a concept to someone else.

A mental model outlines the key characteristics that the student must know to describe or define a concept. The diagram at the beginning of some chapters depicts the mental model for each concept in that chapter.

CONCEPTS	KEY CHARACTERISTICS
Mathematics	
Polygon	Lines (curved or straight, parallel or intersecting), sides (equal or unequal), number of sides, size of angle
Solids	Number of faces, what shape is seen from each side
Patterns	Describing color, size, and shape, color/size/shape sequences
Fractions	Halves, thirds, fourths
Science	
Land Forms/Bodies of Water	Size, shape, height/depth of land, fresh/salt water
Living /Non-Living Things	Growth, food, reproduction, plants/animals
Animals	Type (mammals, birds, fish, reptiles, insects, amphibians), live birth/hatch from eggs, vertebrate/invertebrate, appearance, habitat, life cycle, behavior, protection
Social Studies	
Family Needs	Food, shelter, health care, safety, transportation
Jobs	Types of jobs (provides goods or services, government workers, health care workers), what they do, equipment, special clothing, where they work
Communities	Families, workers (producers/ services), government, transportation, buildings; finding community locations on a map
Country	Cardinal directions, geographical features, (equator, latitude, longitude) climate, Native Americans, Colonial communities

CHAPTER ONE

DESCRIBING SHAPES

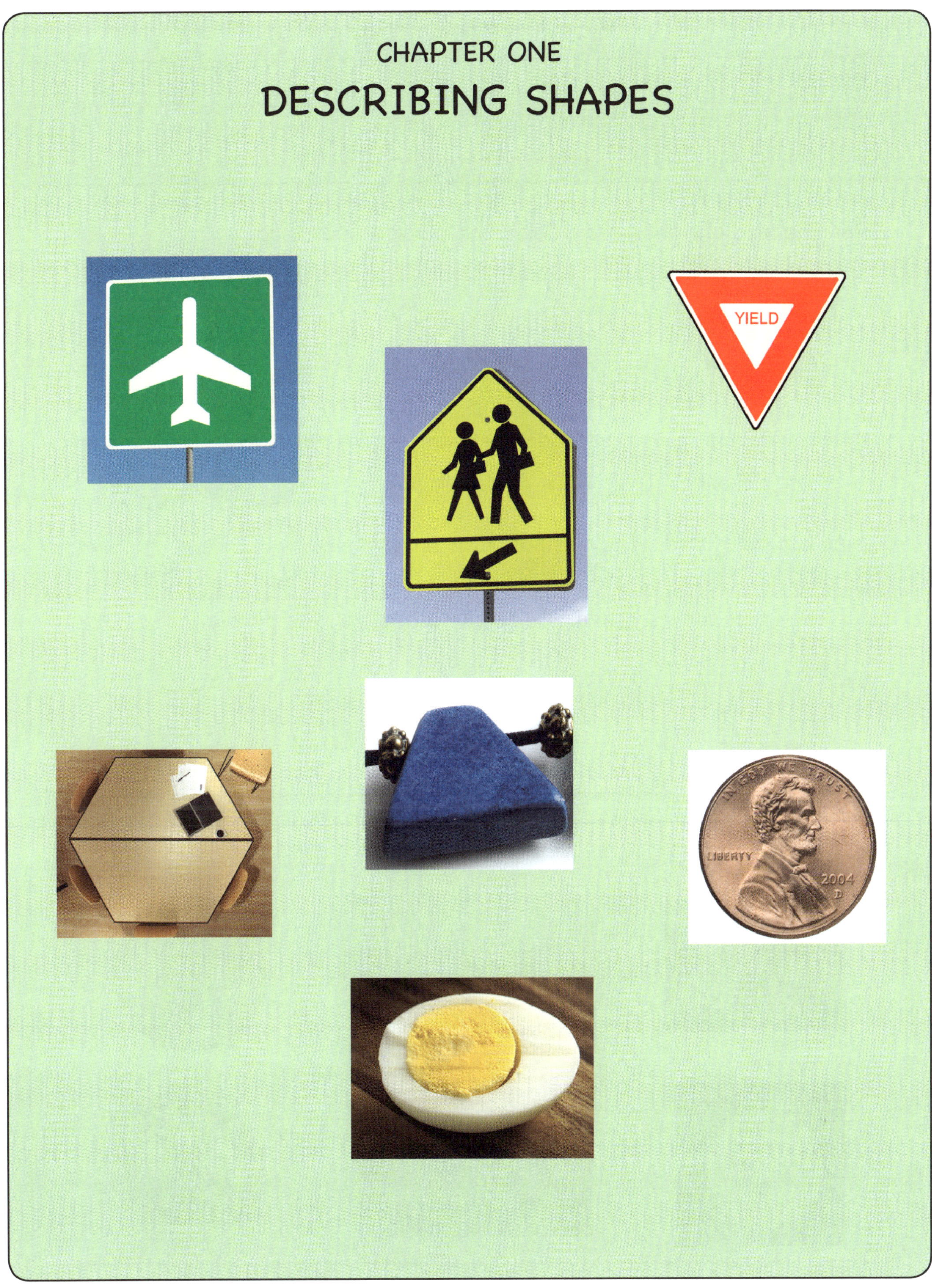

DESCRIBING LINES

A line is a thin mark. It can be straight or curved.

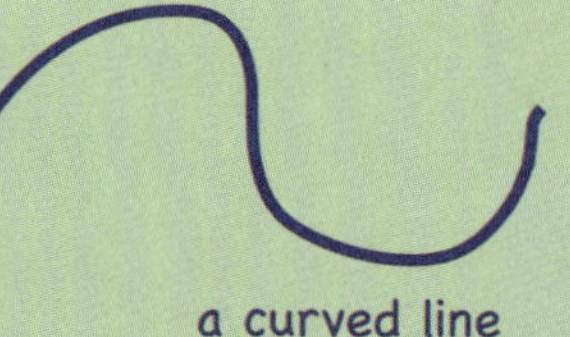

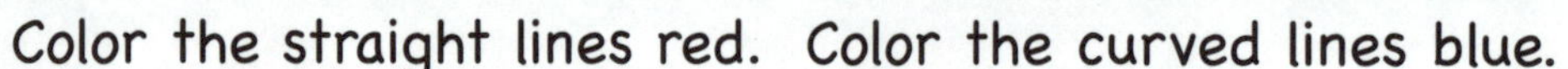

a straight line

a curved line

Color the straight lines red. Color the curved lines blue.

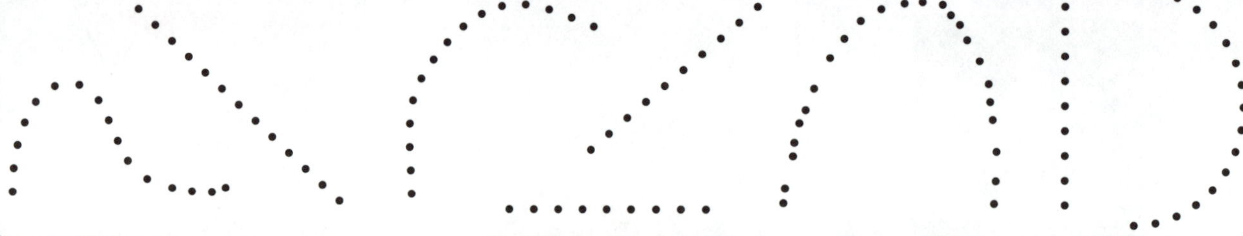

Curves can be open. Their ends do not touch.

Curves can be closed. They do not have ends.

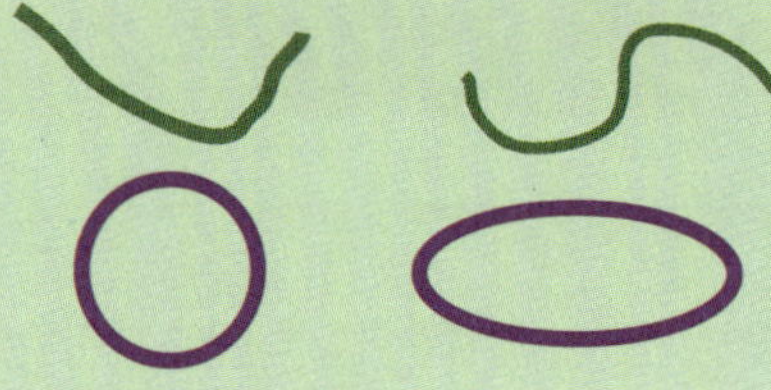

Color the open curves green. Color the closed curves purple.

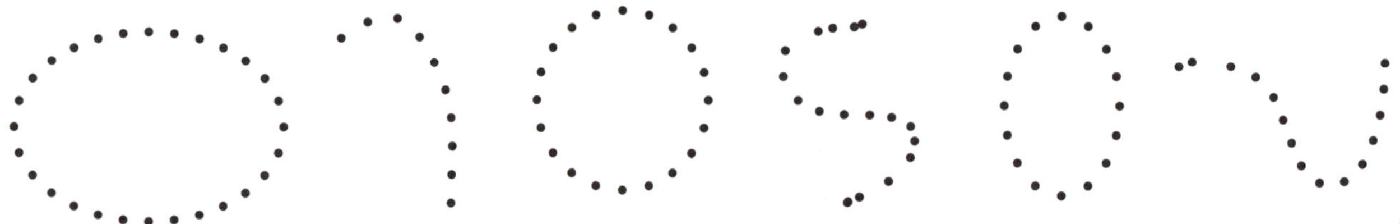

Circle the open curves green. Circle the closed curves purple.

FINDING AND DRAWING CIRCLES AND OVALS

A circle is a closed curve that looks the same from any side.
An oval is a closed curve that looks like a flattened circle.

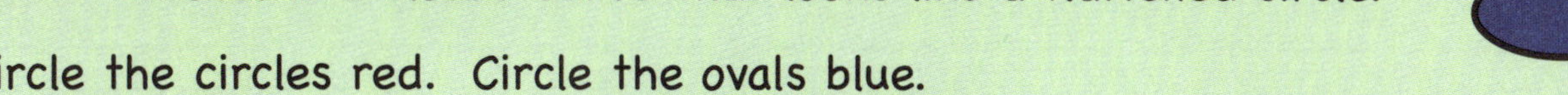

Circle the circles red. Circle the ovals blue.

To make a red circle, draw a curve from each dot to the next one. To make blue ovals, draw a curve from each dot to the next one.

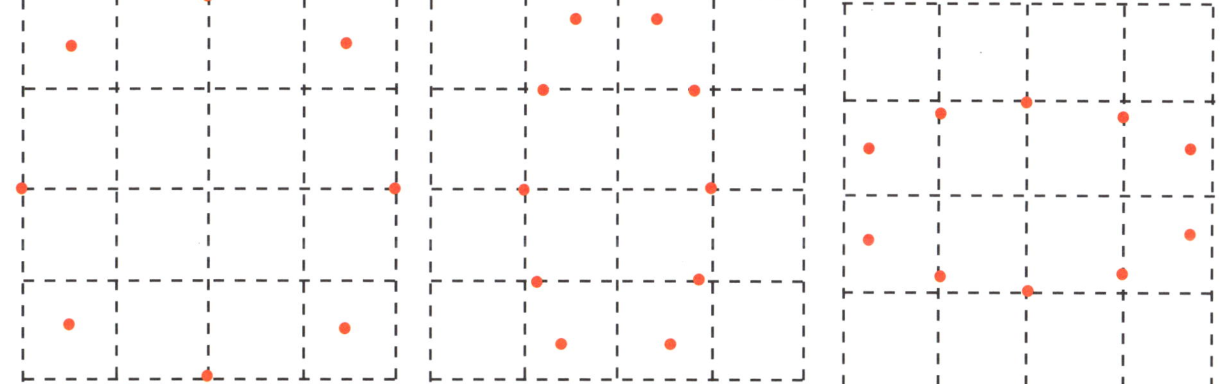

Draw something that has a circle.

Draw something that has an oval.

DESCRIBING LINES

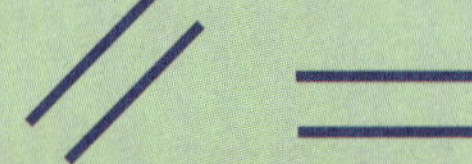

LINES THAT DO NOT TOUCH

Parallel lines do not cross. They are always the same distance apart.

Trace the parallel lines blue. Trace the lines that are not parallel green.

LINES THAT TOUCH

When two straight lines touch, they form an angle. 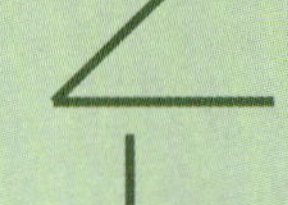

An angle that forms a square corner is a right angle. 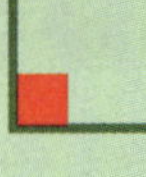

Some angles are wider than a right angle. 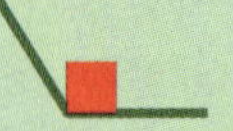

Some angles are thinner than a right angle. 

Circle objects that have parallel lines blue. Circle objects that have angles green.

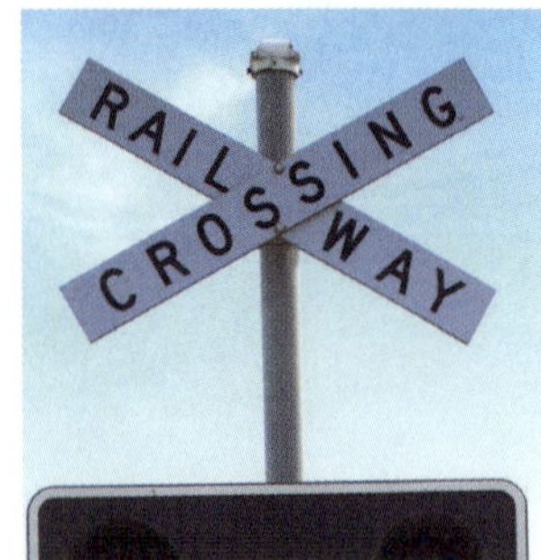

DESCRIBING POLYGONS

When the ends of three or more lines touch, they form shapes called polygons.

Color the polygons red. Mark an "X" through the designs that are not polygons.

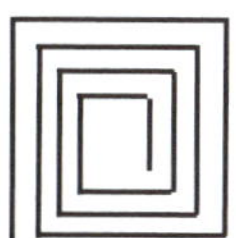
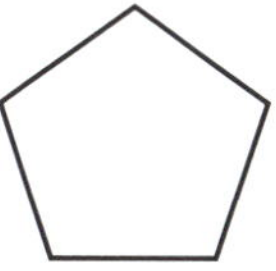

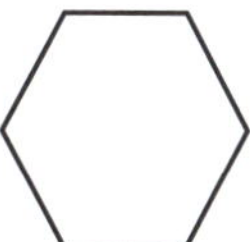

A triangle is a polygon with three sides and three angles.

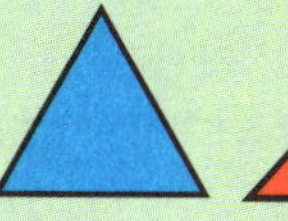

Color the triangles blue. Color the other polygons yellow.

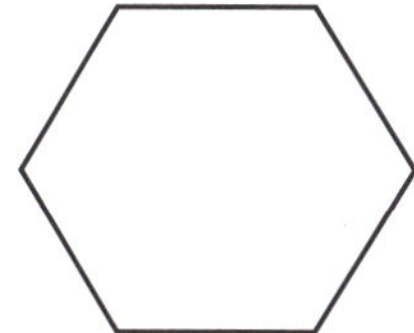
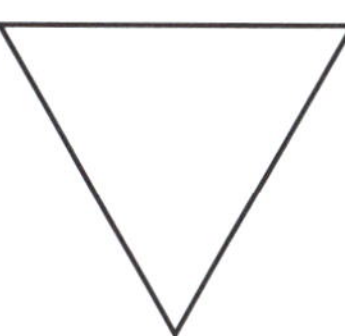

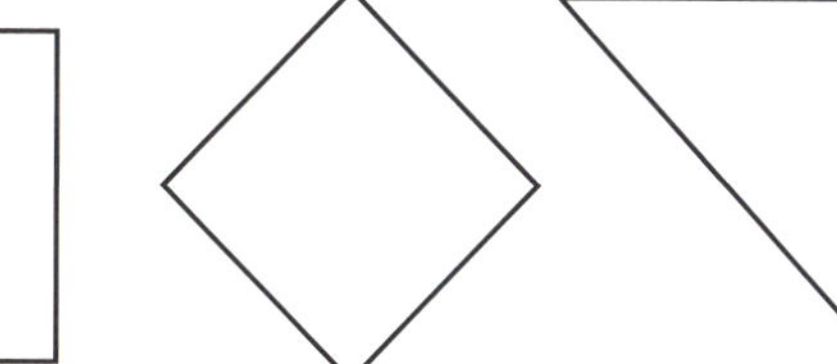

Triangles can have three equal sides.

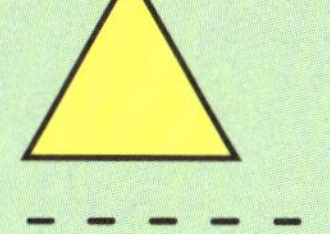

Triangles can have two equal sides. - - - - - -

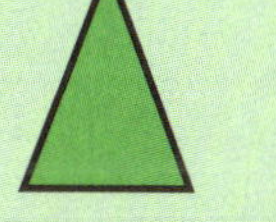

Triangles can have no equal sides. - - - - - - - - - - -

Color the triangles with three equal sides yellow. Color the triangles with two equal sides green. Color the triangles with no equal sides purple.

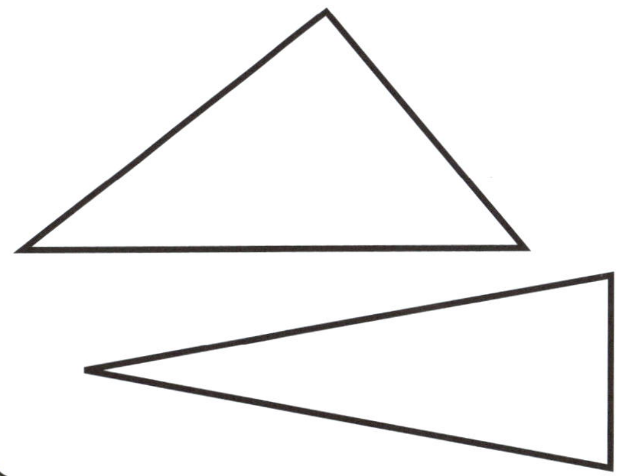
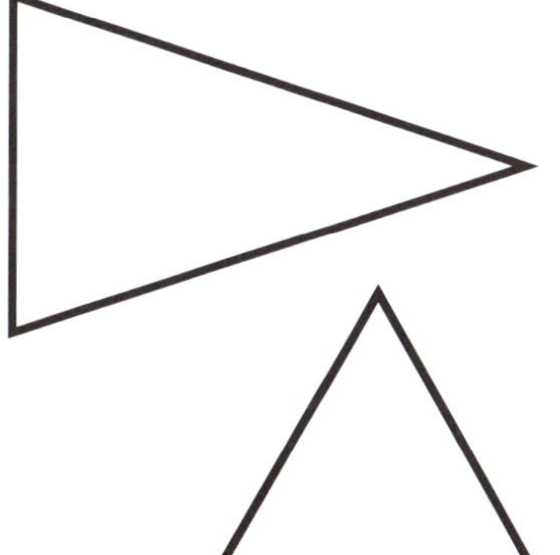

DESCRIBING TRIANGLES

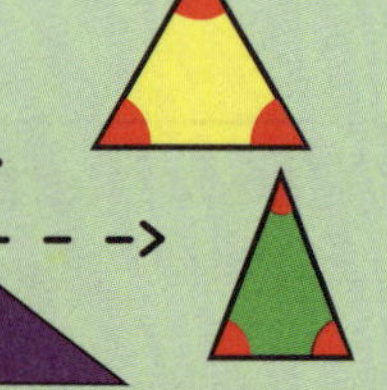

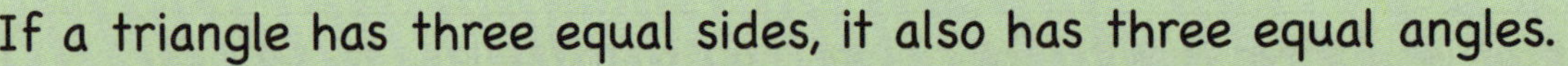
If a triangle has three equal sides, it also has three equal angles.
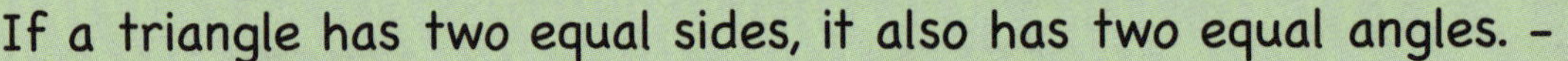
If a triangle has two equal sides, it also has two equal angles. - - - ->
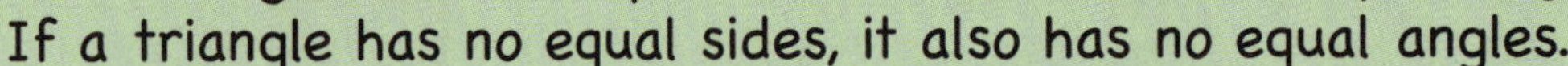
If a triangle has no equal sides, it also has no equal angles.

Color the triangles with three equal angles yellow. Color the triangles with two equal angles green. Color the triangles with no equal angles purple.

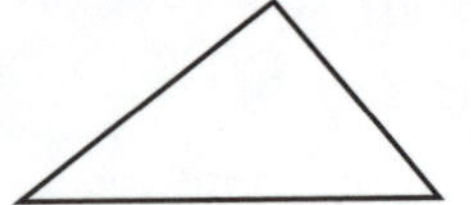  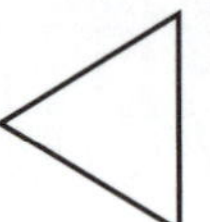 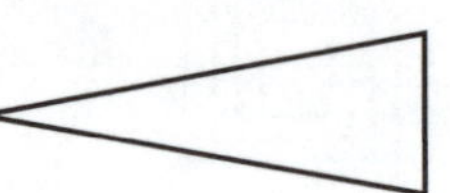  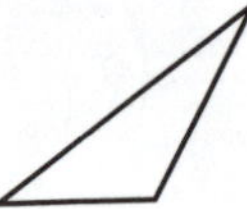

Trace the triangles blue.

   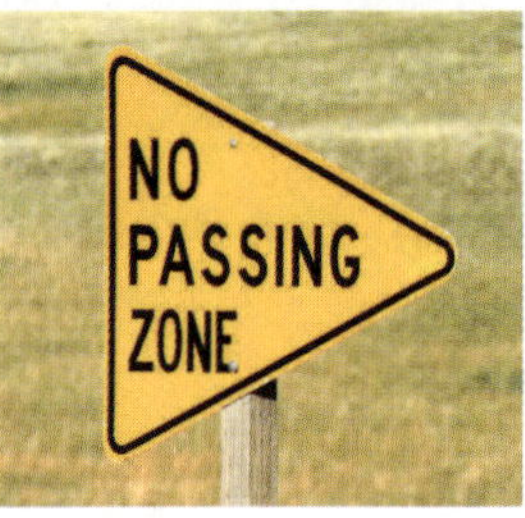

To make a triangle, draw a straight line from one dot to the next dot.

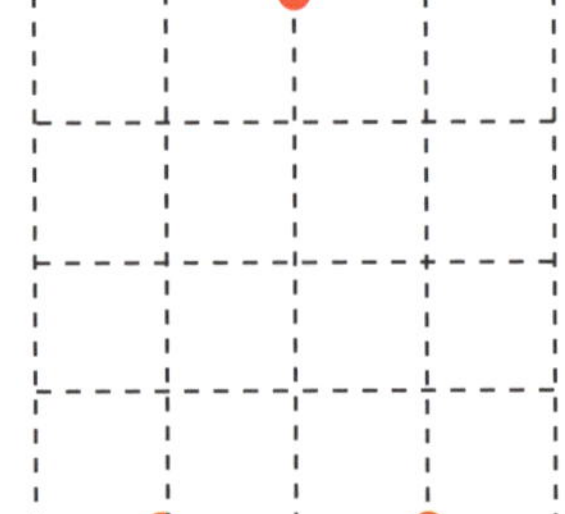 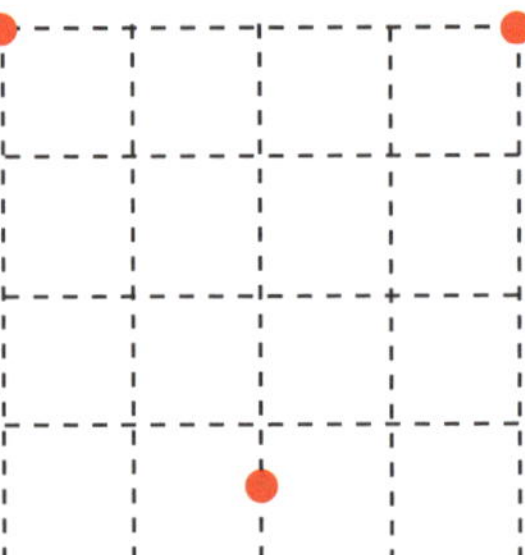 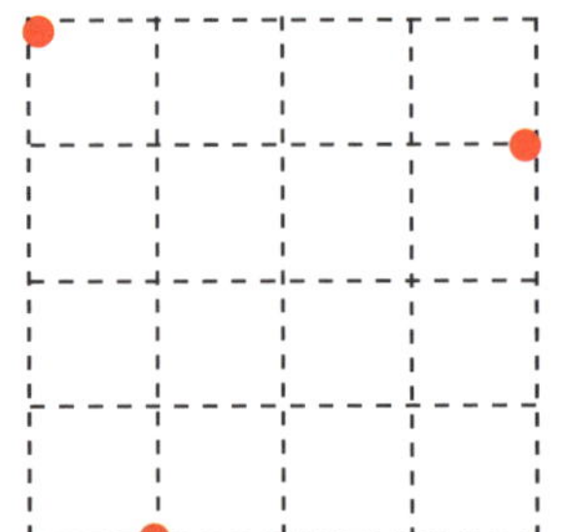 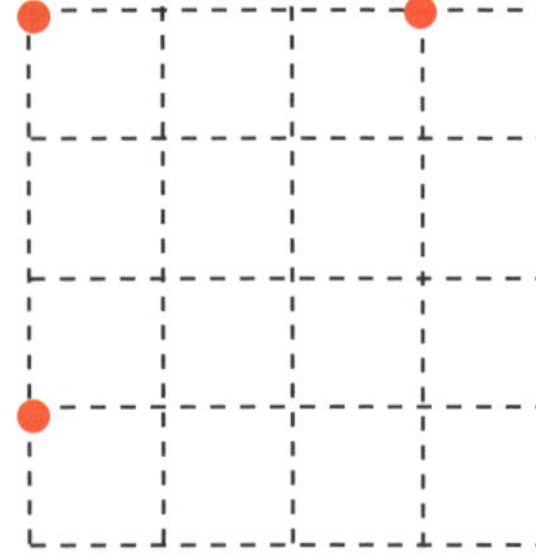

Some triangles have an angle that forms a square corner. That corner is called a "right" angle. That triangle is called a right triangle.

Draw a right triangle. ⟶

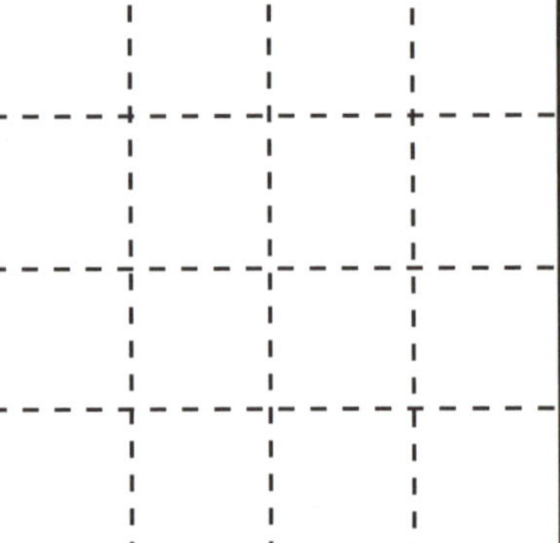

Draw something that has a right triangle.

DESCRIBING QUADRILATERALS

A quadrilateral is a polygon with four sides and four angles.

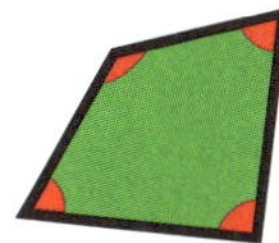

Some quadrilaterals have no equal sides.

Some quadrilaterals have two equal sides.

Some quadrilaterals have four equal sides.

Color the quadrilaterals orange, the other shapes purple.

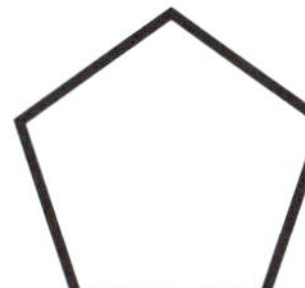
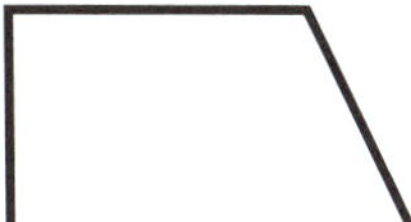

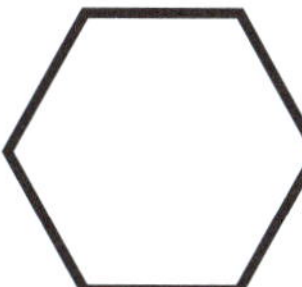

Trace the quadrilaterals orange.

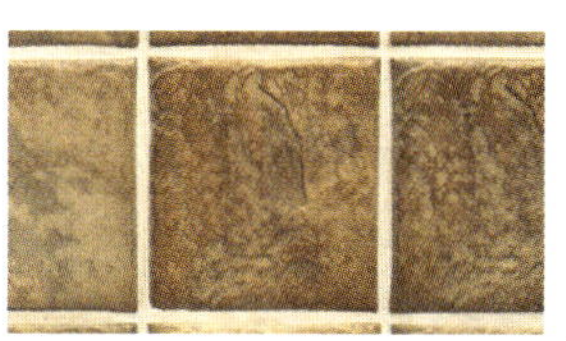

To make a quadrilateral, draw a line from one dot to the next one. Color the quadrilaterals orange.

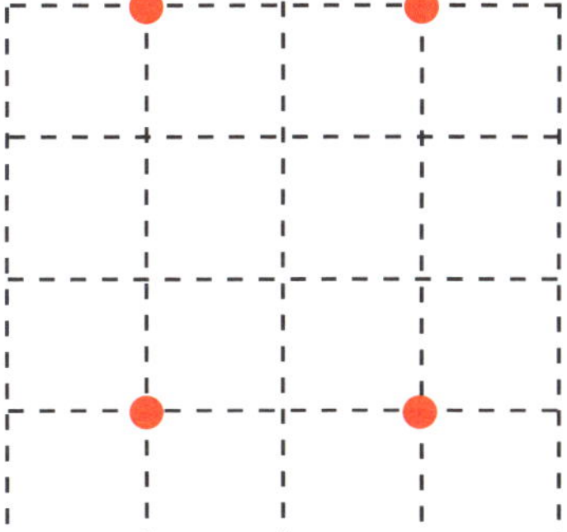
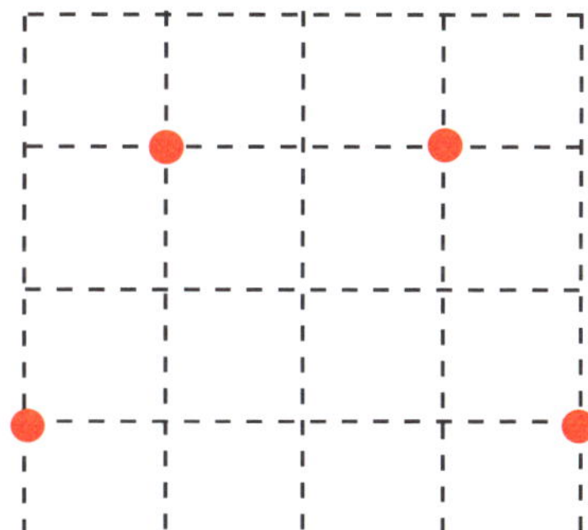
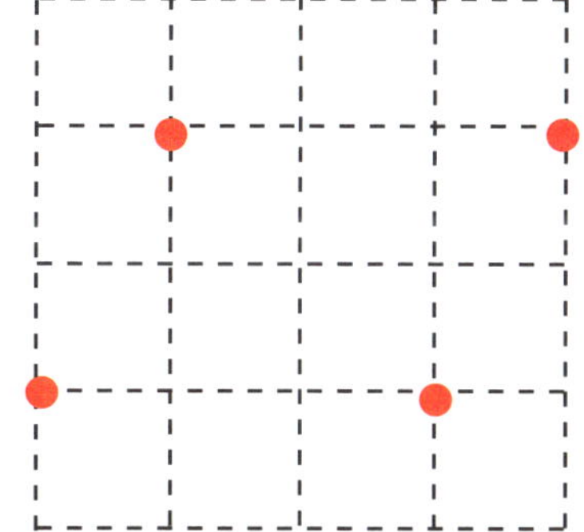

Draw two things that have a quadrilateral.

DESCRIBING TRAPEZOIDS AND PARALLELOGRAMS

Some quadrilaterals have one pair of parallel sides. That quadrilateral is a trapezoid. It looks like a triangle with its top cut off.

Some quadrilaterals have two pairs of parallel sides. That quadrilateral is a parallelogram.

Color the trapezoids green. Color the parallelograms purple.

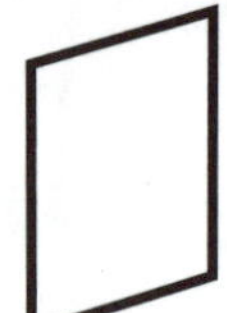     

Trace the trapezoids green. Trace the parallelograms purple.

   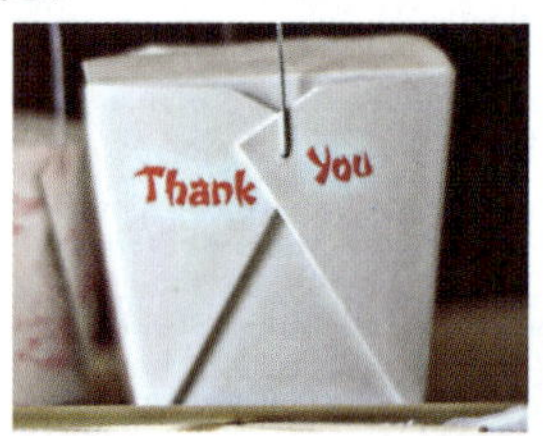

Draw a line from one dot to another. Color the trapezoids green. Color the parallelogram purple.

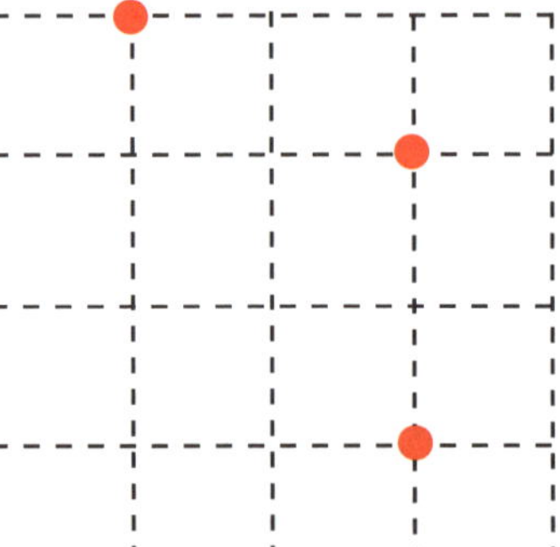 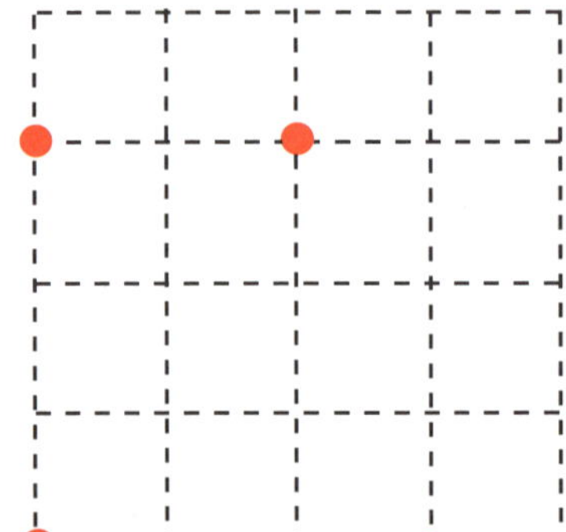 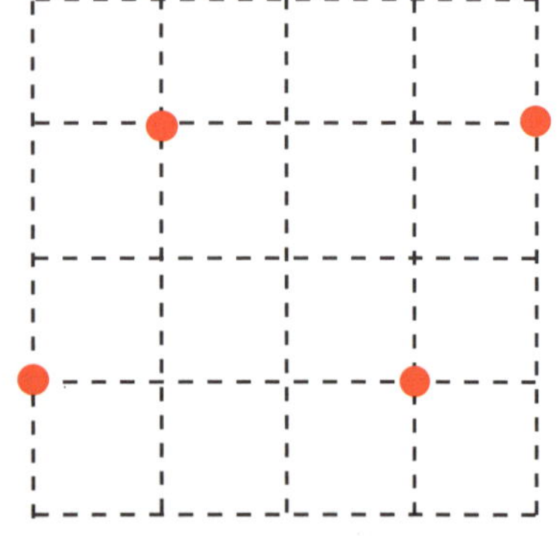

Draw something that has a trapezoid.

Draw something that has a parallelogram.

DESCRIBING RECTANGLES AND SQUARES

A rectangle is a parallelogram with four sides and four right angles. 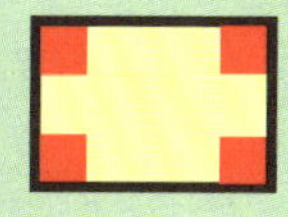

A square is a rectangle with equal sides.

Color the rectangles yellow. Color the squares orange and mark an "X" through the other shapes.

 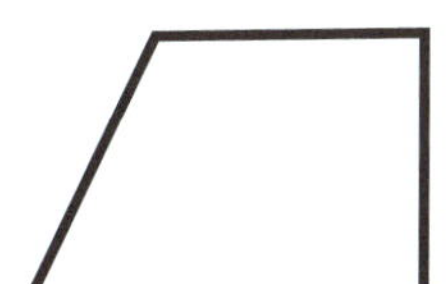    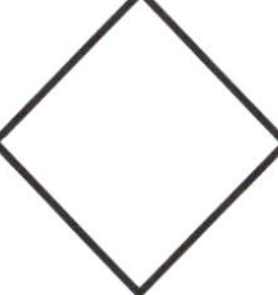

Trace the rectangles yellow. Trace the squares orange.

Draw a line from one dot to the next. Color the rectangles yellow. Color the square orange.

 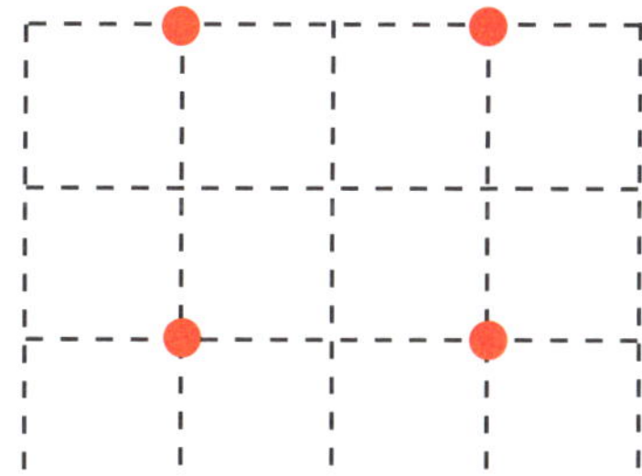 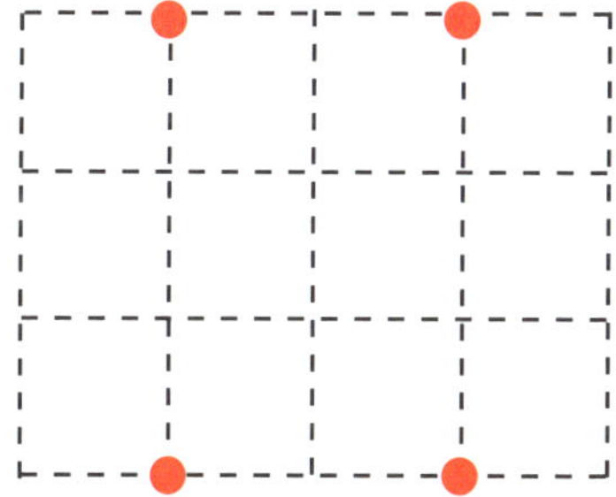

Draw a rectangle.

Draw a square.

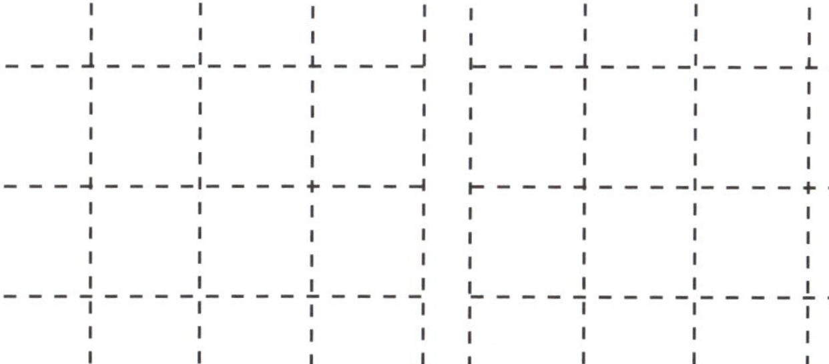

Draw something that has a rectangle or a square.

DESCRIBING PENTAGONS AND HEXAGONS

A pentagon is a polygon that has five sides and five angles.

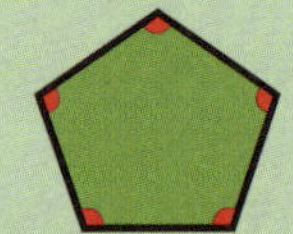

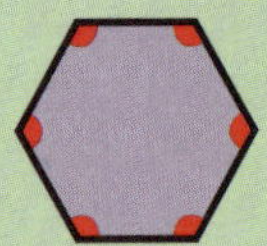

A hexagon is a shape that has six sides and six angles.

Two trapezoids can make a hexagon.

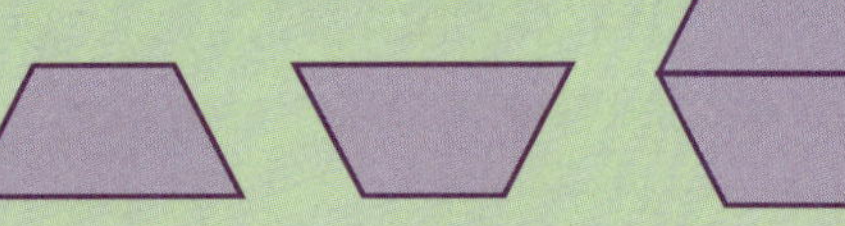

Color the pentagons green. Color the hexagons purple. Mark an "X" through the other shapes.

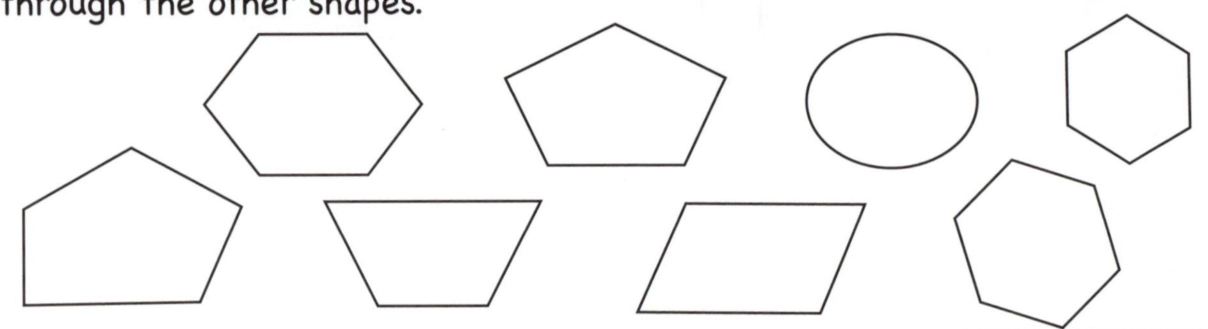

Trace the pentagons green. Trace the hexagons purple.

Draw a line from one dot to the next. Color the pentagons green. Color the hexagon purple.

FINDING POLYGONS IN A DESIGN

		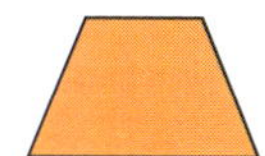			
triangle	parallelogram	trapezoid	pentagon	rectangle	hexagon

Color the triangles red.

Color the rectangle green.

Color the trapezoid orange.

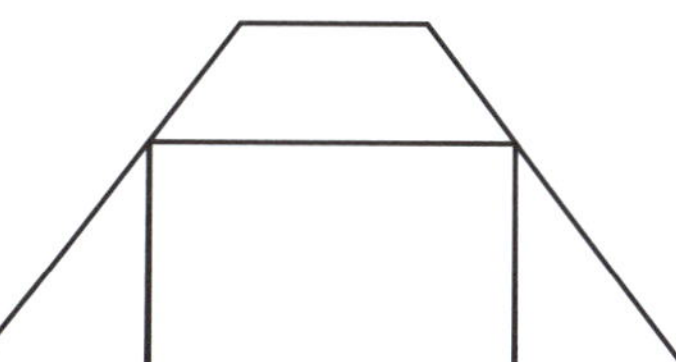

Color the parallelograms yellow.

Color the trapezoids orange.

Color the pentagon purple.

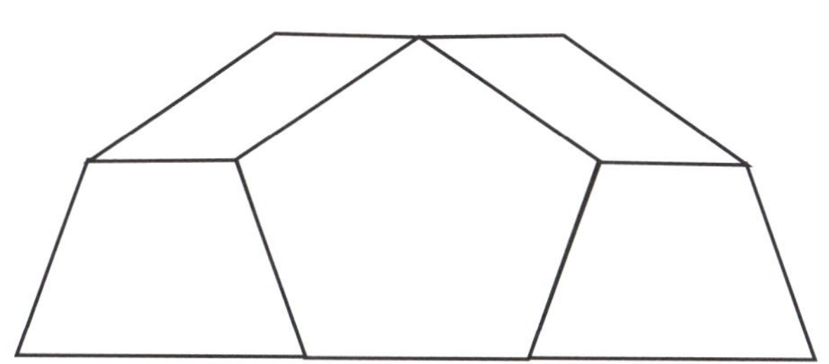

What color is the rectangle? ________________

What color are the triangles? ________________

What color are the squares? ________________

What color is the hexagon? ________________

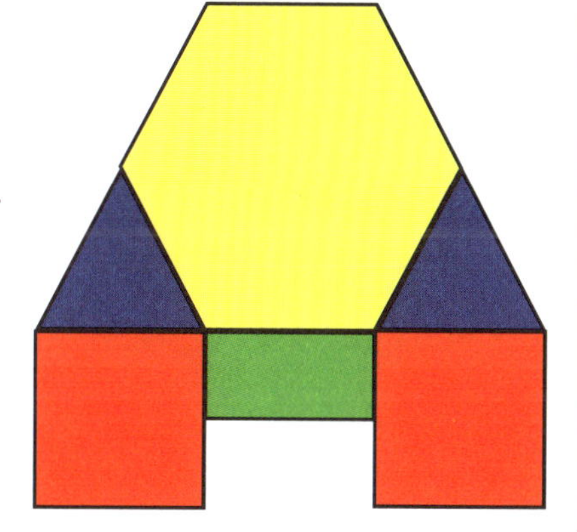

Name the red polygon. ________________

Name the blue polygon. ________________

Name the green polygons. ________________

Name the yellow polygons. ________________

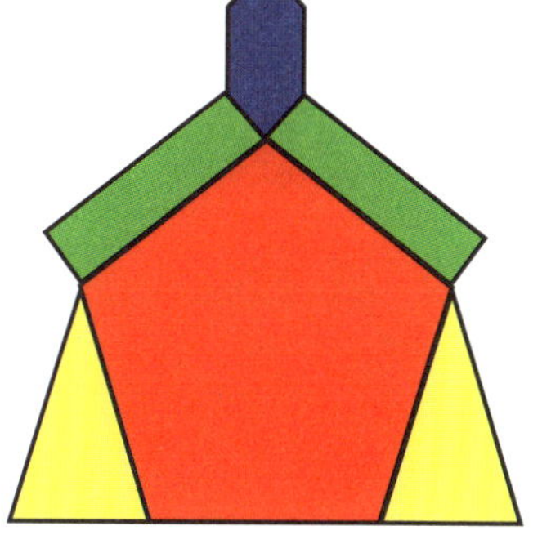

MATCHING SHAPE AND PICTURE

Draw a line from each word to its shape and to its picture.

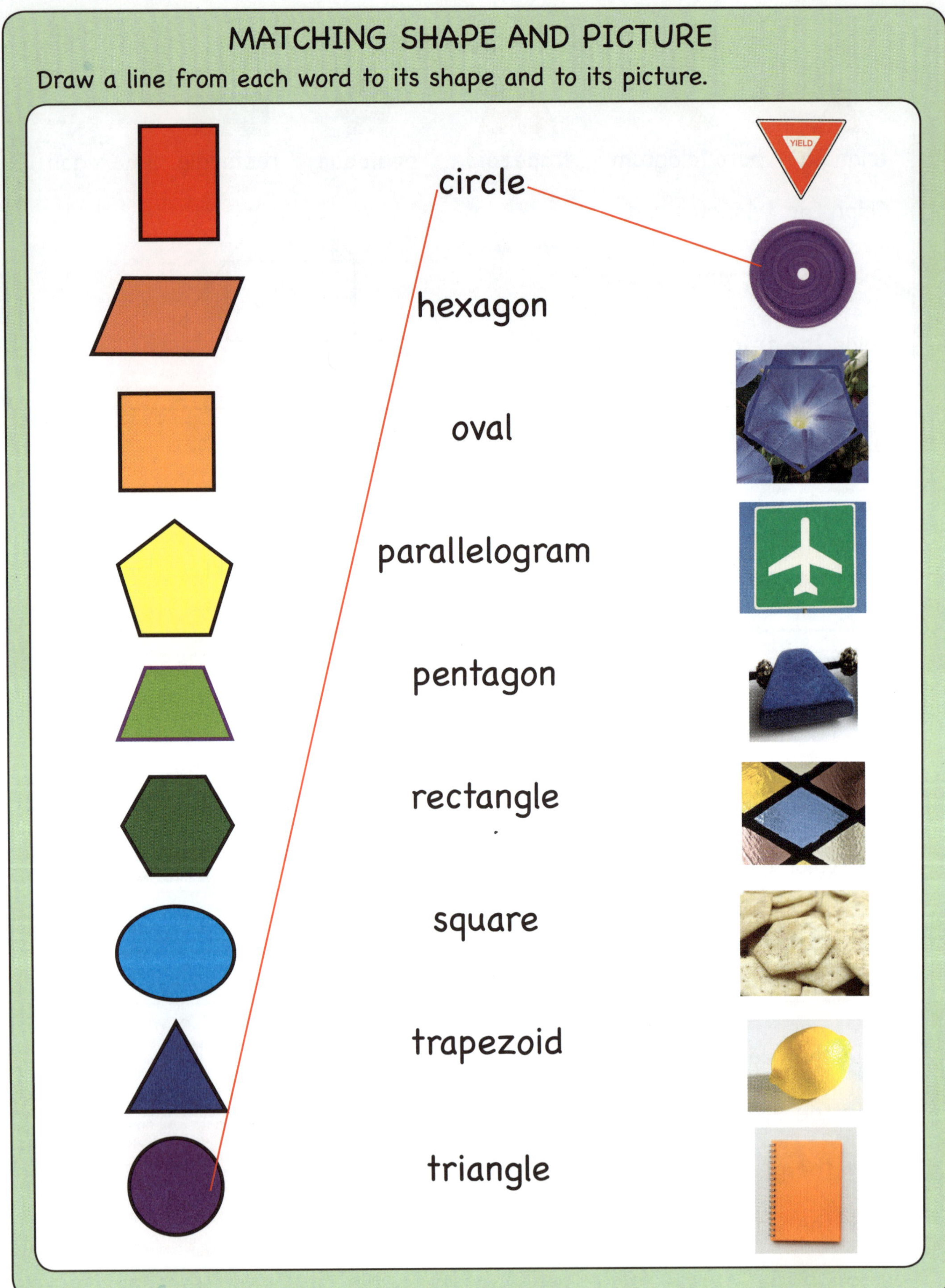

DESCRIBING SHAPES

Use the words in the WORD BOX to describe each shape.

WORD BOX
five, four, hexagon, parallelogram, pentagon, six, three, trapezoid, triangle

This ______________________ has __________ sides and _________ angles.

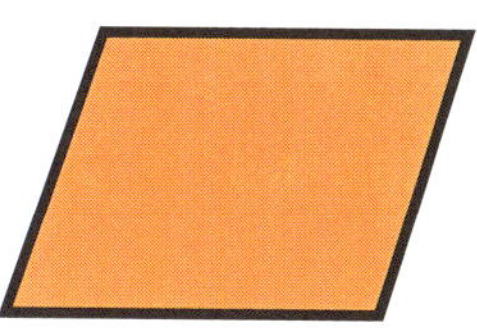

This ______________________ has __________ sides and _________ angles.

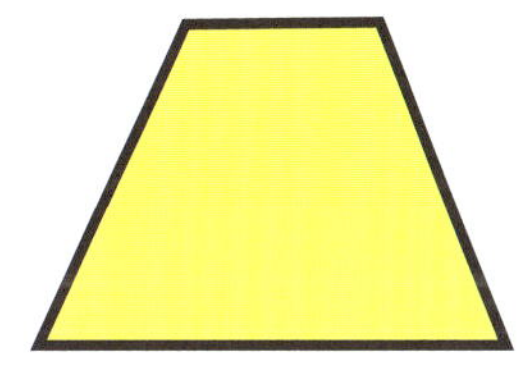

This ______________________ has __________ sides and _________ angles.

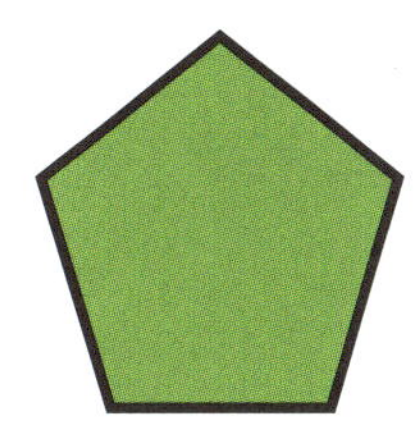

This ______________________ has __________ sides and _________ angles.

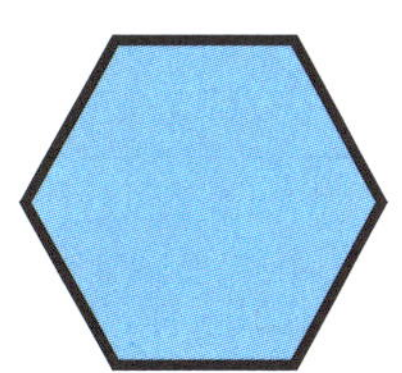

This ______________________ has __________ sides and _________ angles.

DESCRIBING QUADRILATERALS

Some quadrilaterals have one or more pair(s) of parallel sides.

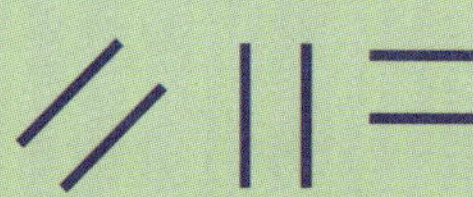

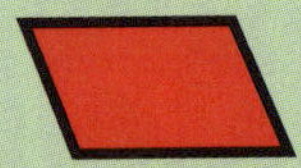

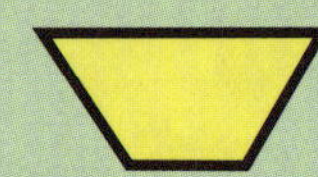

Some quadrilaterals have NO parallel sides. - - ->

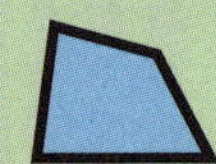

Use the words in the WORD BOX to describe each quadrilateral.

WORD BOX

no, one, two, parallelogram, quadrilateral, rectangle, square, trapezoid

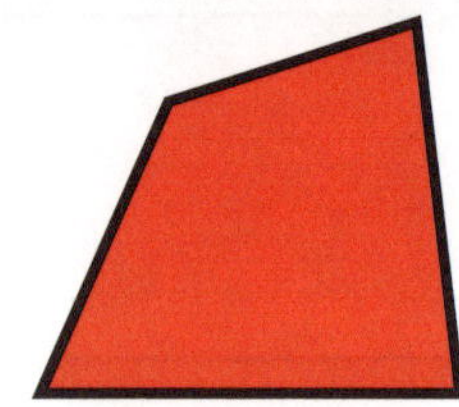

This ______________________ has __________ parallel sides.

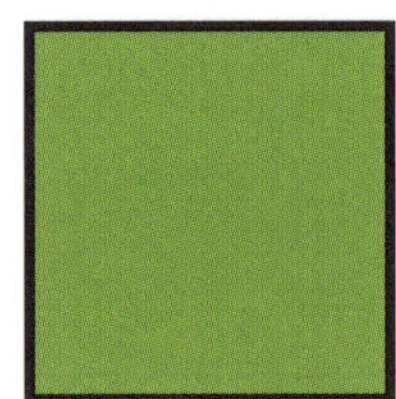

This quadrilateral is a ______________ and has ________ pairs of parallel sides.

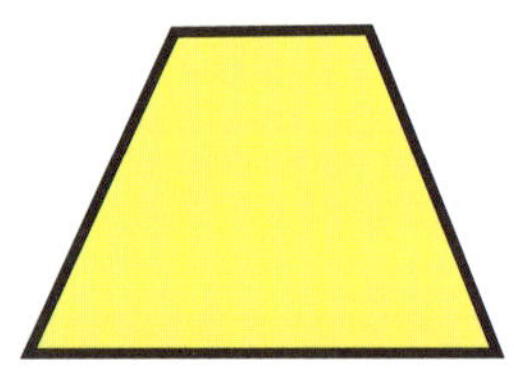

This quadrilateral is a ______________ and has ________ pair of parallel sides.

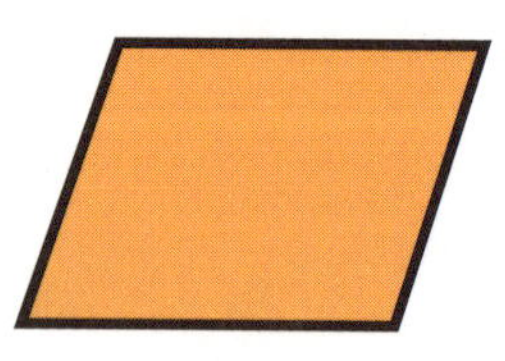

This quadrilateral is a ______________ and has ________ pairs of parallel sides.

This quadrilateral is a ______________ and has ________ pairs of parallel sides.

DESCRIBING QUADRILATERALS

Under each drawing write the name of the quadrilateral.

WORD BOX
angles, four, two, parallelogram, polygon,
quadrilateral, rectangle, square, trapezoid

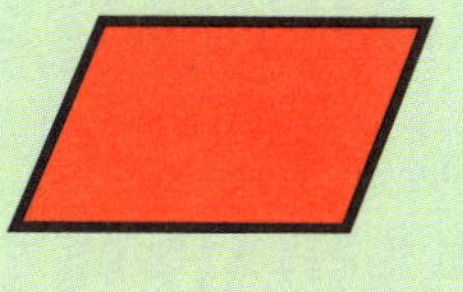
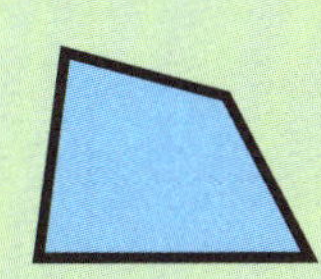
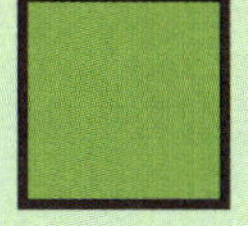

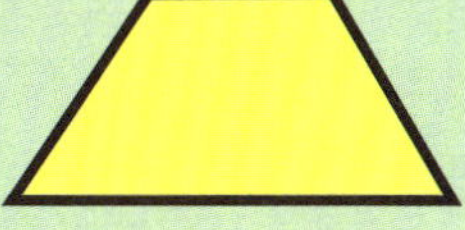

________ quadrilateral ________ ________ ________

Write the words to describe these quadrilaterals.

Any ____________ that has four sides is a ______________. The blue quadrilateral has no equal sides and no equal __________.

The yellow ____________ has one pair of parallel sides (top and bottom). The red ______________ has two pair of parallel sides (═ and / /).

The purple _____________ has ______ pairs of parallel sides and ________ right angles. The green __________ has ________ pairs of parallel sides.

and also has ________ right angles.

DESCRIBING POLYGONS

In each box, underline all the words that apply to the polygon.

EXAMPLE

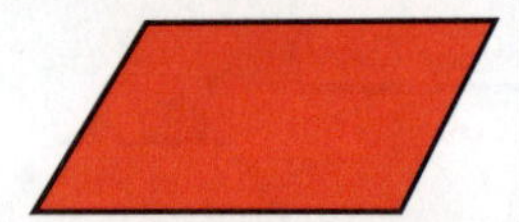

This polygon is a:
parallelogram
quadrilateral
rectangle
square
trapezoid

This polygon is a:
parallelogram
quadrilateral
rectangle
square
trapezoid

This polygon is a:
parallelogram
quadrilateral
rectangle
square
trapezoid

This polygon is a:
parallelogram
quadrilateral
rectangle
trapezoid
triangle

This polygon is a:
parallelogram
quadrilateral
rectangle
square
trapezoid

This polygon is a:
parallelogram
quadrilateral
rectangle
square
trapezoid

This polygon is a:
hexagon
pentagon
quadrilateral
square
triangle

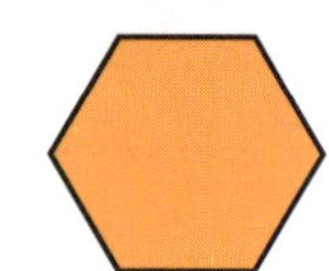

This polygon is a:
circle
hexagon
pentagon
quadrilateral
square

Put a check mark in each box which applies to the polygon.

	 (trapezoid)	 (rectangle)	 (square)	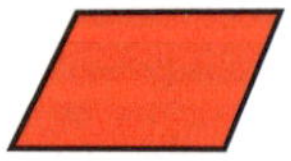 (parallelogram)
PARALLELOGRAM				
QUADRILATERAL				
RECTANGLE				
SQUARE				
TRAPEZOID				

DRAWING EQUAL SHAPES

Use the grid to draw a shape the same size and shape. Then color your drawing.

EXAMPLE

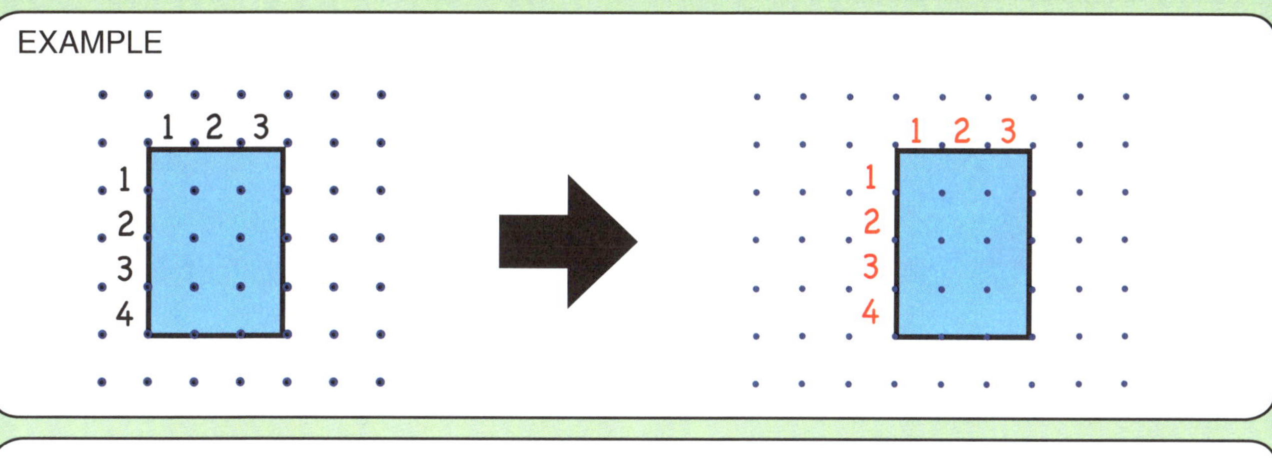

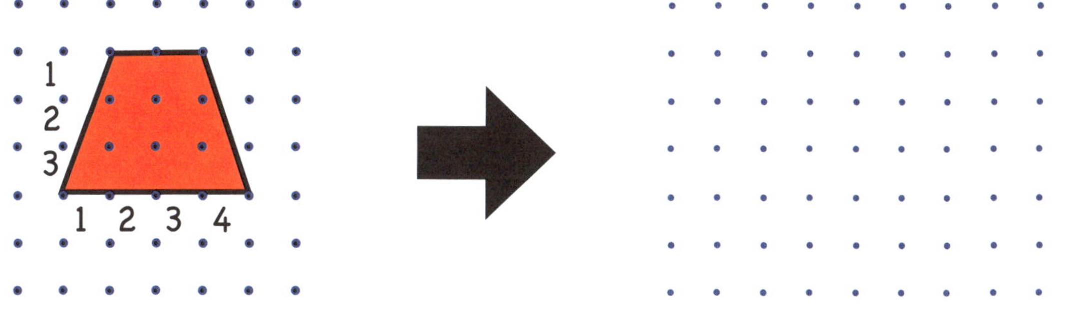

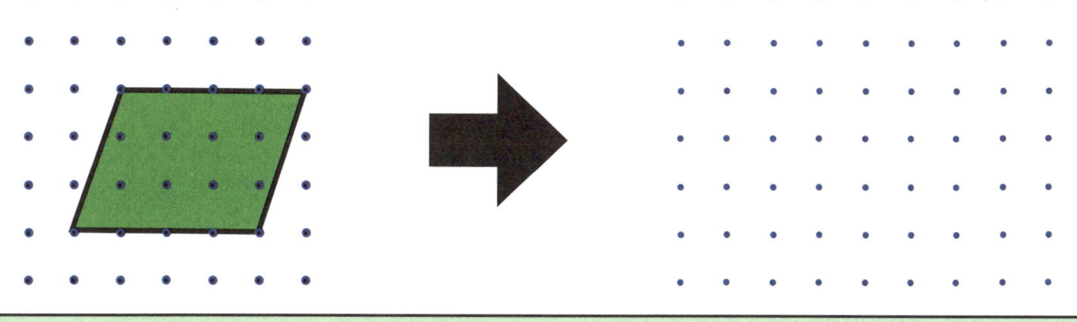

DRAWING SHAPES

We call shapes "small" or "large" compared to each other. Draw and color the shape named at the top of each box.

small, red trapezoid	large, yellow trapezoid	small, green square
large, blue square	small, orange triangle	large, purple triangle
small, green circle	large, brown circle	small, red rectangle
large, green rectangle	small, blue hexagon	large, purple hexagon

FINDING SHAPES

Circle any shape that matches one of the parts of the shape in the box at the left.

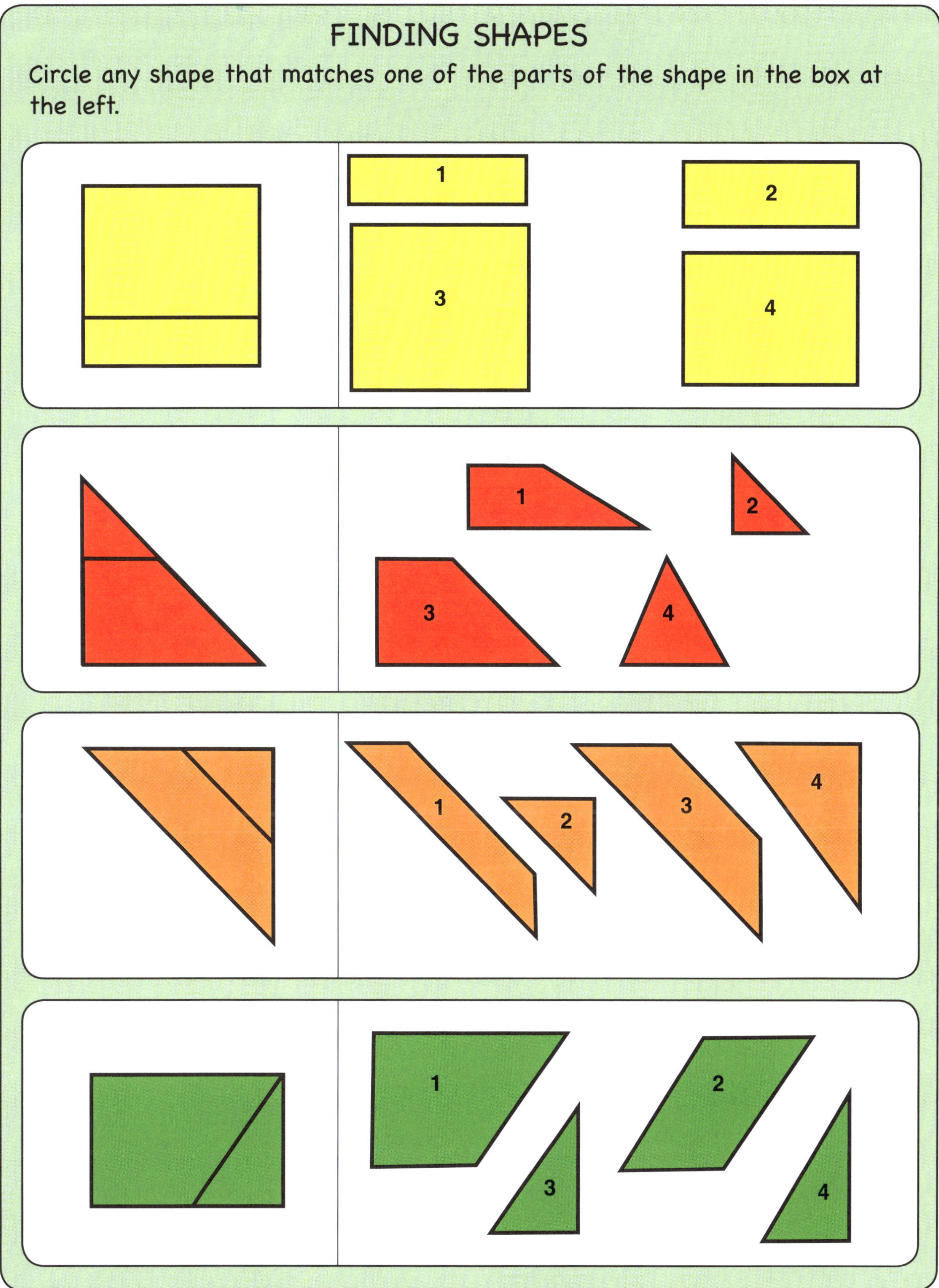

FINDING SHAPES THAT COMPLETE A SQUARE

Circle the shape that completes the big square.

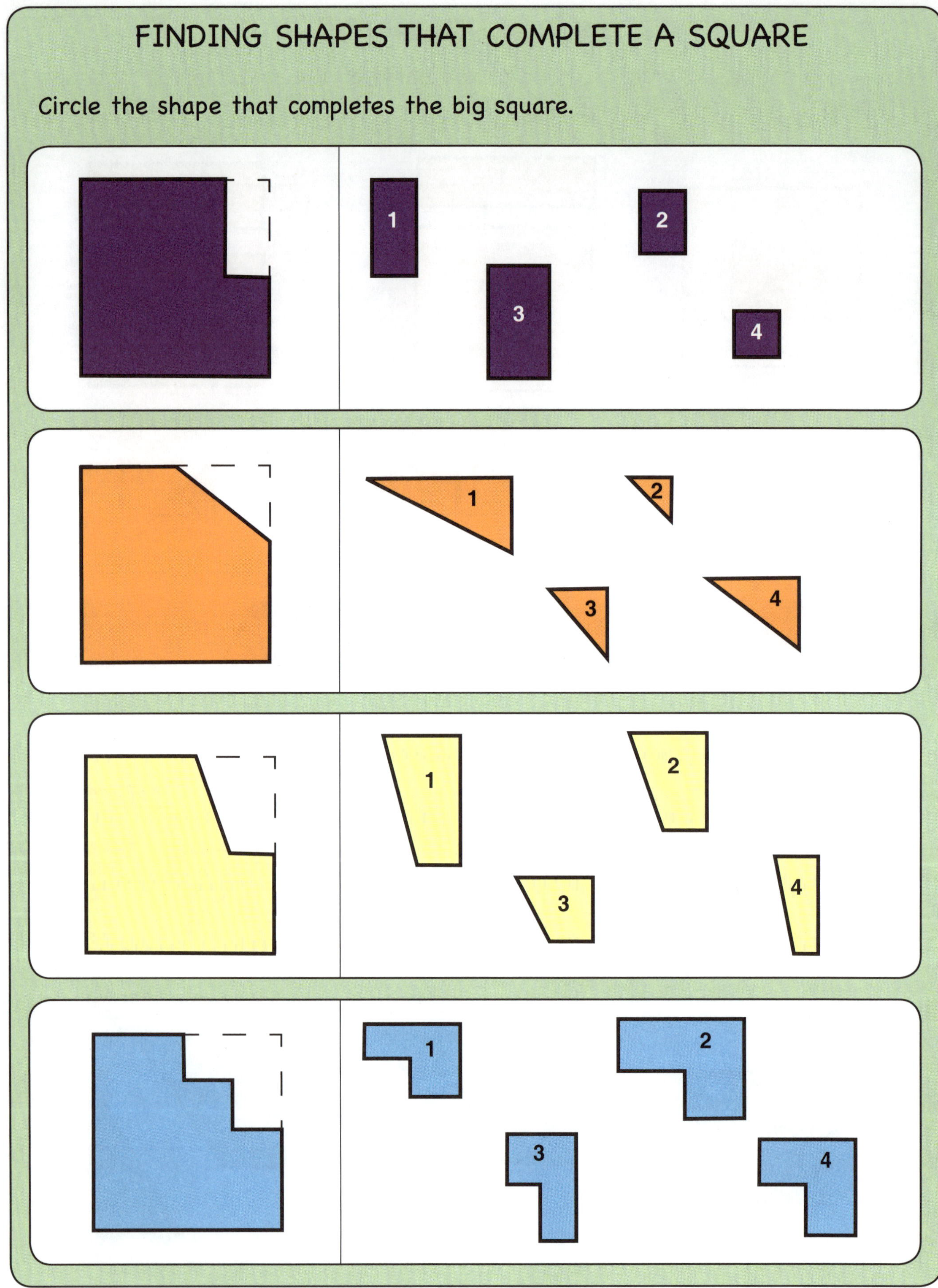

COMBINING SHAPES

Mark an "X" over the shapes that **CANNOT** be formed by joining the two shapes in the box.

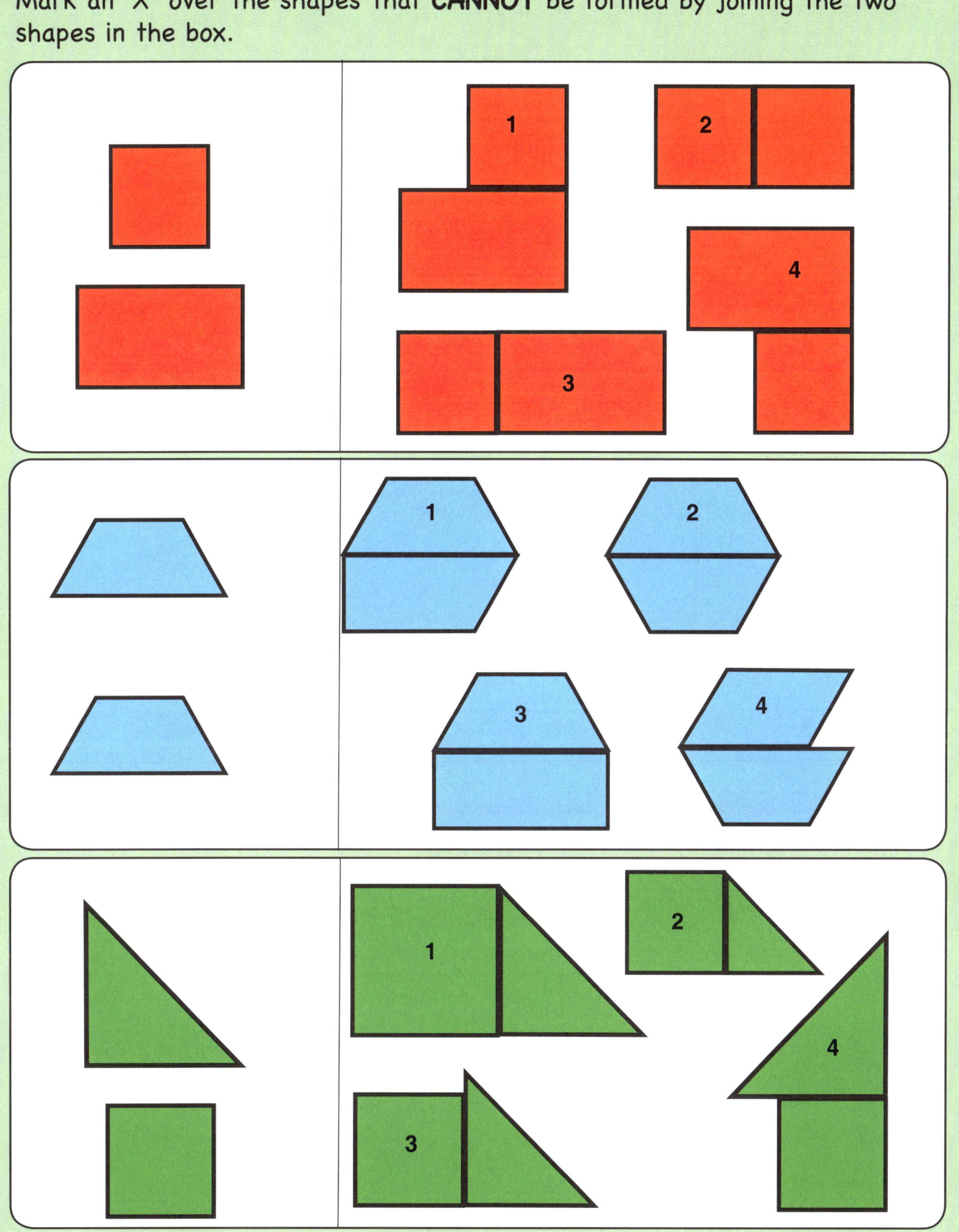

DRAWING PICTURES BY COMBINING SHAPES

Combine circles and rectangles to draw a truck.

Combine a trapezoid and triangles to draw a sailboat.

Combine a triangle and rectangles to draw a house.

DESCRIBING SOLIDS

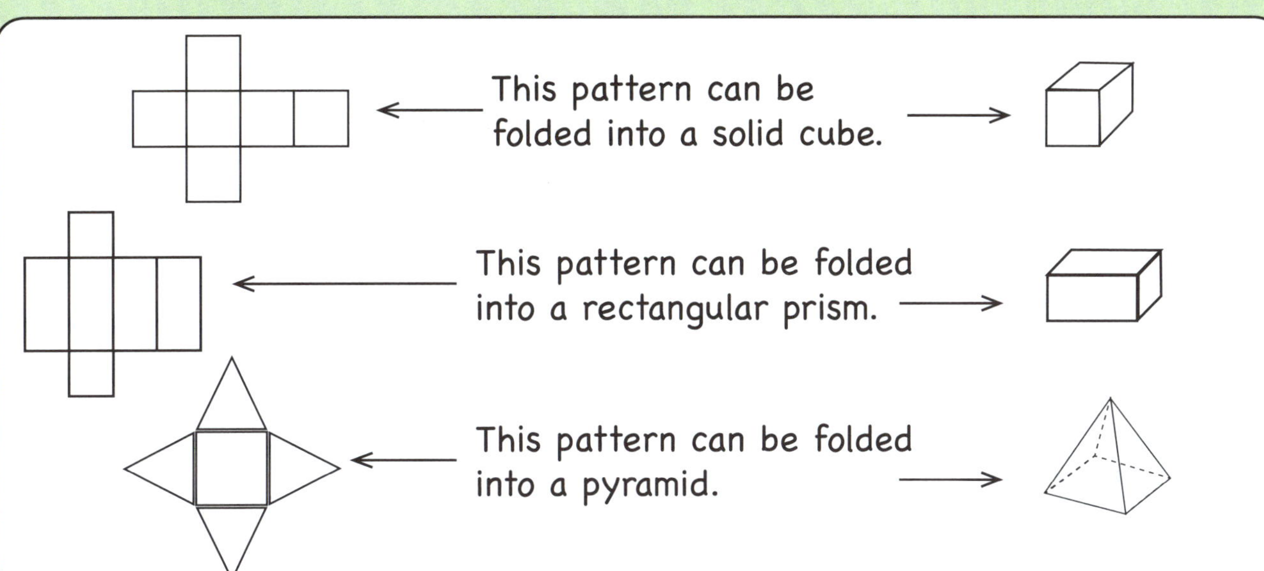

Draw a line from each picture to the word that describes its shape.

cubes

pyramid

rectangular prism

This object is a ______________________ __________.

This object is a ____________________.

This object is a ______________________.

DESCRIBING SOLIDS

A flat rectangle can be formed into a solid ball called a sphere.

A flat rectangle can also be rolled into a solid tube called a cylinder.

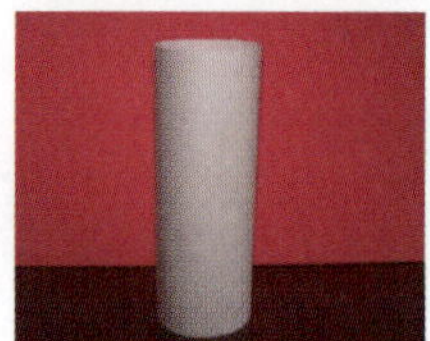

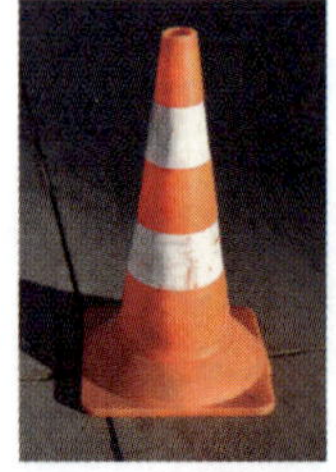

A flat triangle can be formed into a pointed solid called a cone.

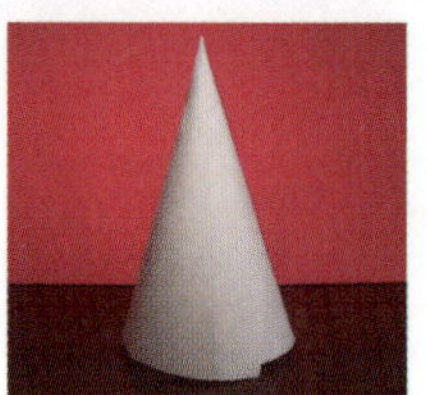

Draw line from each picture to the word that describes its shape.

cone

cylinders

sphere

This object is a ______________________.

This object is a ______________________.

This object is a ______________________.

DESCRIBING SOLIDS

WORD BOX
cube, cylinder, prism, pyramid

Use words in the WORD BOX to name each solid. Then draw a line from the picture of each solid to the drawing of the solid.

_______________ _______________ _______________ _______________

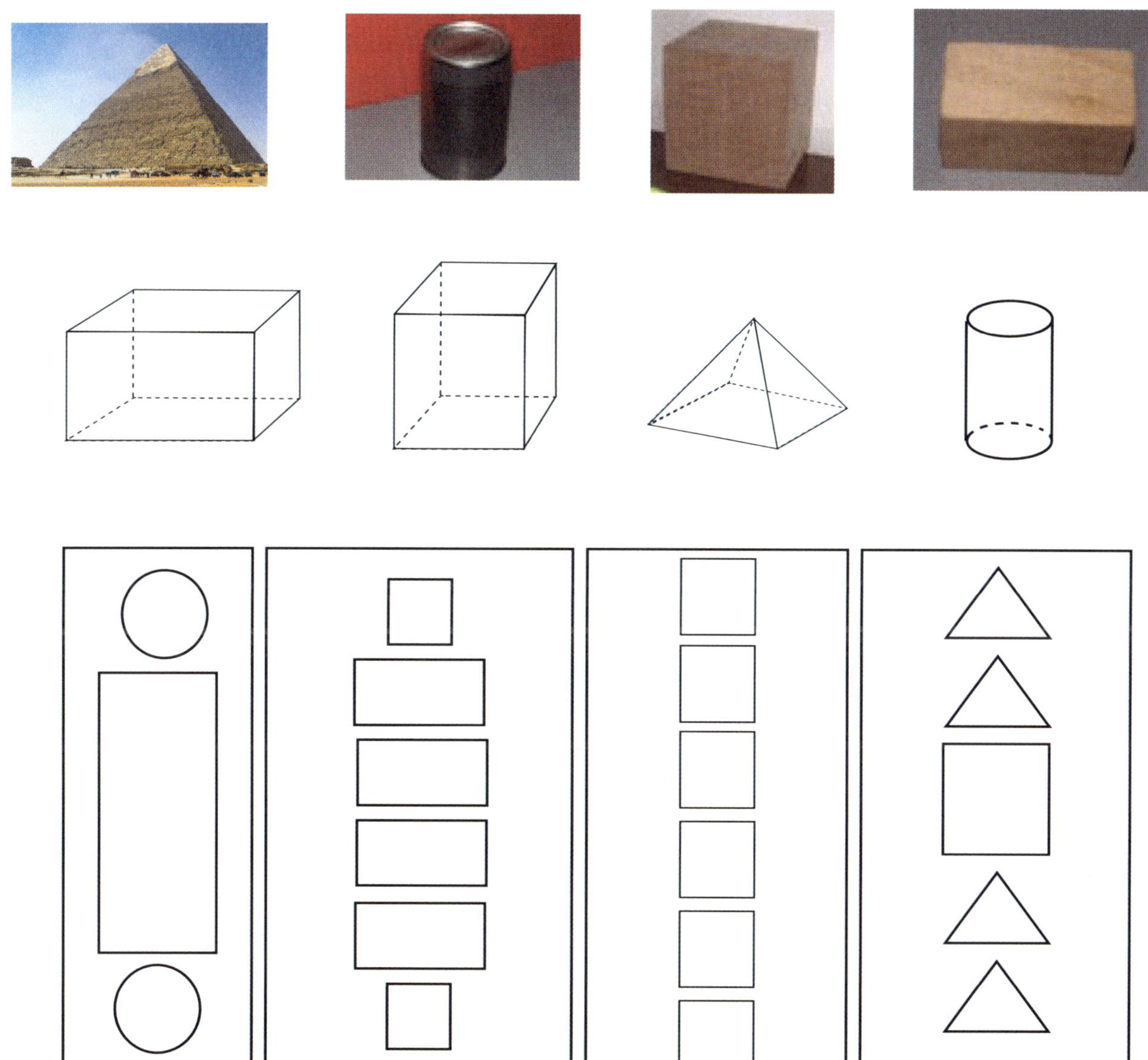

Draw a line from each drawing of the solid to the box that shows the sides of the solids.

COMBINING SOLIDS

Many things are combinations of solids. Describe the following objects using words from the WORD BOX.

WORD BOX
cone, cubes, cylinder, cylinders, sphere

This light is a ________________

on a ____________________.

This steeple is a ________________

on a ____________________.

This glass has three ________________

inside a ____________________.

This wedding cake is made

with three short

____________________.

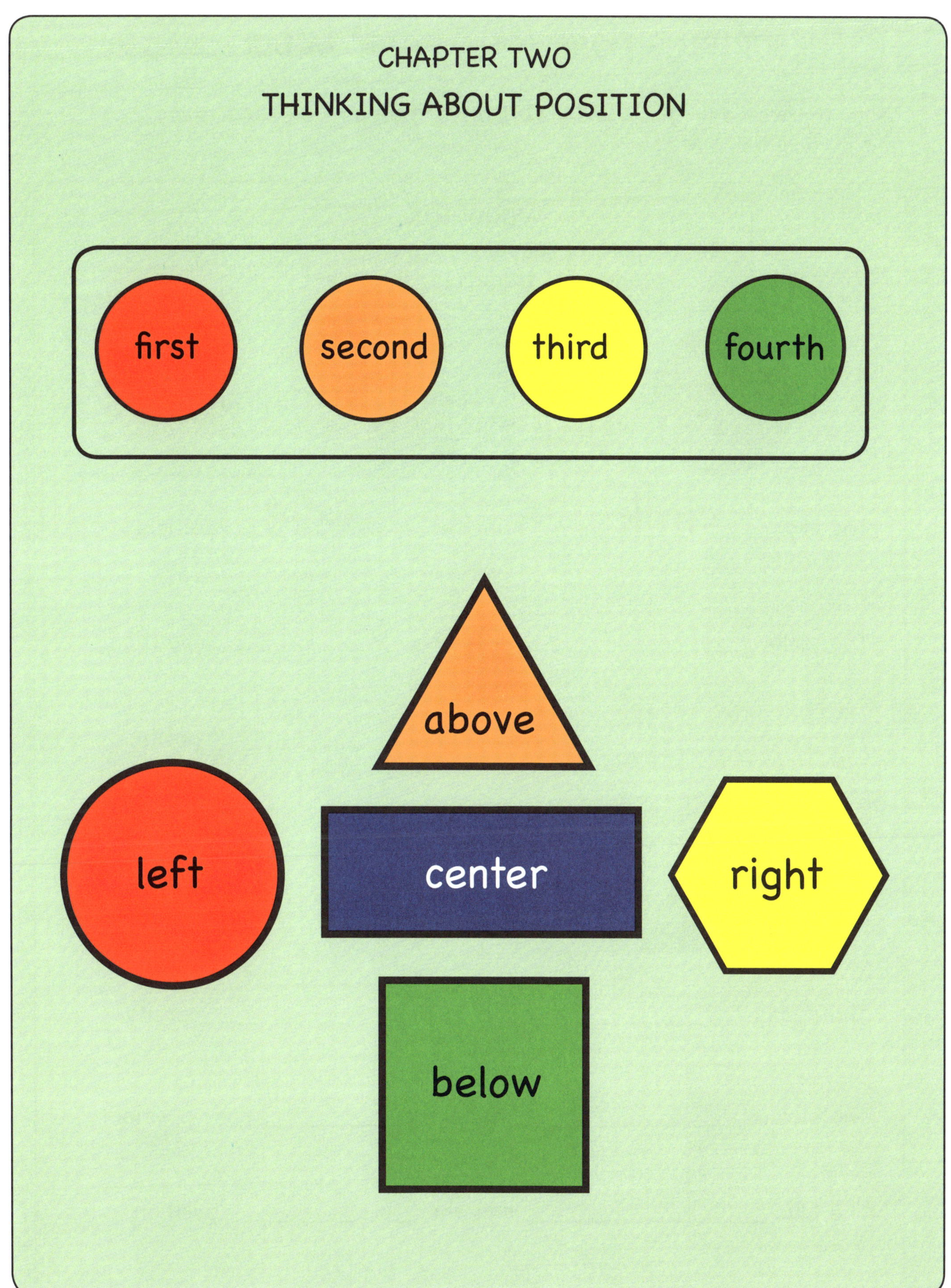
CHAPTER TWO
THINKING ABOUT POSITION
first
second
third
fourth
above
left
center
right
below

DESCRIBING POSITION - FIRST, MIDDLE, LAST

Using the words in the WORD BOX, write the name of each shape and its position.

WORD BOX
circle, first, hexagon, last, middle, rectangle, square, trapezoid, triangle

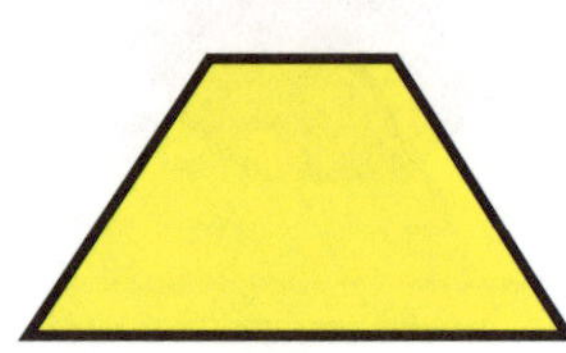

The red circle (name) is in the first position.

The yellow ________ (name) is in the ________ position.

The green ________ (name) is in the ________ position.

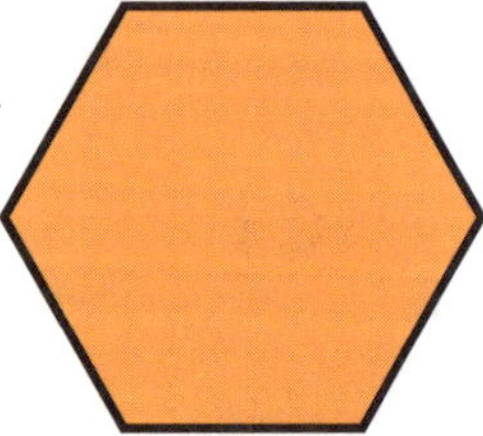

The orange ________ (name) is in the ________ position.

The purple ________ (name) is in the ________ position.

The blue ________ (name) is in the ________ position.

DESCRIBING POSITION – FIRST, SECOND, THIRD, FOURTH

Using the words in the WORD BOX, write the name of each shape and its position or color.

WORD BOX
circle, fourth, green, hexagon, orange,
red, second, square, third, trapezoid

The blue ________________ (name) is in the ______________ position.

The yellow ________________ (name) is in the ______________ position.

The green ________________ (name) is in the ______________ position.

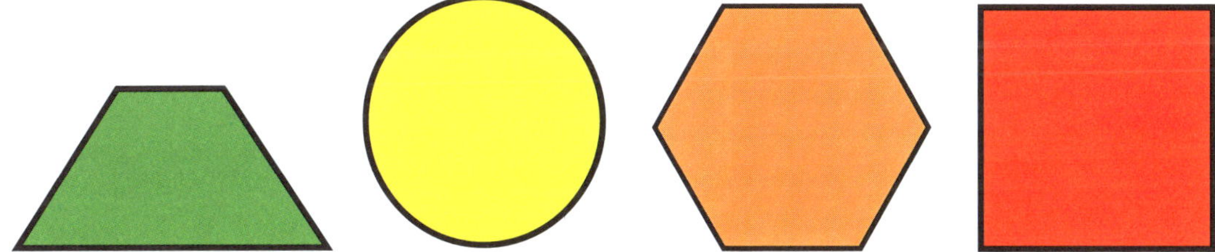

The polygon in the first position is a ____________ (color) ______________ (name).

The polygon in the third position is a ____________ (color) ______________ (name).

The polygon in the fourth position is a ____________ (color) ______________ (name).

SHOWING POSITION - LEFT, CENTER, RIGHT

left **center** **right**

Draw a red square to the left of the triangle.

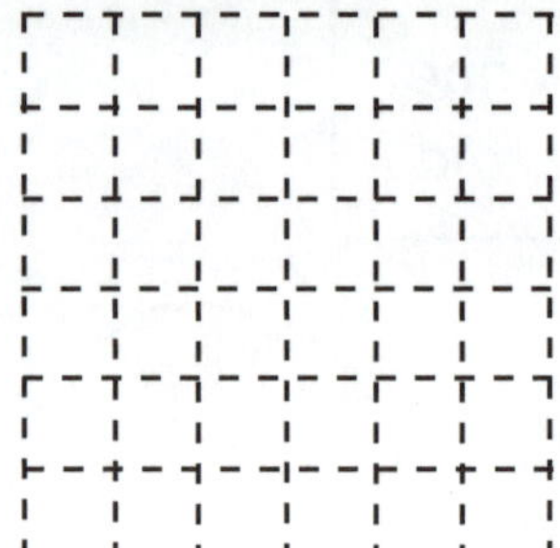

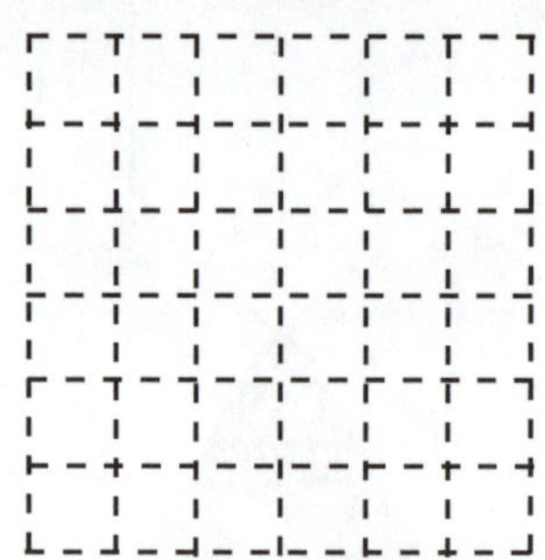

Draw a green triangle to the right of the square.

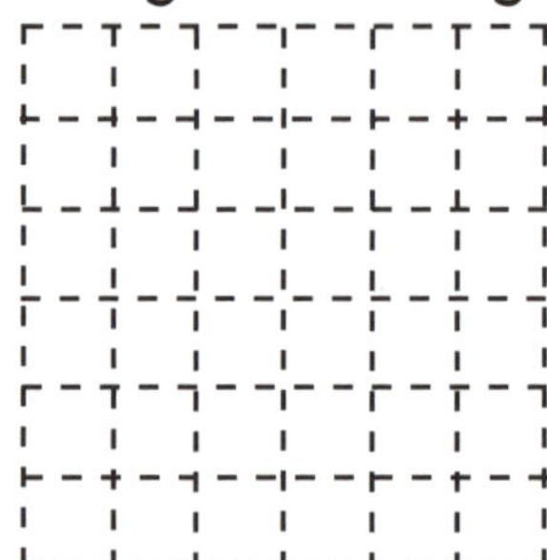
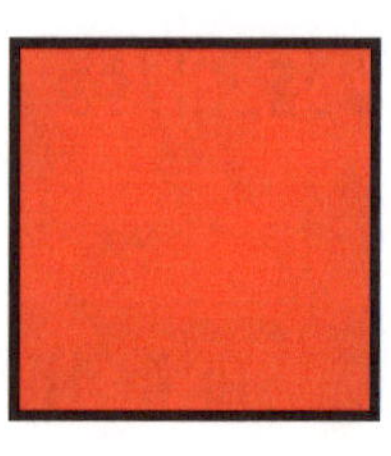
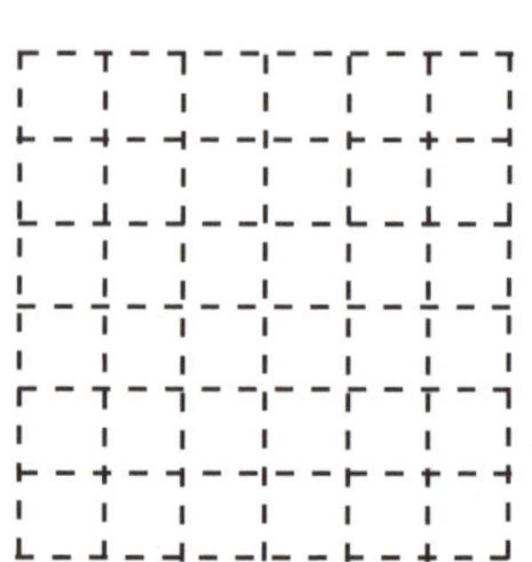

Draw an orange rectangle in the center and a purple hexagon on the left.

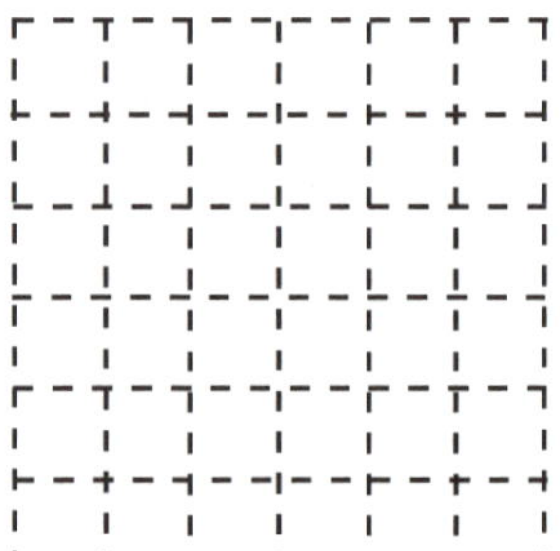
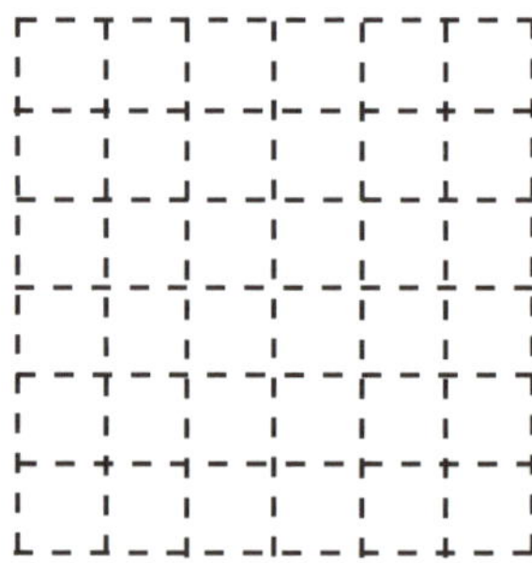
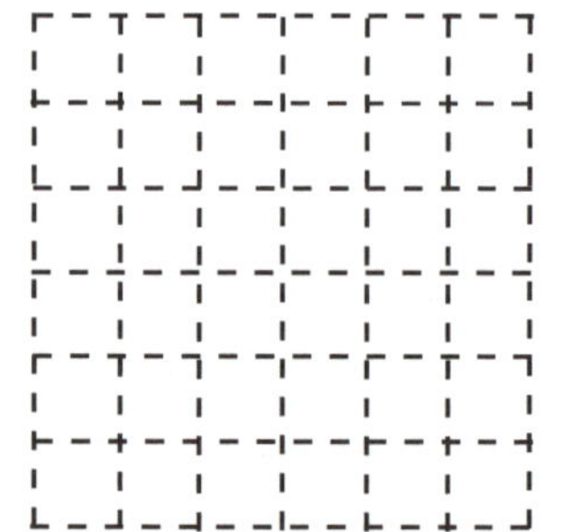

Draw a blue circle to the right of the hexagon and a red oval on the left.

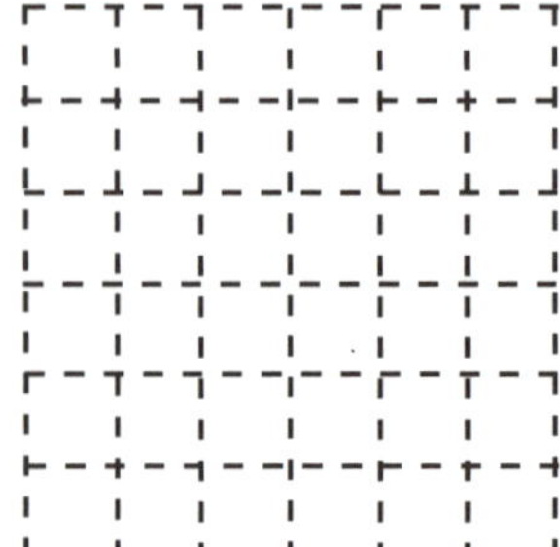

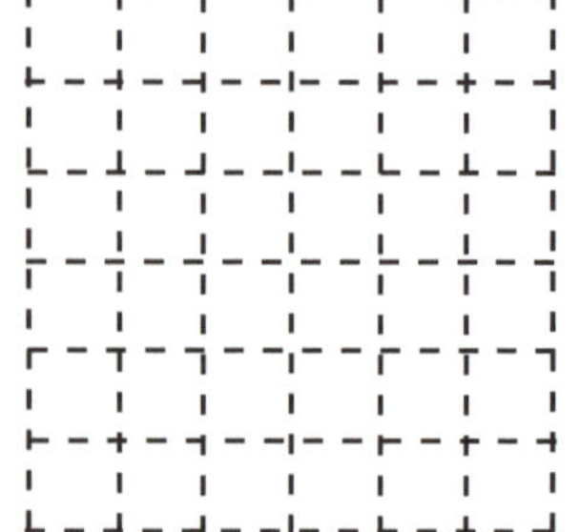

SHOWING POSITION - ABOVE, BELOW

Draw a blue square above the yellow circle.

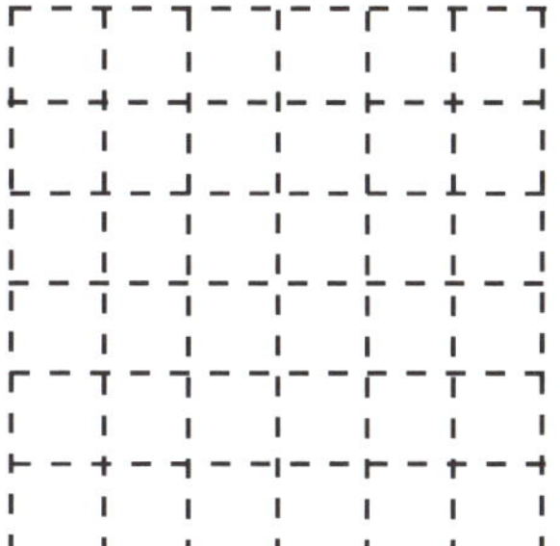

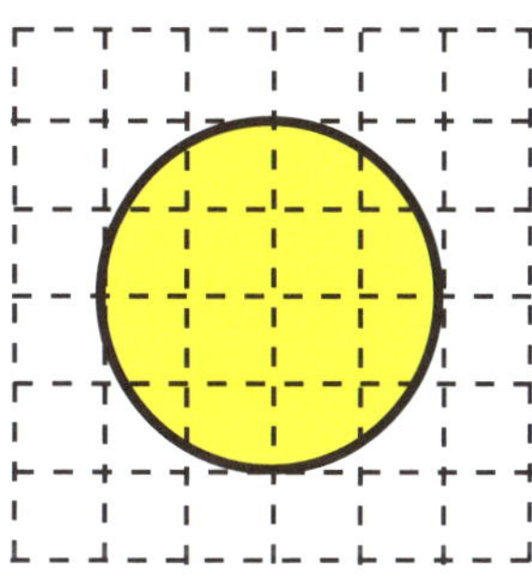

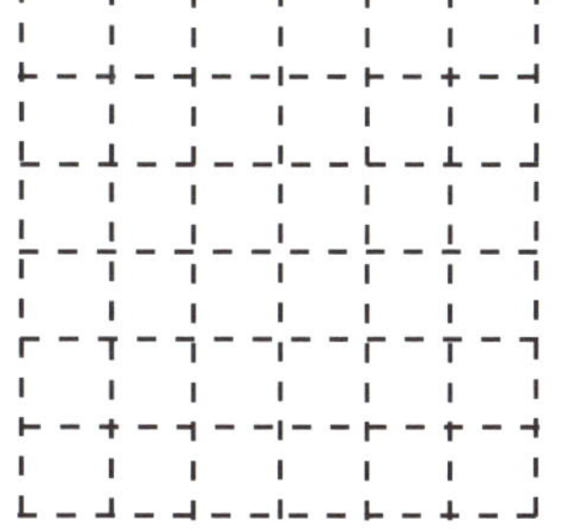

Draw a red square in the middle box and an orange triangle below it.

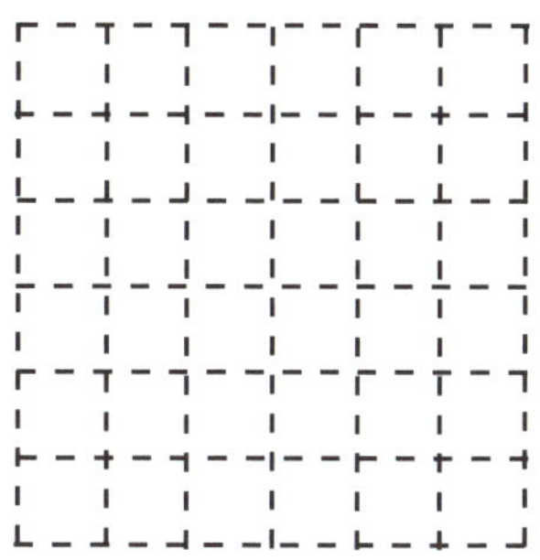

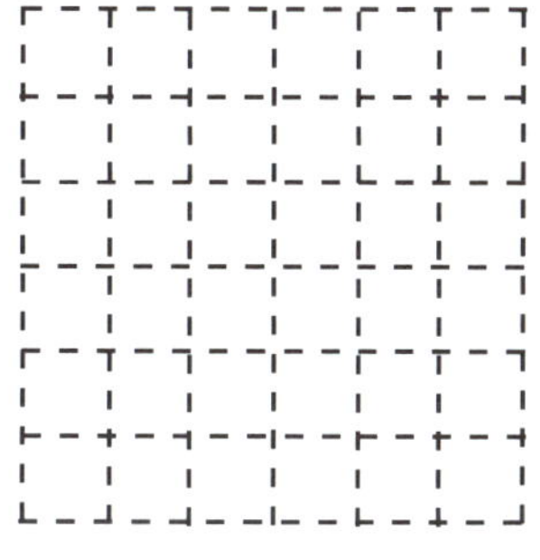

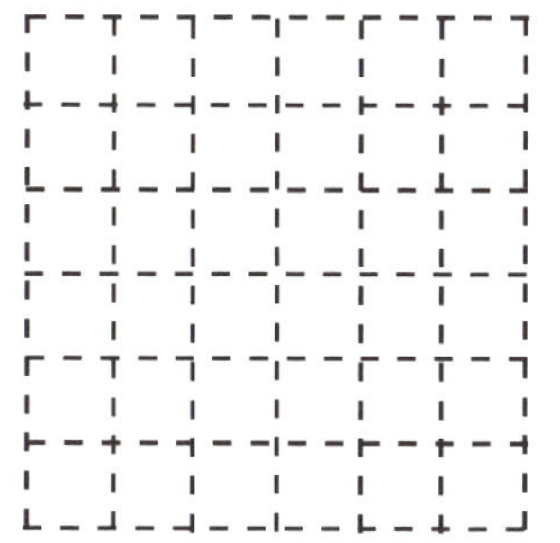

Draw a red triangle above the purple trapezoid and a green circle below it.

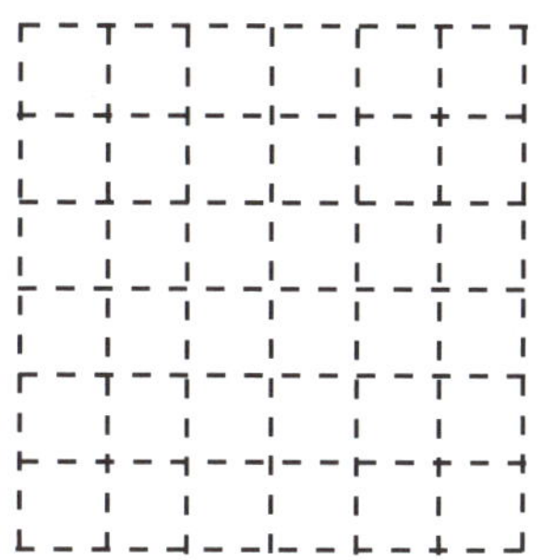

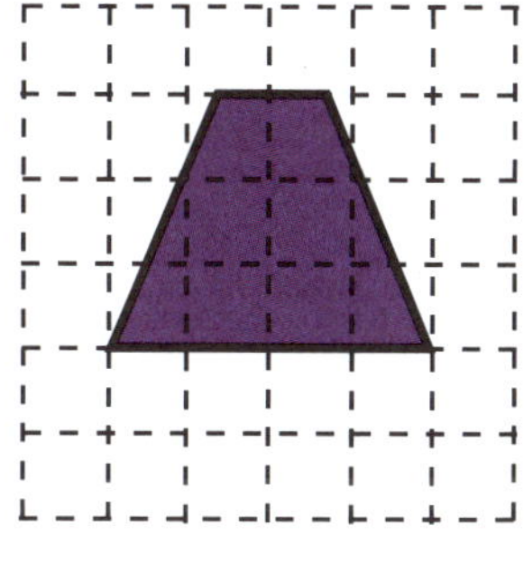

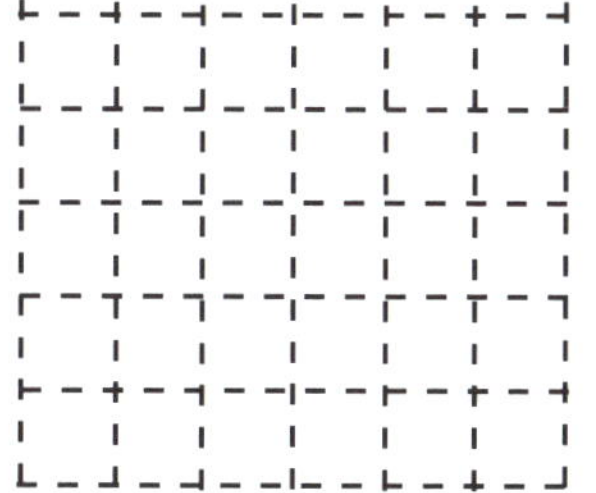

WRITING POSITION WORDS

Use the words in the WORD BOX to finish this paragraph that describes the positions of five shapes.

WORD BOX
above, below, left, right

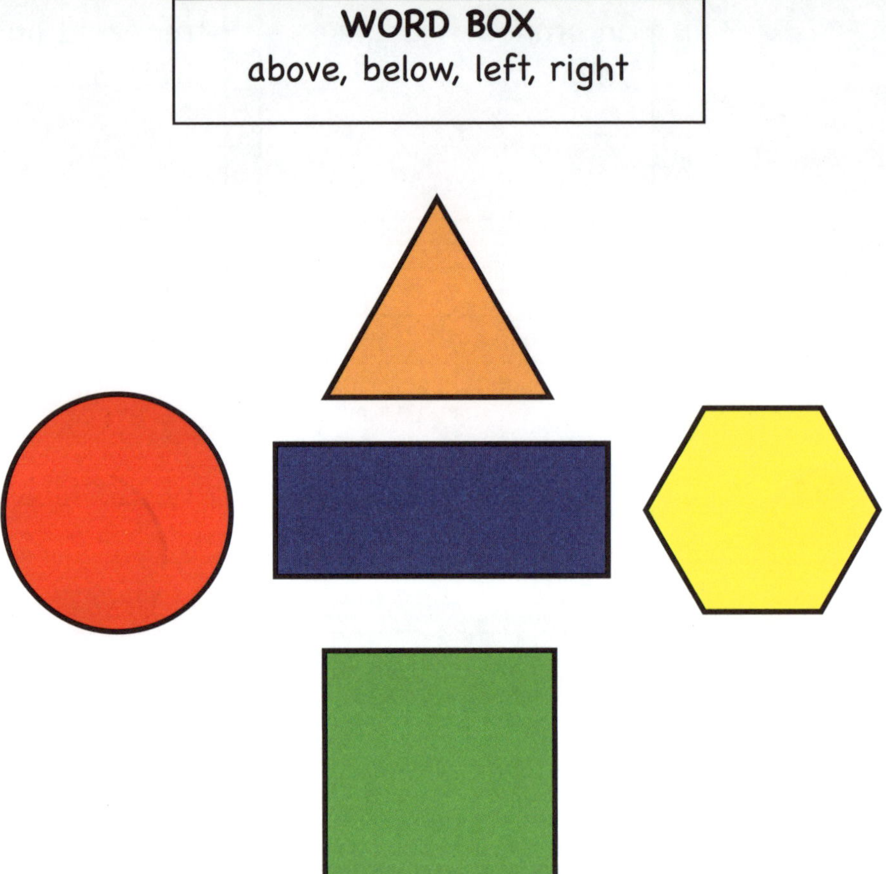

The rectangle is ____________ the square and ____________ the triangle. The hexagon is on the ____________ of the rectangle. The circle is on the ____________ of the rectangle.

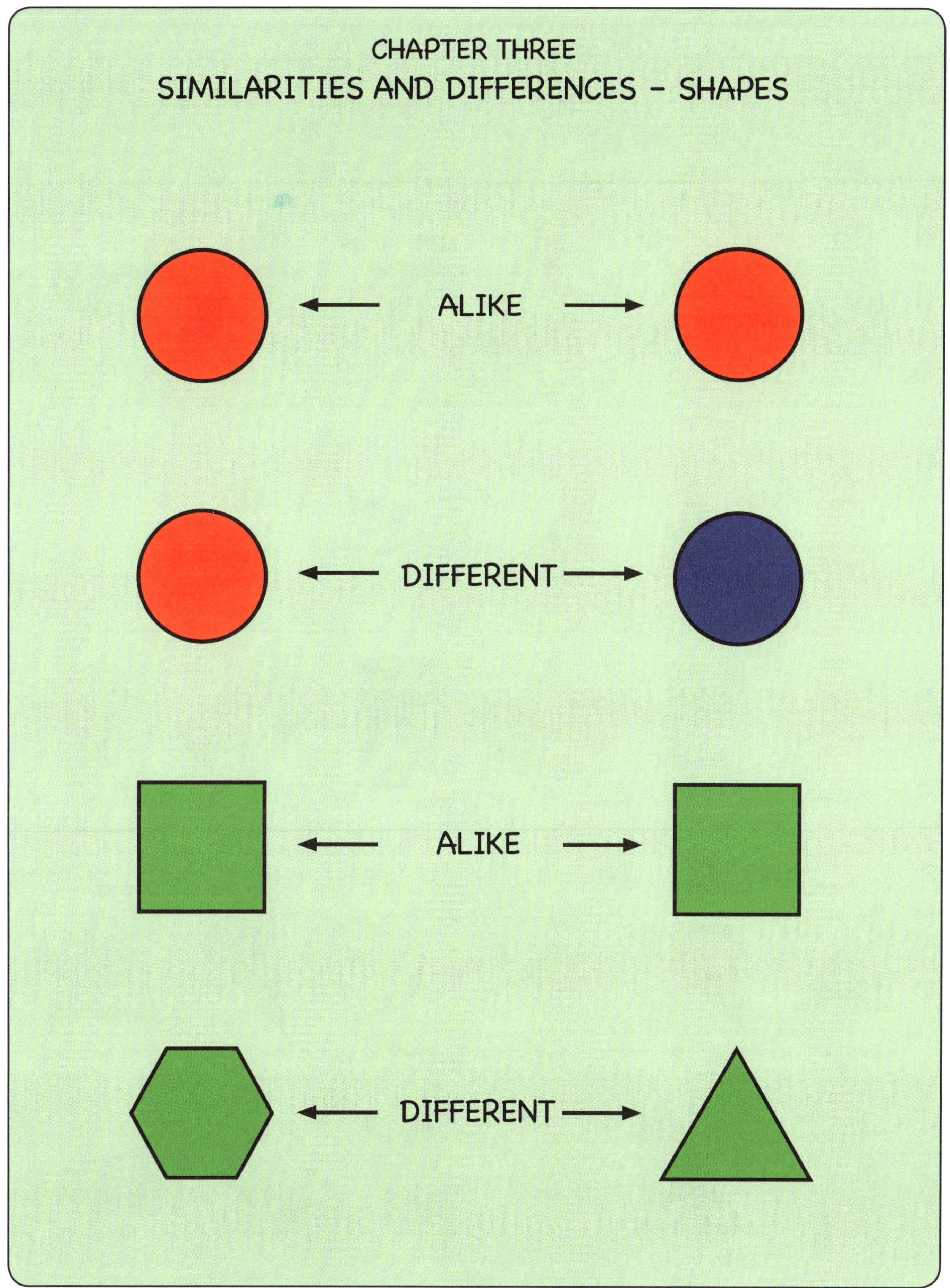
CHAPTER THREE
SIMILARITIES AND DIFFERENCES – SHAPES
ALIKE
DIFFERENT
ALIKE
DIFFERENT

FINDING EQUAL SHAPES

Cross out the shapes in each row that are not equal to the first one. An equal shape may be turned to a different position.

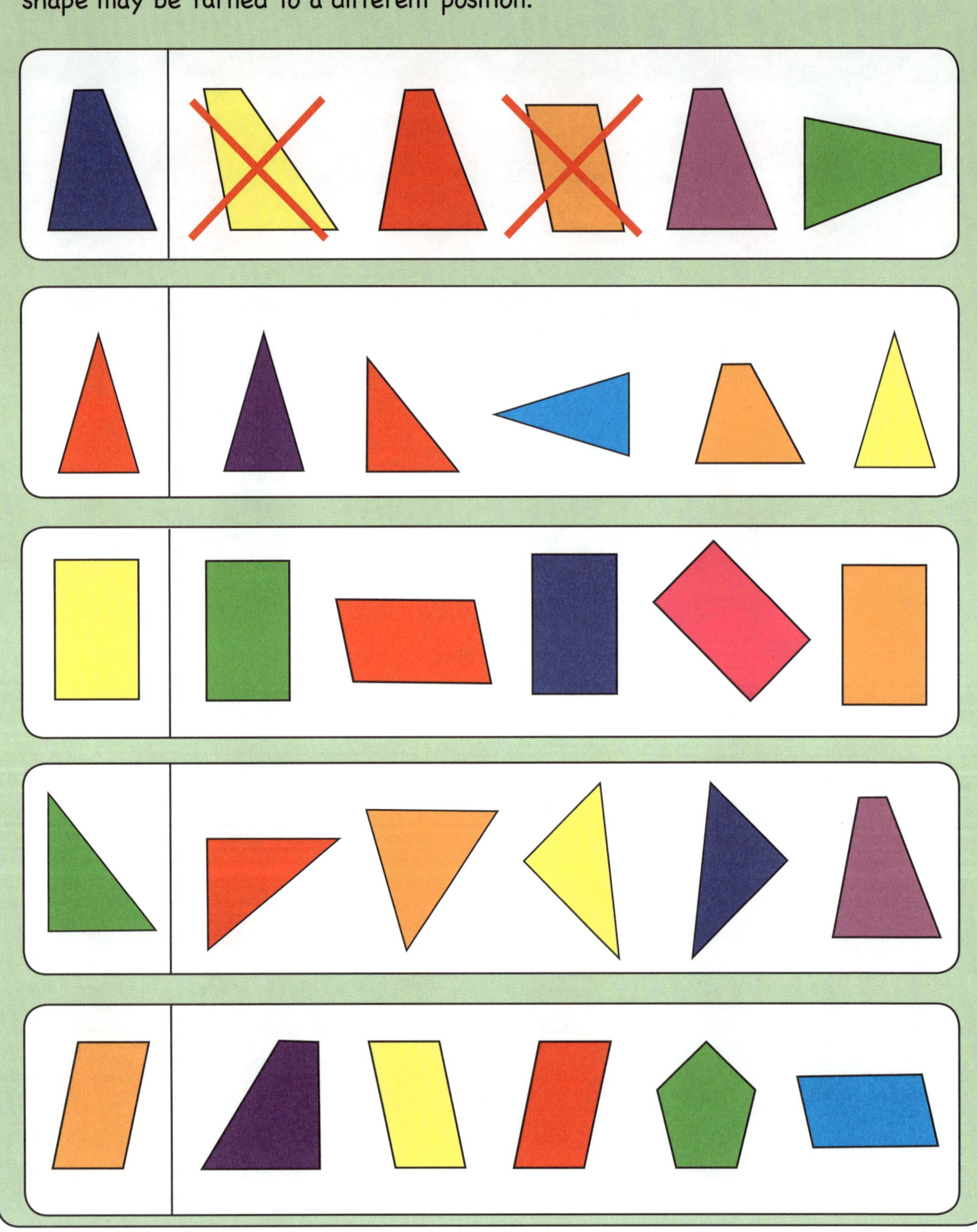

COMPARING SHAPES

Write "S" for same or "D" for different for color, shape, and size.

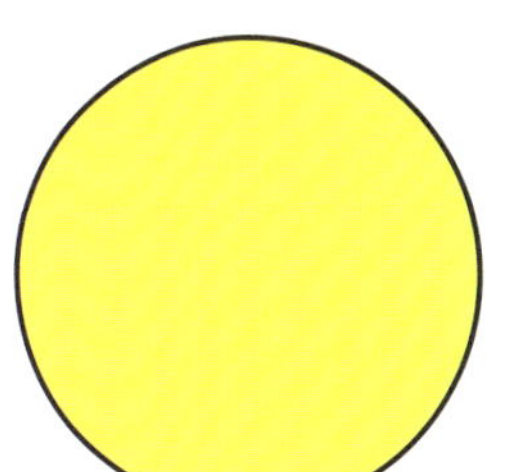
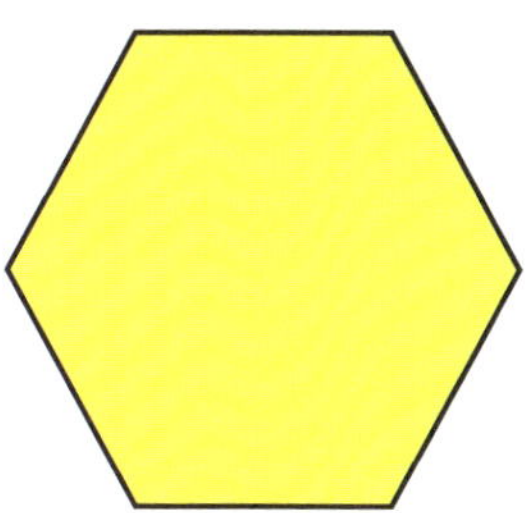

color S
shape D
size S

color ______
shape ______
size ______

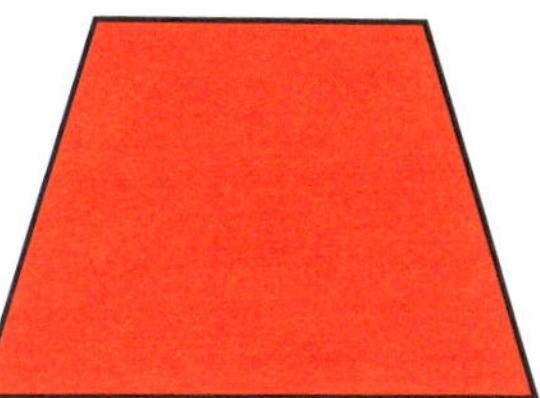

color ______
shape ______
size ______

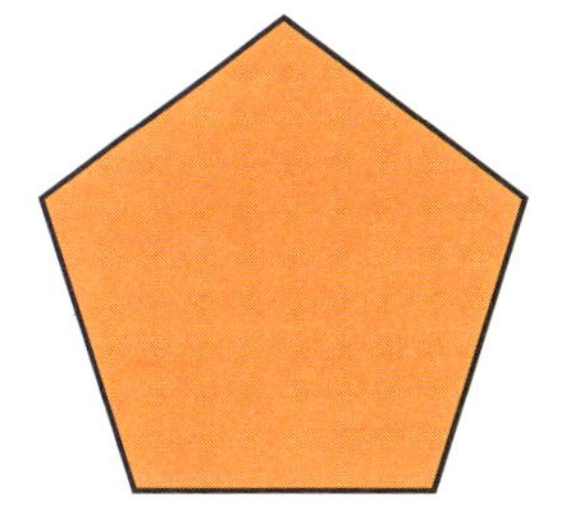
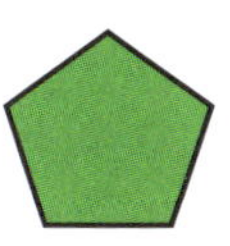

color ______
shape ______
size ______

color ______
shape ______
size ______

COMPARING SHAPES

Use the words from the WORD BOX to complete each sentence that describes how the shapes are ALIKE and DIFFERENT.

WORD BOX
color, circle, green, hexagon, orange, parallelogram, pentagon, rectangle, red, shape, size, small, square, trapezoids

Both the ____________ and the ______________ are ____________,

but their _____________ and ____________ are different.

Both the _________________ and the ____________________ are

__________ and ____________, but their ____________ is different.

Both polygons are _________________, but their _______________

and ________________ are different.

Both the _________________ and the ____________________ are

__________ and ____________, but their ____________ is different.

DRAWING A DIFFERENT SHAPE

In each box draw and color a polygon to fit the directions.

EXAMPLE

Draw and color a polygon that has the same size, but different shape and color.

Draw and color a polygon that has the same color, but different size and shape.

Draw and color a polygon that has the same shape, but a different size and color.

Draw and color a polygon that has the same size, but a different shape and color.

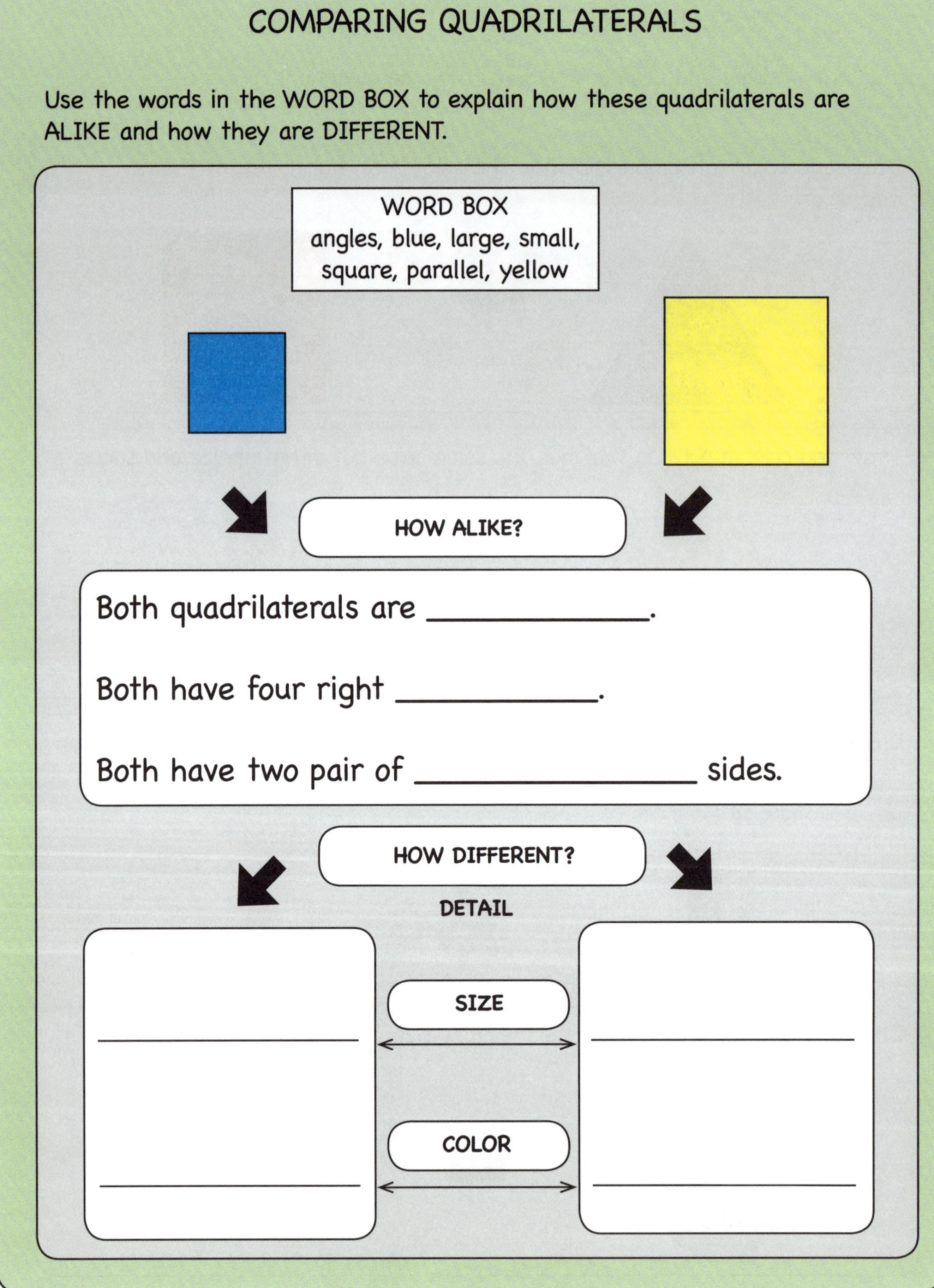
COMPARING QUADRILATERALS
Use the words in the WORD BOX to explain how these quadrilaterals are ALIKE and how they are DIFFERENT.
WORD BOX
angles, blue, large, small, square, parallel, yellow
HOW ALIKE?
Both quadrilaterals are ____________.
Both have four right ____________.
Both have two pair of ______________ sides.
HOW DIFFERENT?
DETAIL
SIZE
COLOR

DIVIDING SHAPES INTO TWO EQUAL PARTS

The colored shapes below are the same size. Color the blank shape to show these two equal parts.

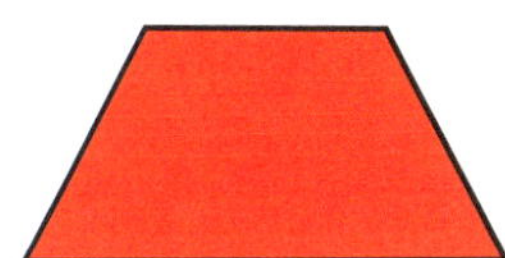   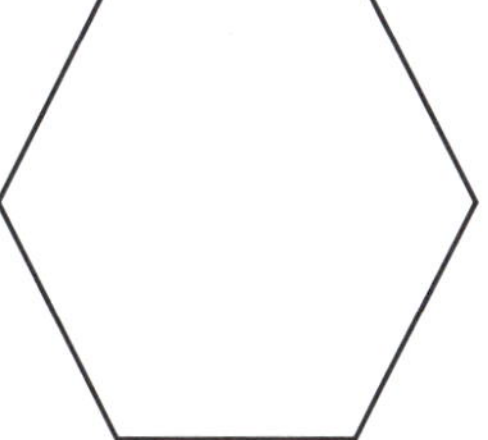

Each of these squares is divided into two equal parts called halves. One half is written 1/2.

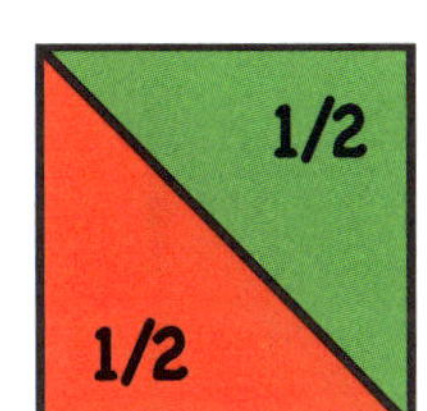

Show other ways that these squares can be divided into two equal parts. Color one half red and the other half green.

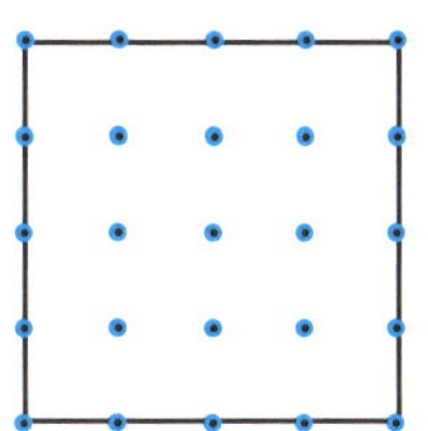 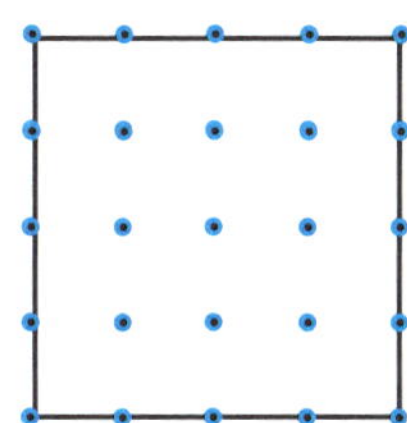

Divide each of the polygons into two equal parts. Color one half red and the other half green. Write 1/2 on each half.

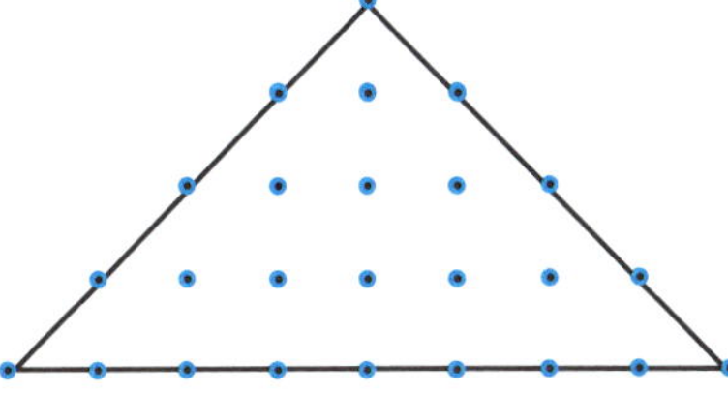 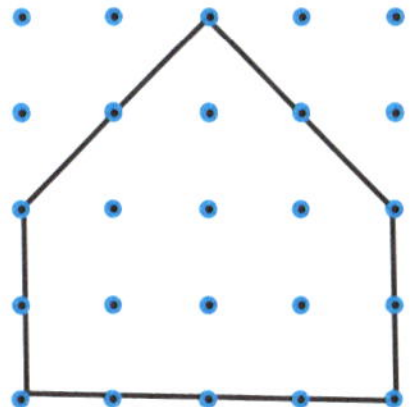 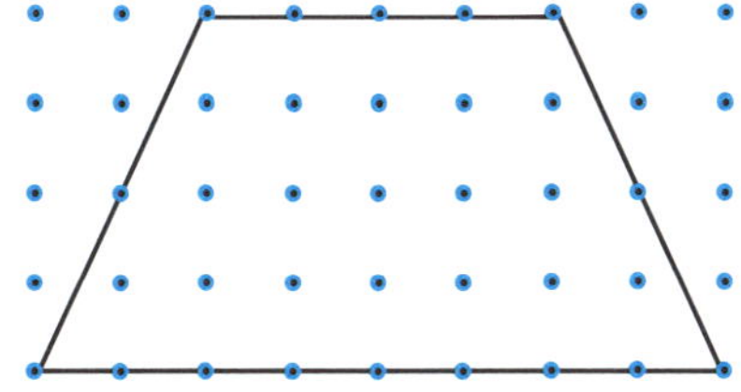

Show two ways you can divide each pair of shapes into halves. Color one half red and the other half green. Write 1/2 on each half.

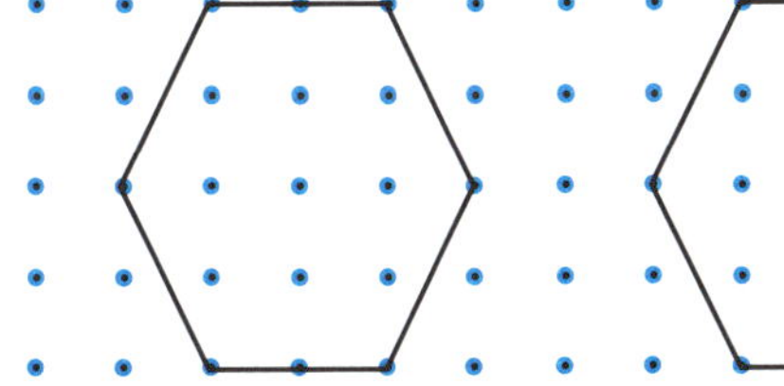 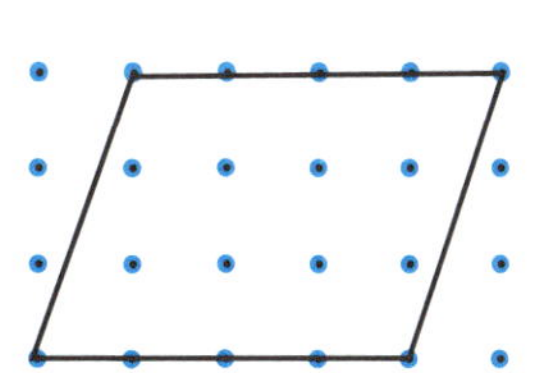 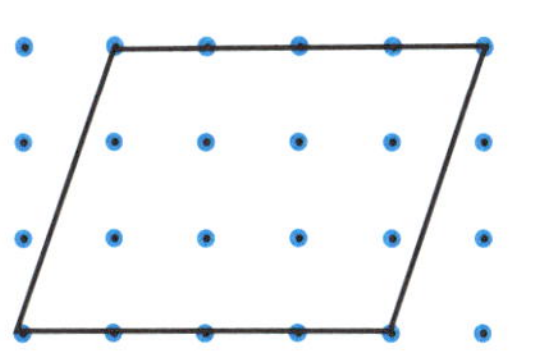

DIVIDING SHAPES INTO THREE EQUAL PARTS

The colored shapes below are the same size. Color the blank shape to show these three equal parts.

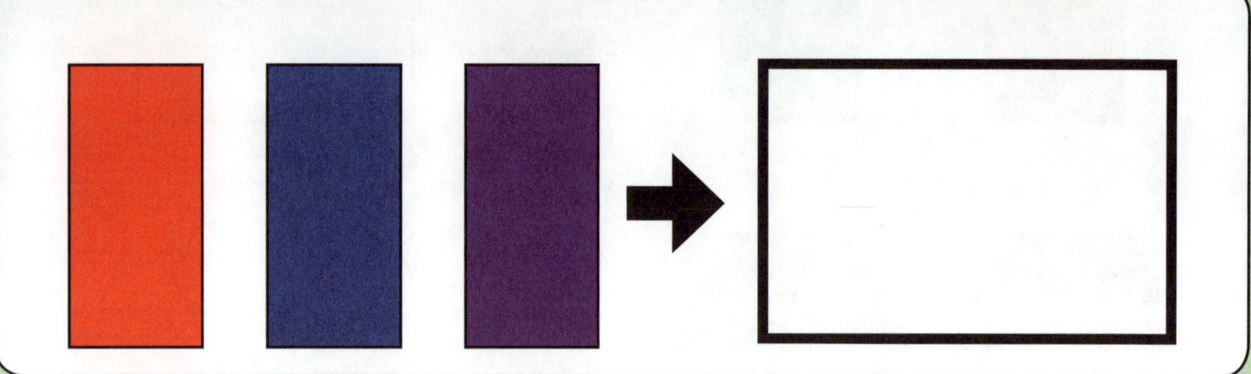

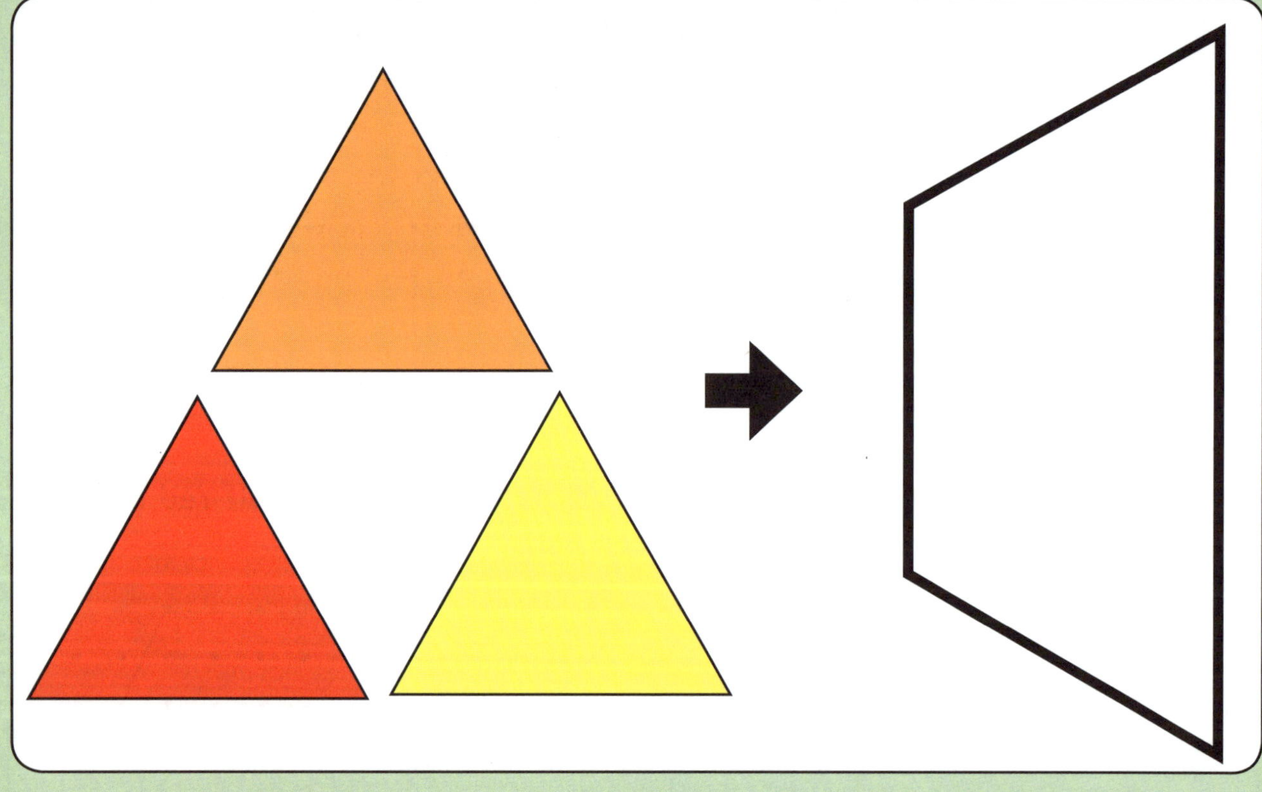

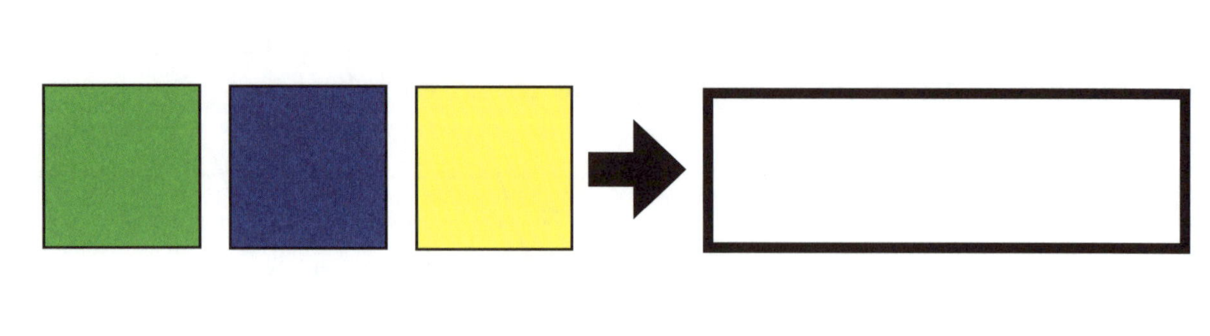

DIVIDING SHAPES INTO THREE EQUAL PARTS

Each of these squares is divided into three equal parts called thirds.

Each square is one-third blue, one-third green, and one-third red. One-third is written 1/3.

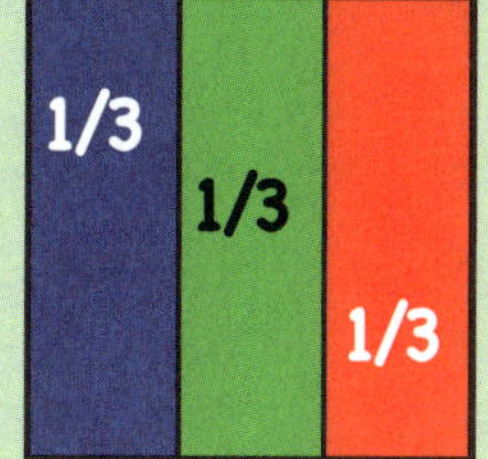

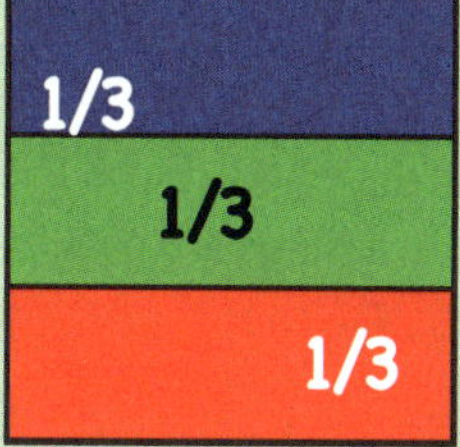

Divide the rectangles into thirds. Color one-third blue, one-third green, and one-third red. Write 1/3 on each third.

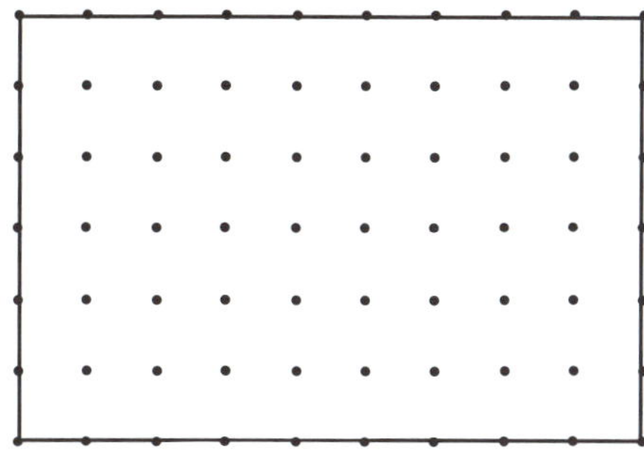

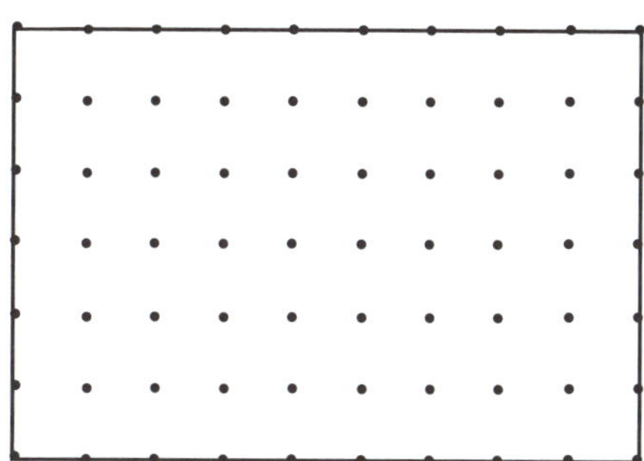

Divide the rectangles into thirds. Color one-third blue, one-third green, and one-third red. Write 1/3 on each third.

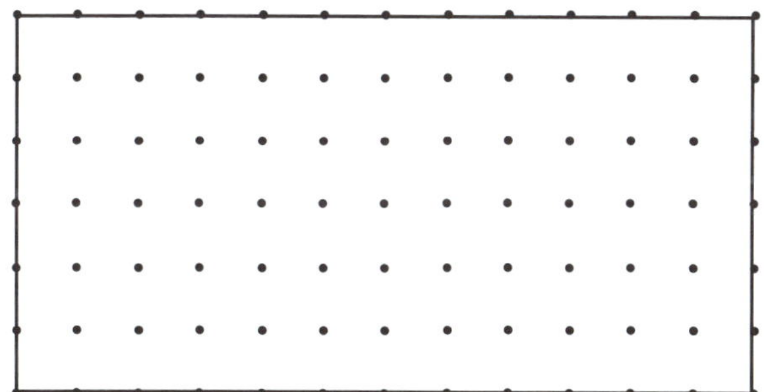

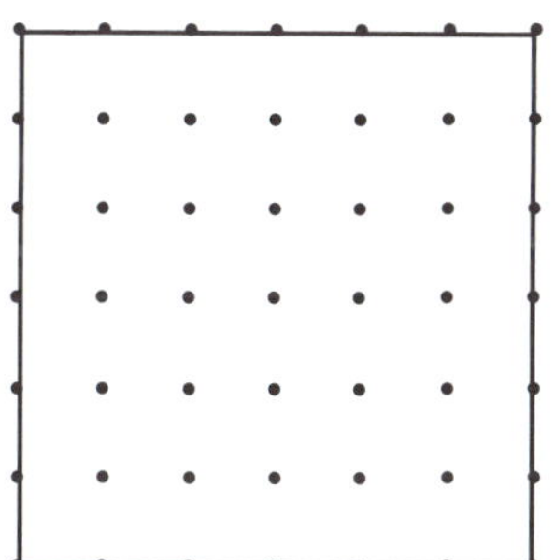

Divide the trapezoid into thirds by copying the triangle onto the trapezoid. Color one-third blue, one-third green, and one-third red. Write 1/3 on each third.

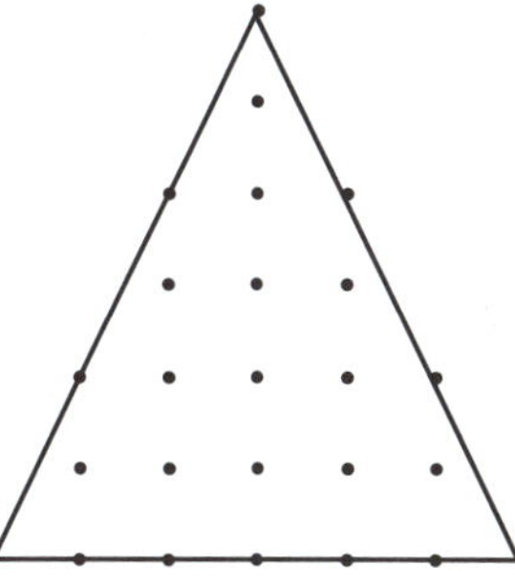

DIVIDING SHAPES INTO FOUR EQUAL PARTS

Each of these squares is divided into four equal parts called fourths.

Each square is one-fourth red, one-fourth orange, one-fourth yellow, and one-fourth green. One-fourth is written 1/4.

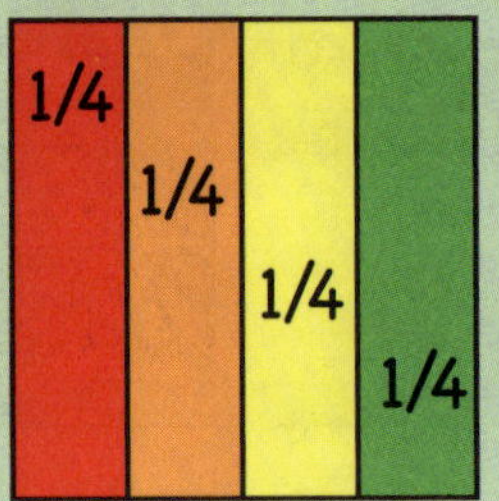

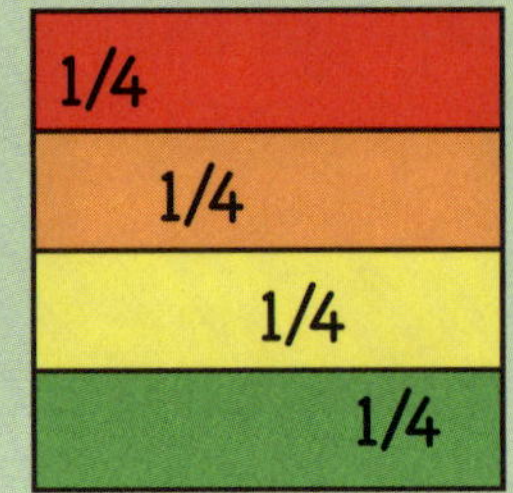

Divide the rectangles into fourths. Color one-fourth red, one-fourth orange, one-fourth yellow, and one-fourth green. Write 1/4 on each fourth.

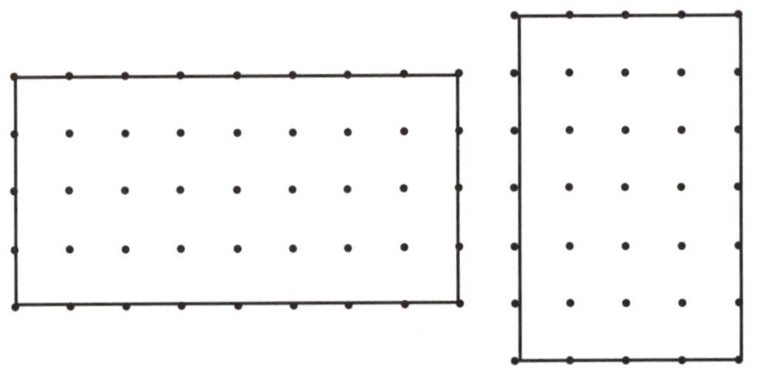

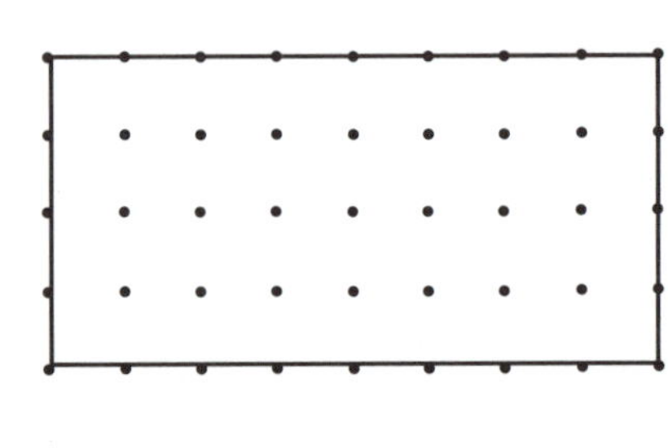

Divide the shapes into fourths. Color one-fourth red, one-fourth orange, one-fourth yellow, and one-fourth green. Write 1/4 on each fourth.

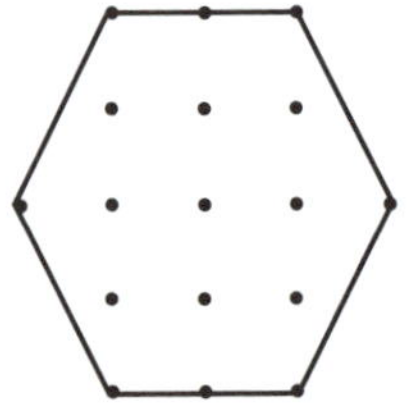

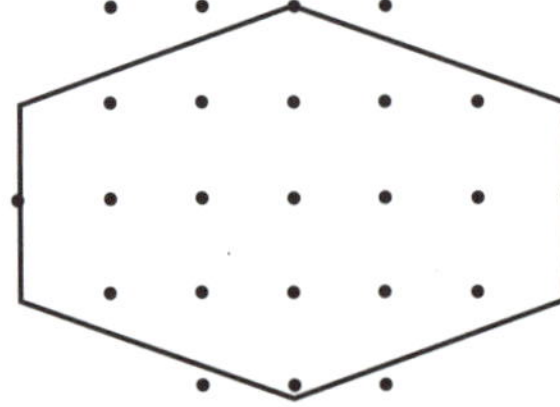

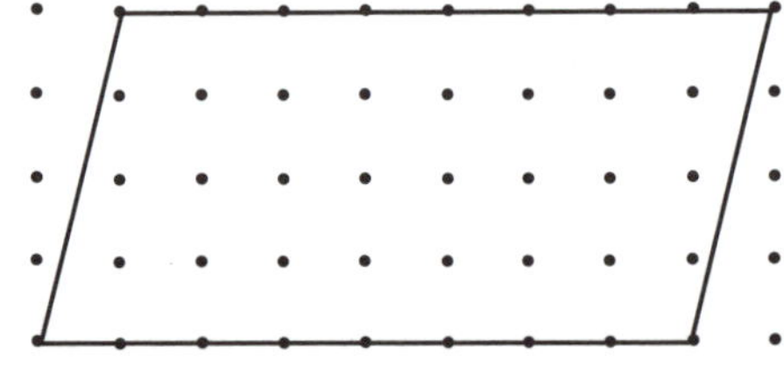

Draw a rectangle around one-half of the candy bar.

Draw a rectangle around one-fourth of the candy bar.

COUNTING PARTS OF A RECTANGLE

When you divide rectangles or squares into equal squares, you can count the parts it contains.

Trace eight small, equal squares. Color one-half of them red and one-half of them green.

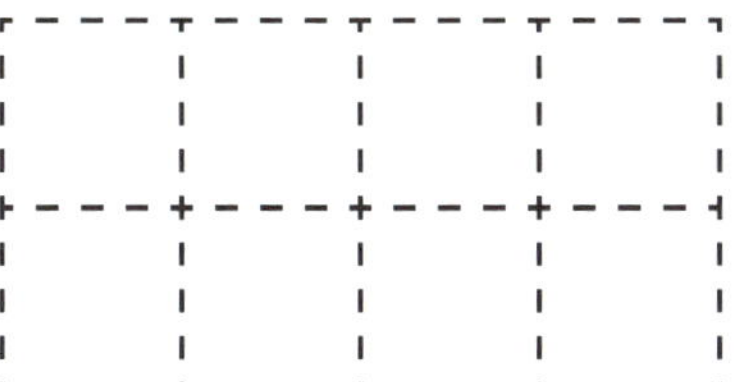

Trace twelve small, equal squares. Color one-third of them blue, one-third of them green, and one-third of them red.

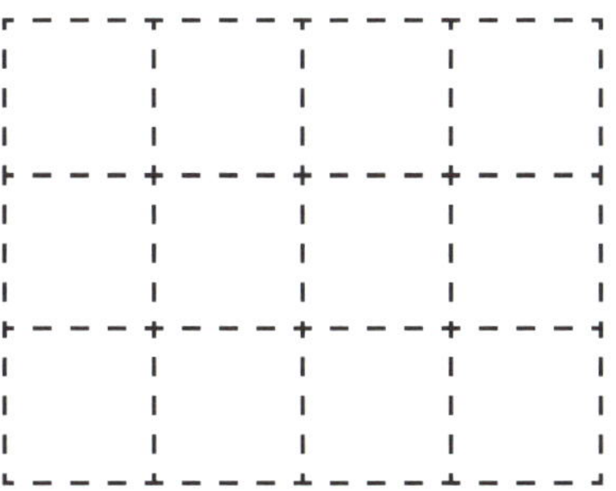

Trace nine small, equal squares. Color one-third of them blue, one-third of them green, and one-third of them red.

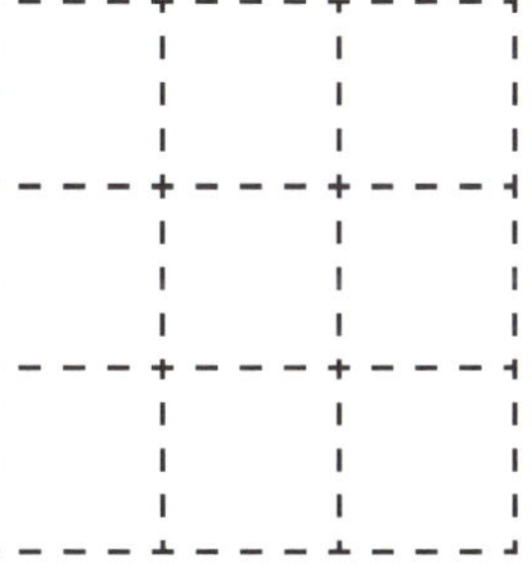

Trace sixteen small, equal squares. Color one-fourth of them red, one-fourth of them orange, one-fourth of them yellow, and one-fourth of them green.

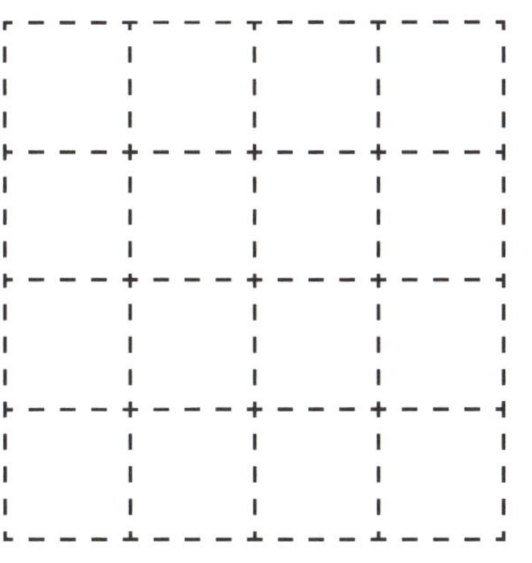

CHAPTER FOUR

RECOGNIZING PATTERNS

WHAT COMES NEXT?

Color the last box or boxes to continue each sequence (pattern).

These sequences are made by adding or subtracting a square. Color the next stack to continue the sequence.

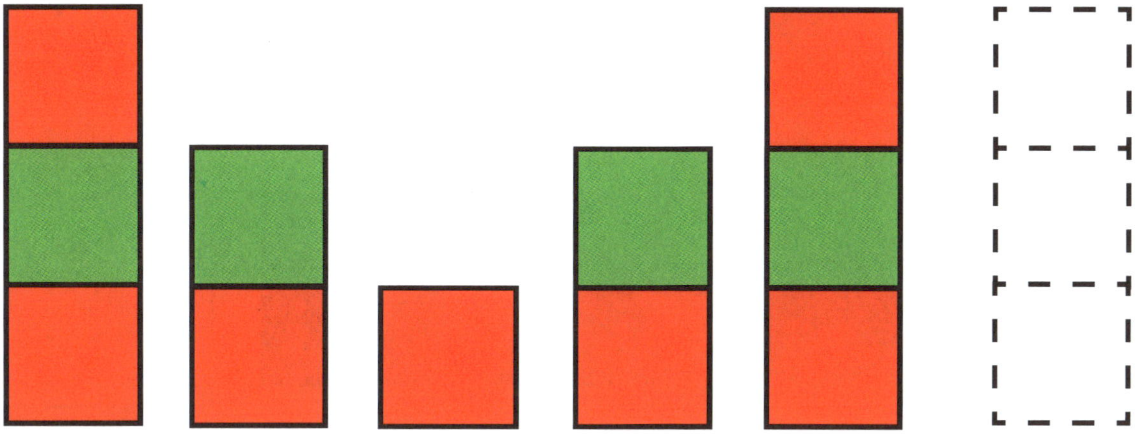

WHAT COMES NEXT?

Circle the shape that comes next.

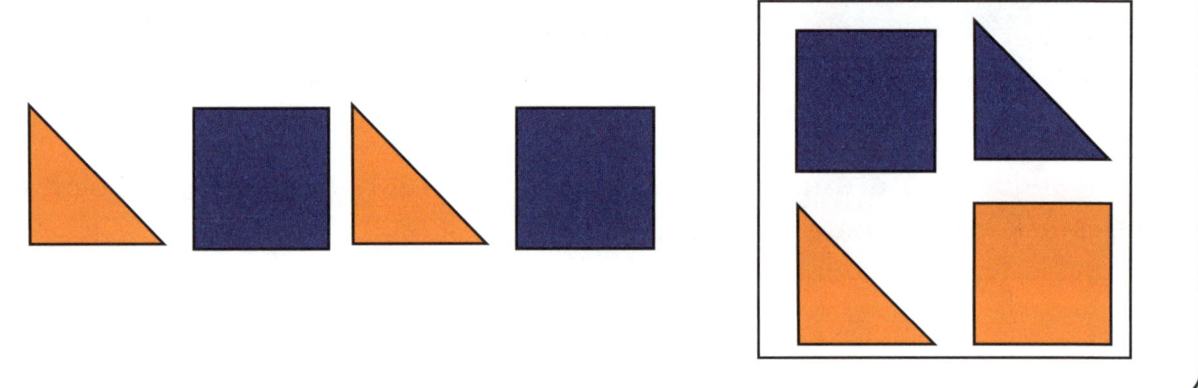

Draw and color the shape that continues the sequence.

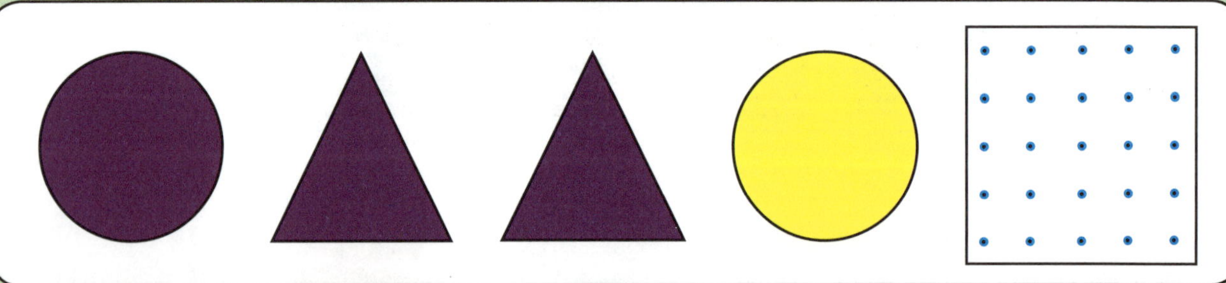

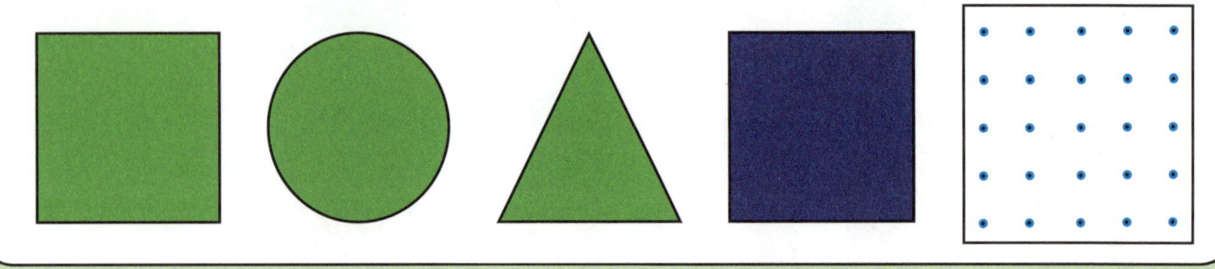

DRAWING A SEQUENCE OF POLYGONS

Count the number of sides of each of these polygons. Then draw them on the diagram to show the increasing number of sides.

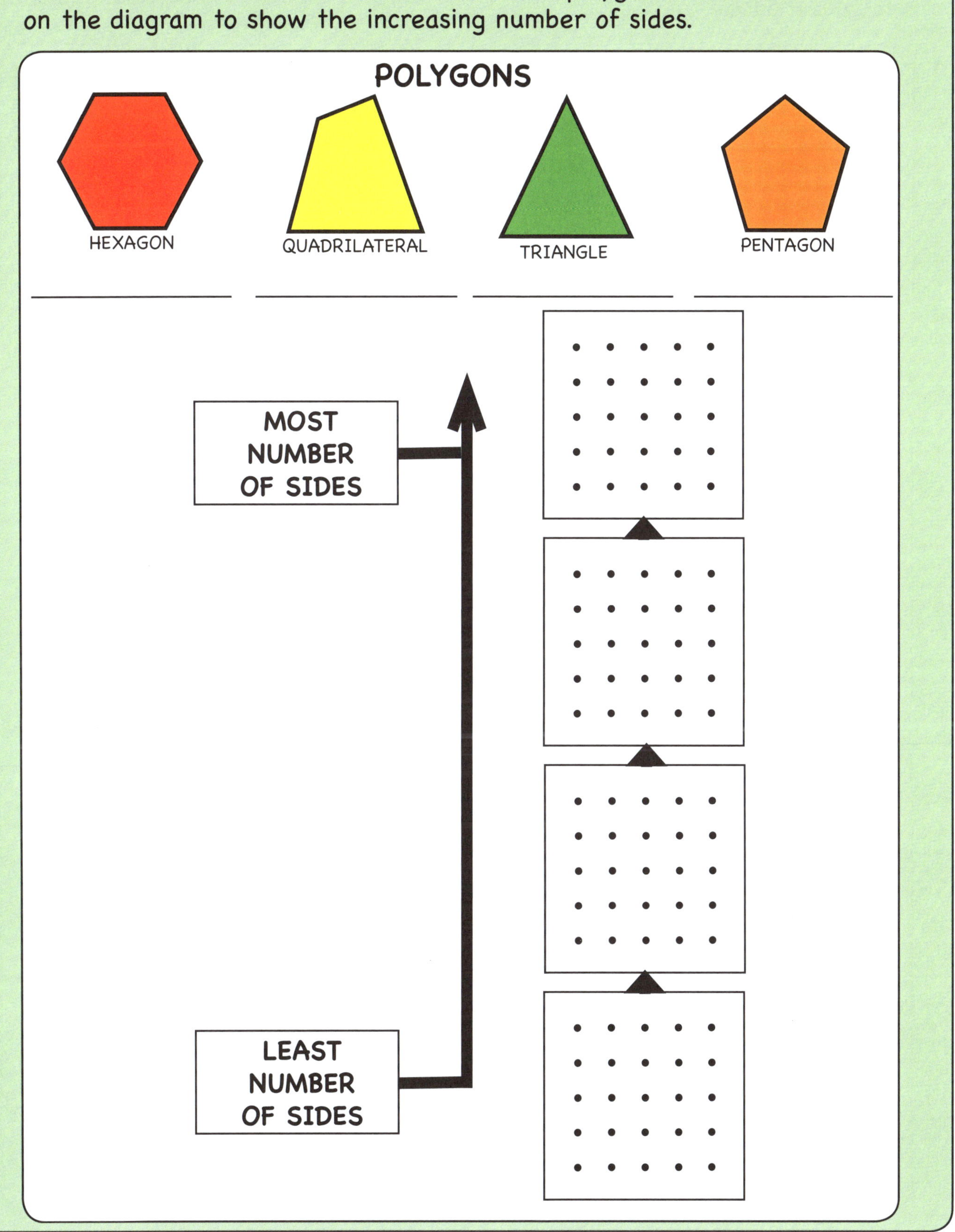

DESCRIBING A SEQUENCE OF SHAPES

Use the words in the WORD BOX to write a sentence that describes each sequence.

WORD BOX
blue, red, sequence, yellow

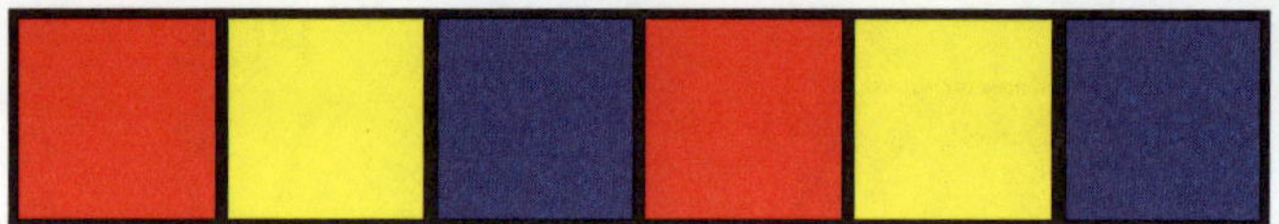

DESCRIPTION

This ________________ of squares is red, yellow, blue,

________________, ________________, ________________.

WORD BOX
circle, green, orange, square

DESCRIPTION

____

____

____

WORD BOX
large, purple, red, small, triangle

DESCRIPTION

____

____

____

____

SHOWING A SEQUENCE OF FRACTIONS

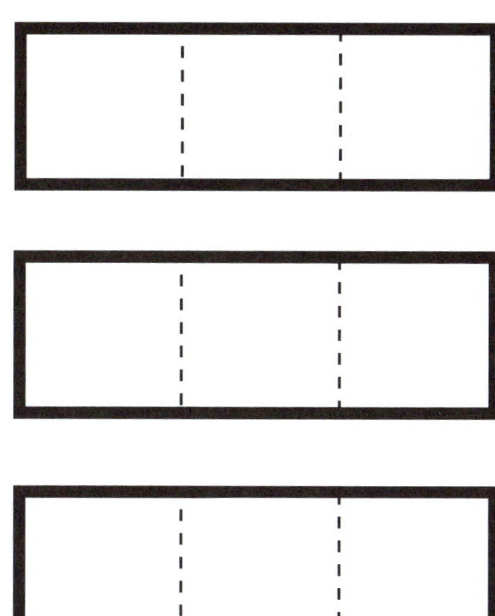

Color one-third of the rectangle green. Mark the green part as 1/3 of the rectangle.

Color two-thirds of the rectangle green. Mark each green square as 1/3 of the rectangle. The green part is 2/3 of the rectangle.

Color the boxes green to show the next fraction in the sequence. Mark each green square as the fraction 1/3. The rectangle is 3/3 green.

Color one-fourth of the rectangle yellow. Mark the yellow part as 1/4 of the rectangle.

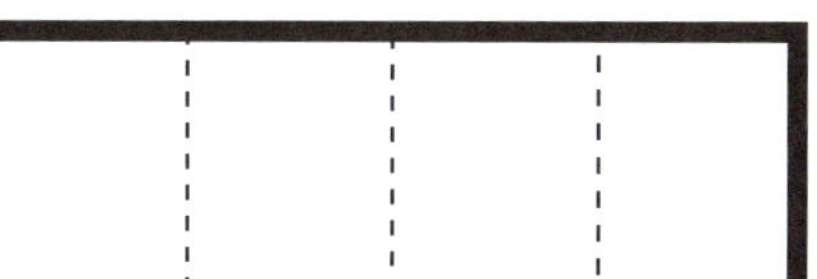

Color two-fourths of the rectangle yellow. Mark each yellow part as 1/4 of the rectangle. The yellow part is 2/4 of the rectangle.

Color three-fourths of the rectangle yellow. Mark each yellow part as 1/4 of the rectangle. The yellow part is 3/4 of the rectangle.

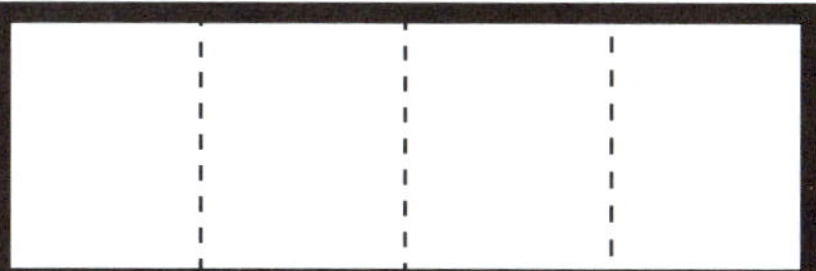

Color the boxes yellow to show the next fraction in the sequence. Mark each yellow square as the fraction 1/4. The rectangle is 4/4 yellow.

SHOWING A SEQUENCE OF FRACTIONS

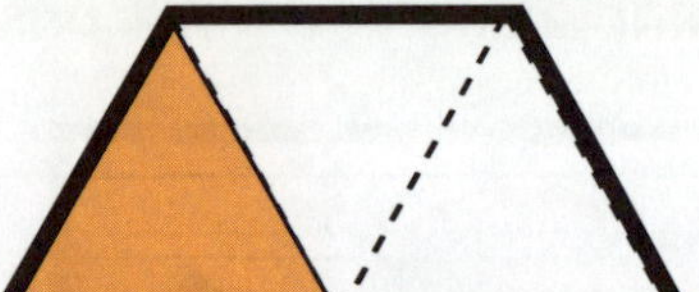

The orange part is ____________ of the trapezoid.

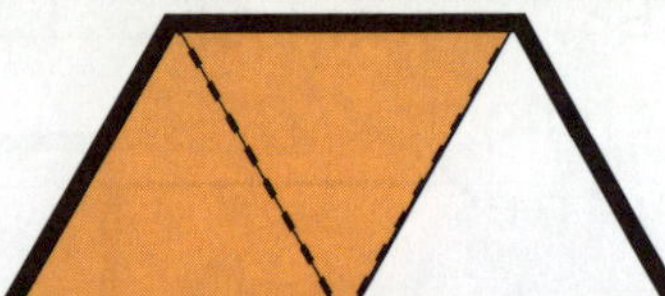

The orange part is ____________ of the trapezoid.

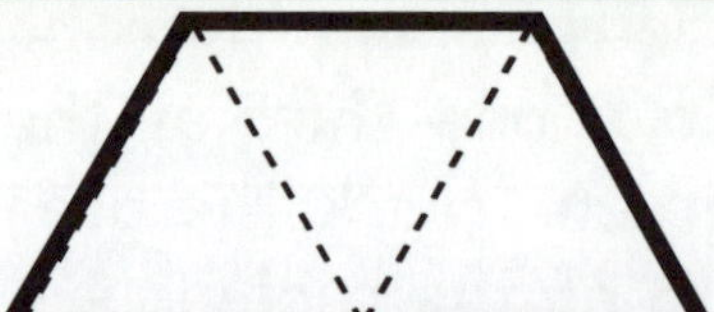

Color the triangles to show the next fraction in the sequence. Mark each part as a fraction.

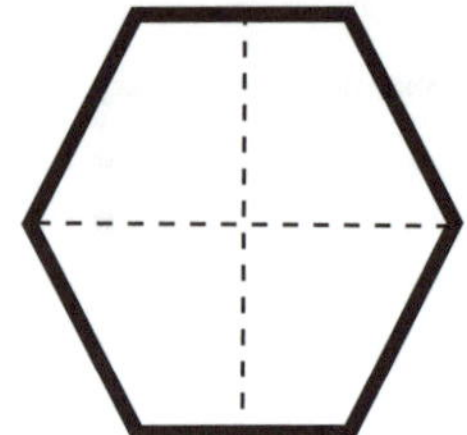

Color the hexagon one-fourth (1/4) blue.

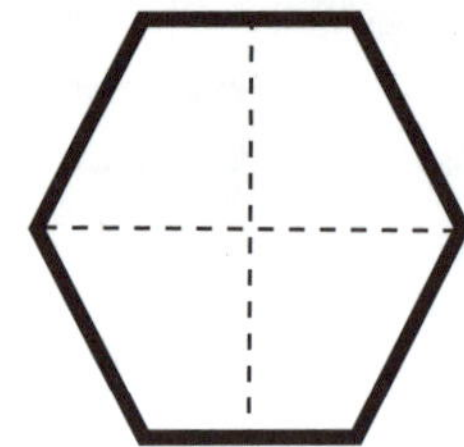

Color the hexagon two-fourths (2/4) blue.

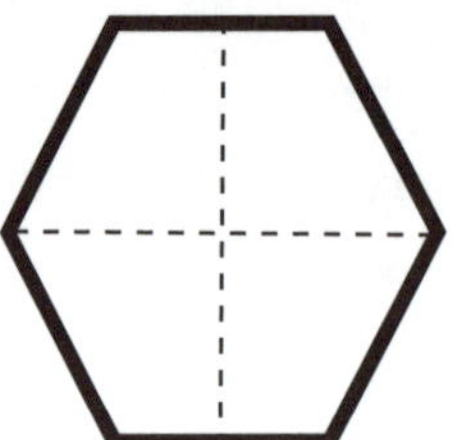

Color these hexagons to continue the sequence of fractions.

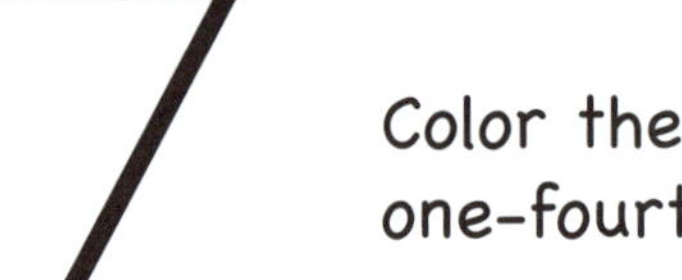

Color the first parallelogram one-fourth (1/4) red.

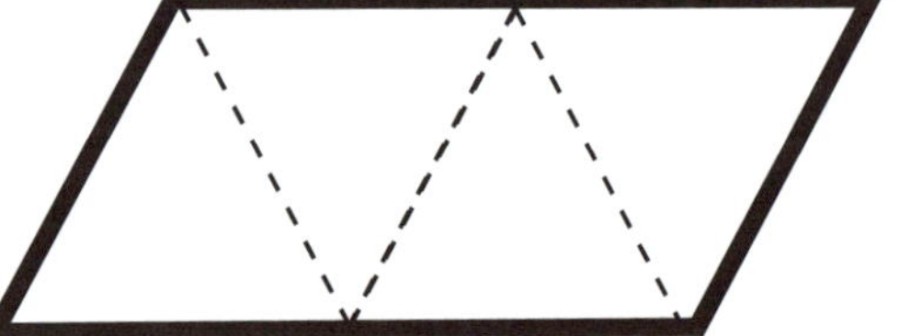

Color the second parallelogram two-fourths (2/4) red.

Color the third parallelogram to continue this series of fractions.

Color the fourth parallelogram to continue this series of fractions. Mark each part as a fraction.

TUMBLING

Circle the shape that shows how it will look as it tumbles to the next position.

EXAMPLE

DIRECTION OF TUMBLING

DIRECTION OF TUMBLING

DIRECTION OF TUMBLING

DIRECTION OF TUMBLING

TUMBLING

Color the shape to show how it will look as it tumbles to the next position.

DIRECTION OF TUMBLING

DIRECTION OF TUMBLING

DIRECTION OF TUMBLING

DIRECTION OF TUMBLING

DIRECTION OF TUMBLING

TUMBLING

Draw the shape that shows how it will look as it tumbles to the next position.

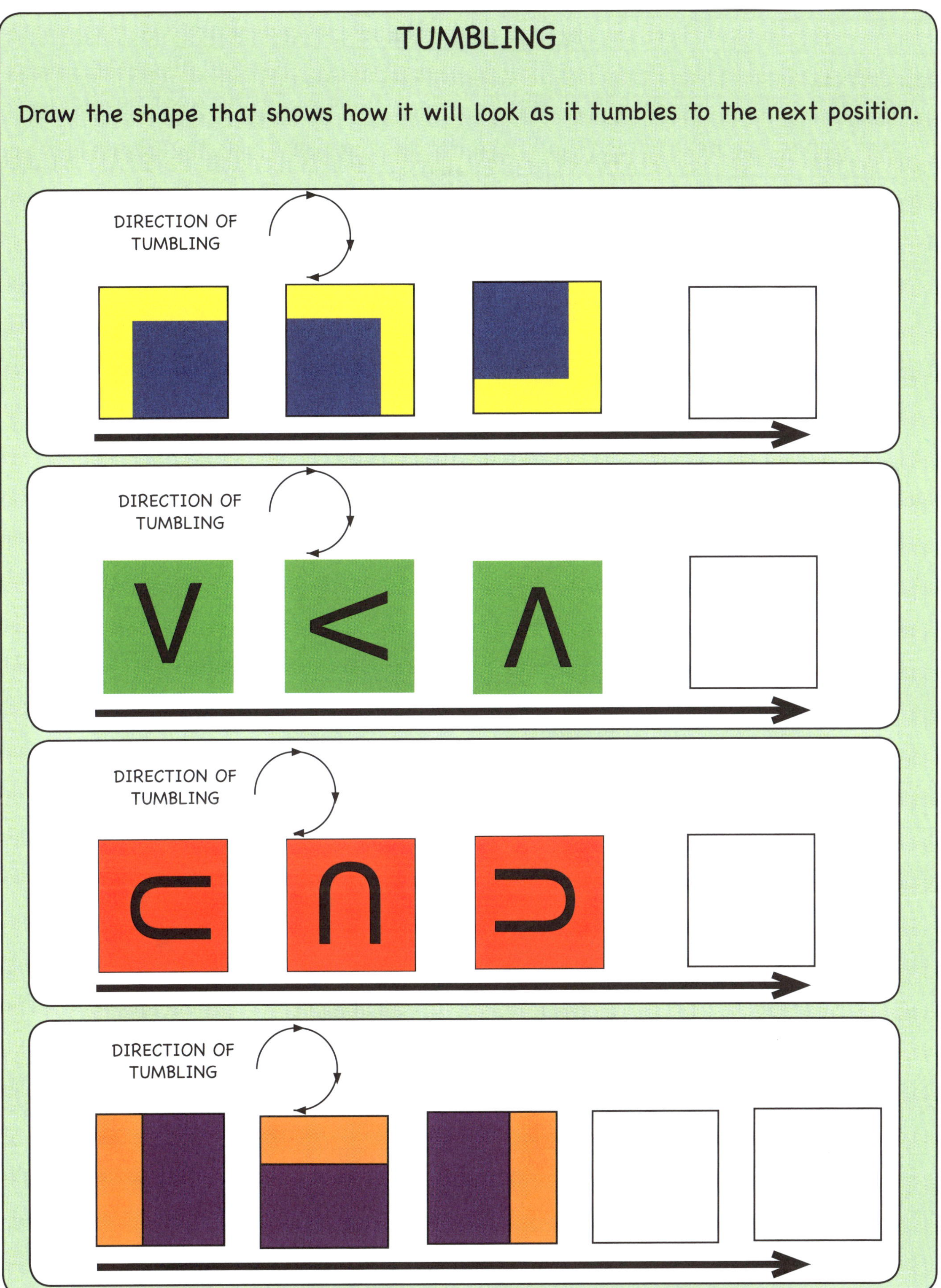

PAPER FOLDING

The shape on the left shows a sheet of paper with holes punched in it. The paper has been folded along the dotted line. How will the paper look when it is unfolded? Circle the correct answer.

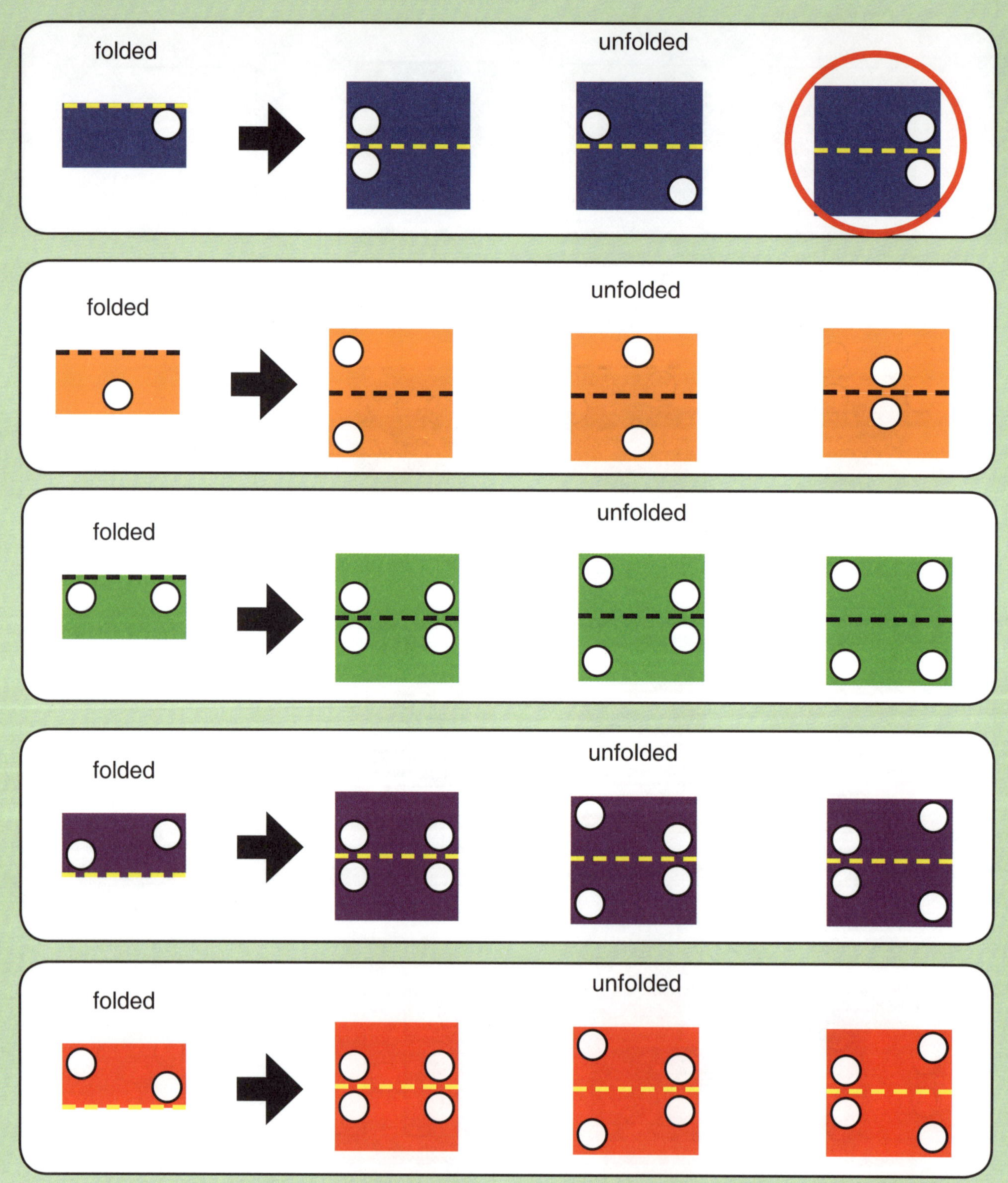

PAPER FOLDING

The shape on the left shows a sheet of paper with holes punched in it. How will the paper look when it is folded along the dotted line? Circle the correct answer.

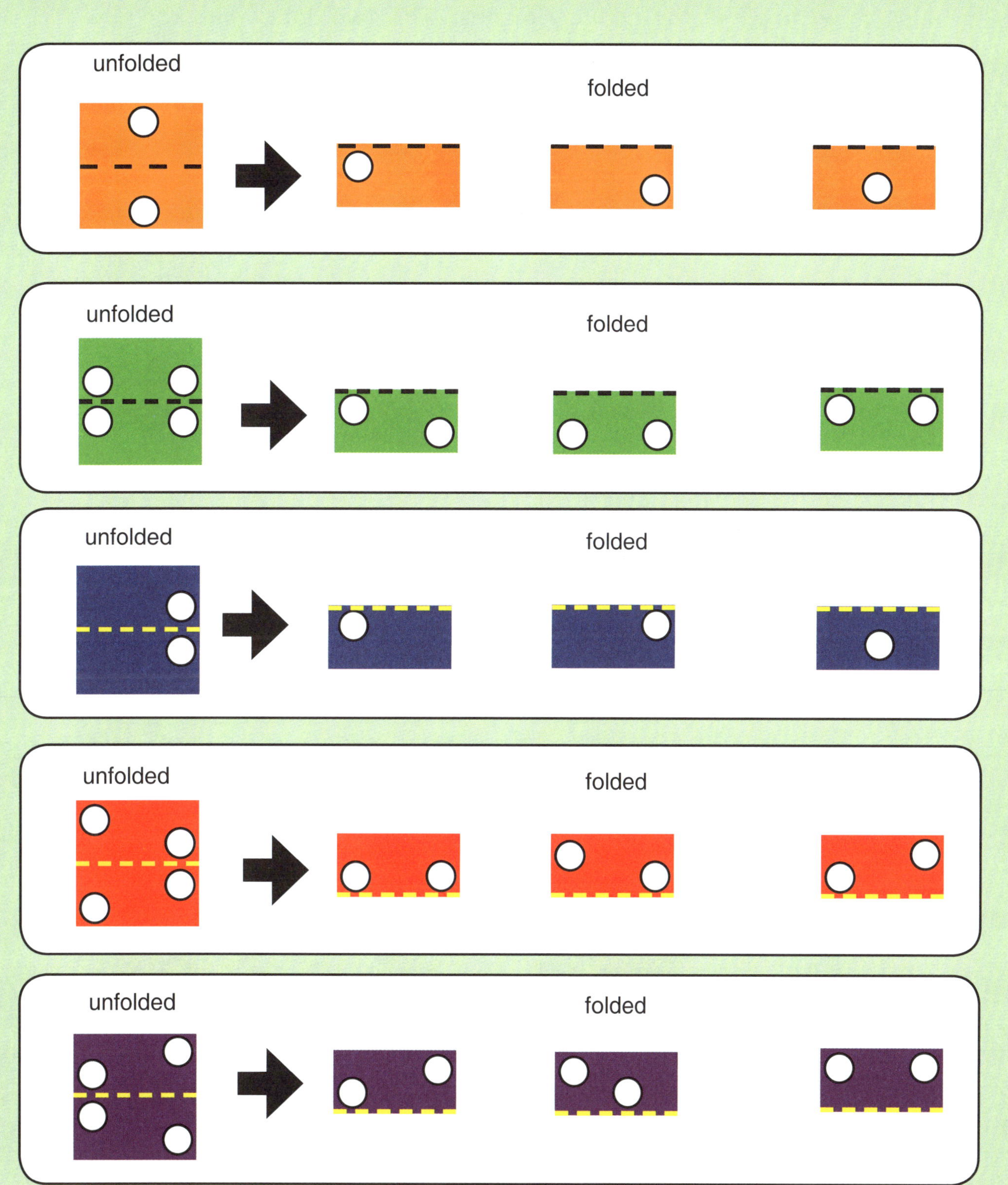

ANALOGIES WITH SHAPES

An ANALOGY is a comparison of two things.

The four shapes below show an analogy. To understand an analogy, it helps to write what the analogy means. The two dots stand for how the two shapes are changed. Four dots stand for the word LIKE.

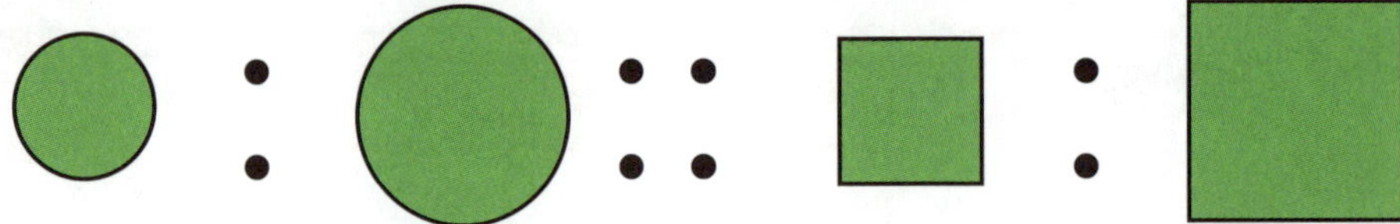

The green circle becomes larger LIKE the green square becomes larger.

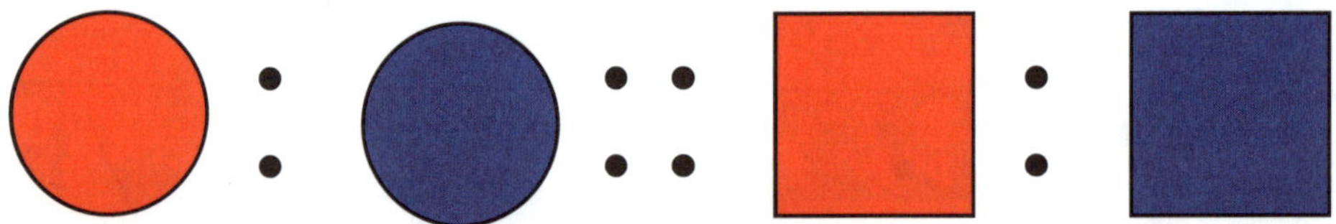

The red circle becomes blue LIKE the red square becomes blue.

The orange circle becomes ______________ LIKE the yellow square becomes______________.

The square changes ______________ and ______________ LIKE the circle changes ______________ and ______________.

ANALOGIES WITH SHAPES

Circle the shape that completes each analogy. Then explain the analogy to your partner or teacher.

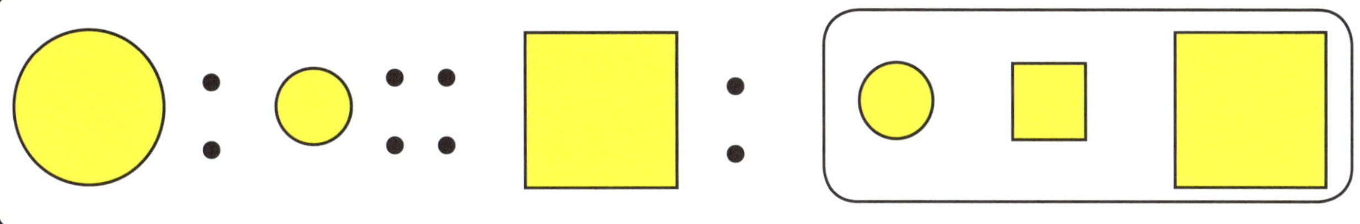

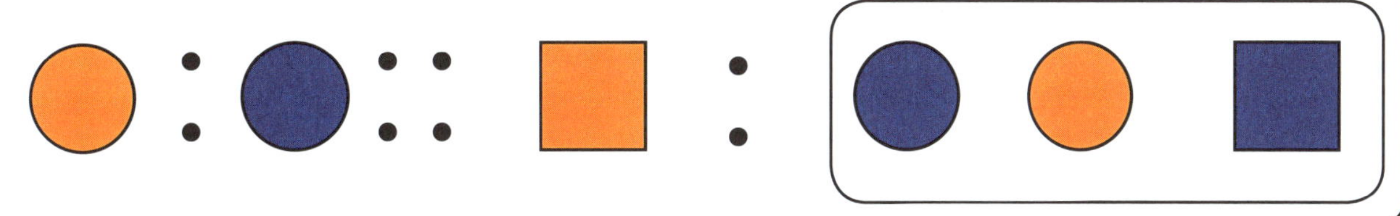

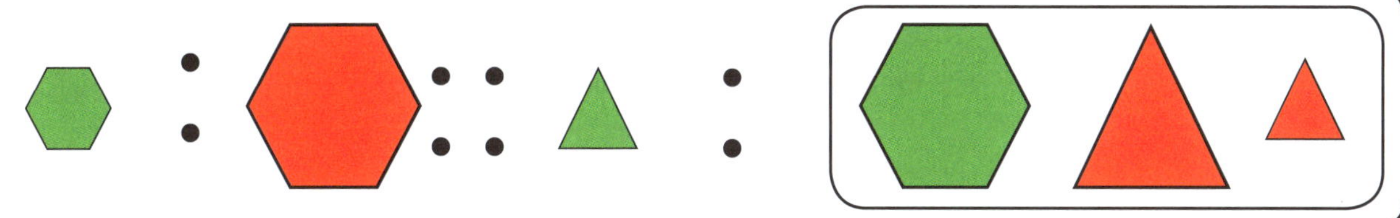

Some analogies show change in direction.

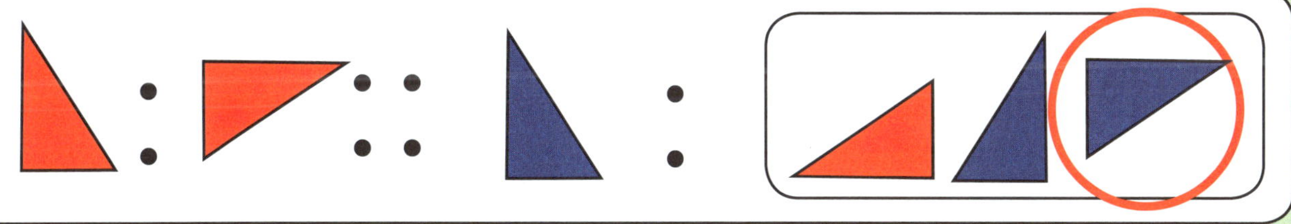

ANALOGIES WITH SHAPES

Some analogies show change in the number of parts.

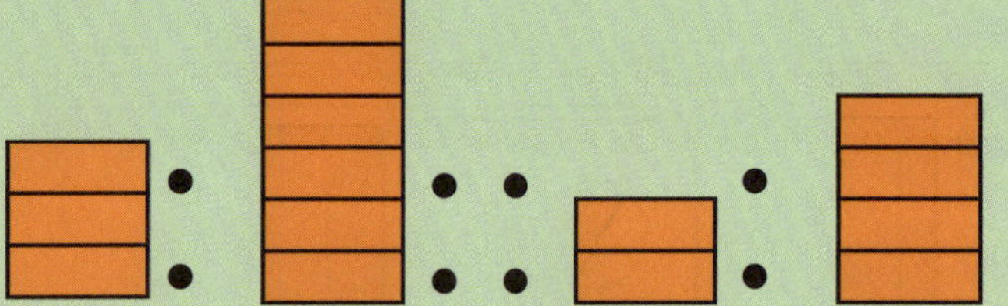

Three blocks double to become six blocks LIKE two blocks double to become four blocks.

Circle the shape that completes the analogy. Then explain the analogy to your partner or teacher.

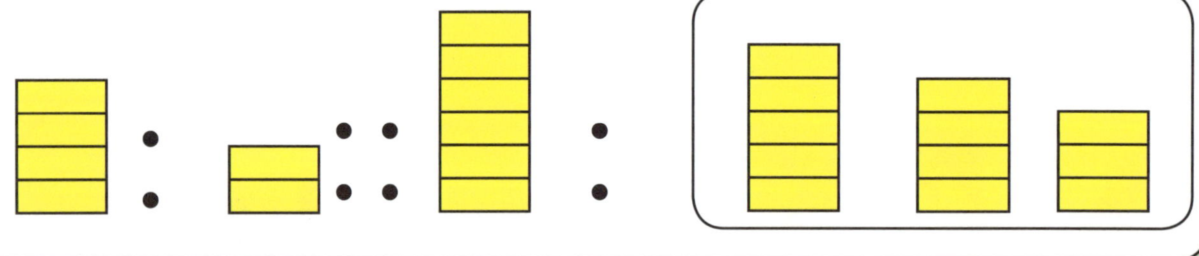

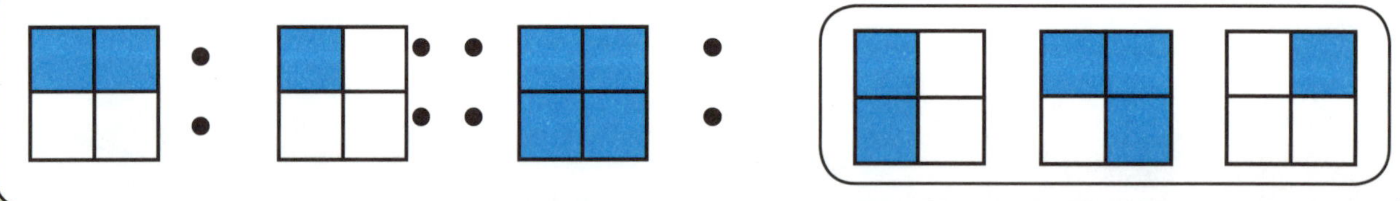

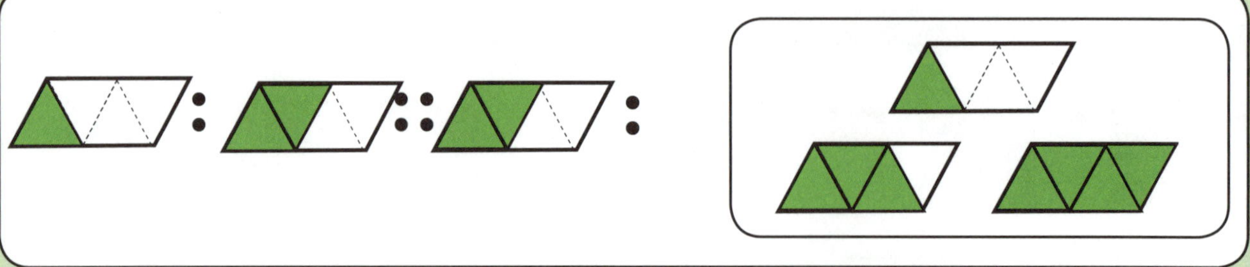

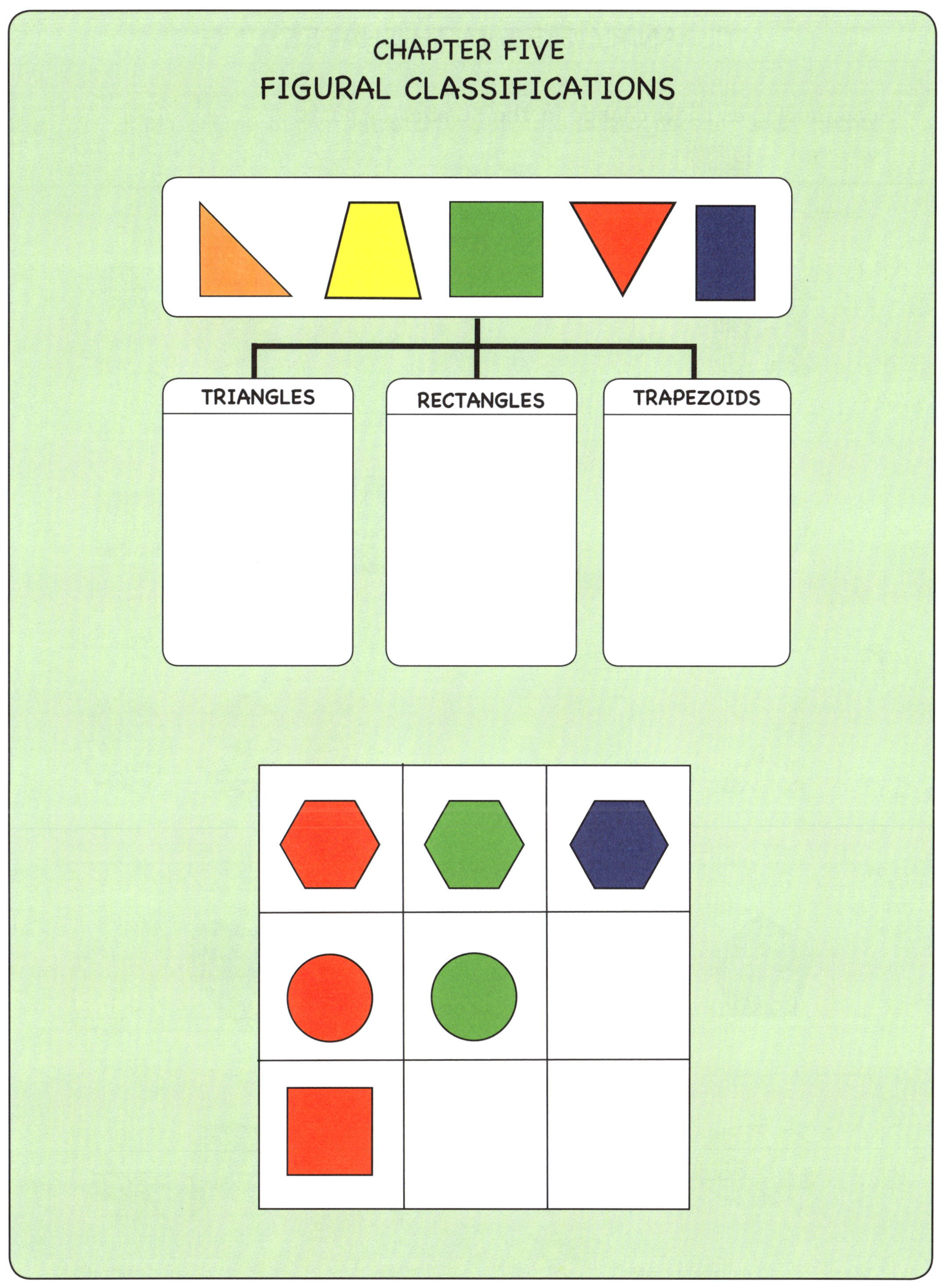
CHAPTER FIVE
FIGURAL CLASSIFICATIONS
TRIANGLES
RECTANGLES
TRAPEZOIDS

CLASSIFYING SHAPES - MATCHING

Draw a line from each shape on the left to the group on the right in which it belongs.

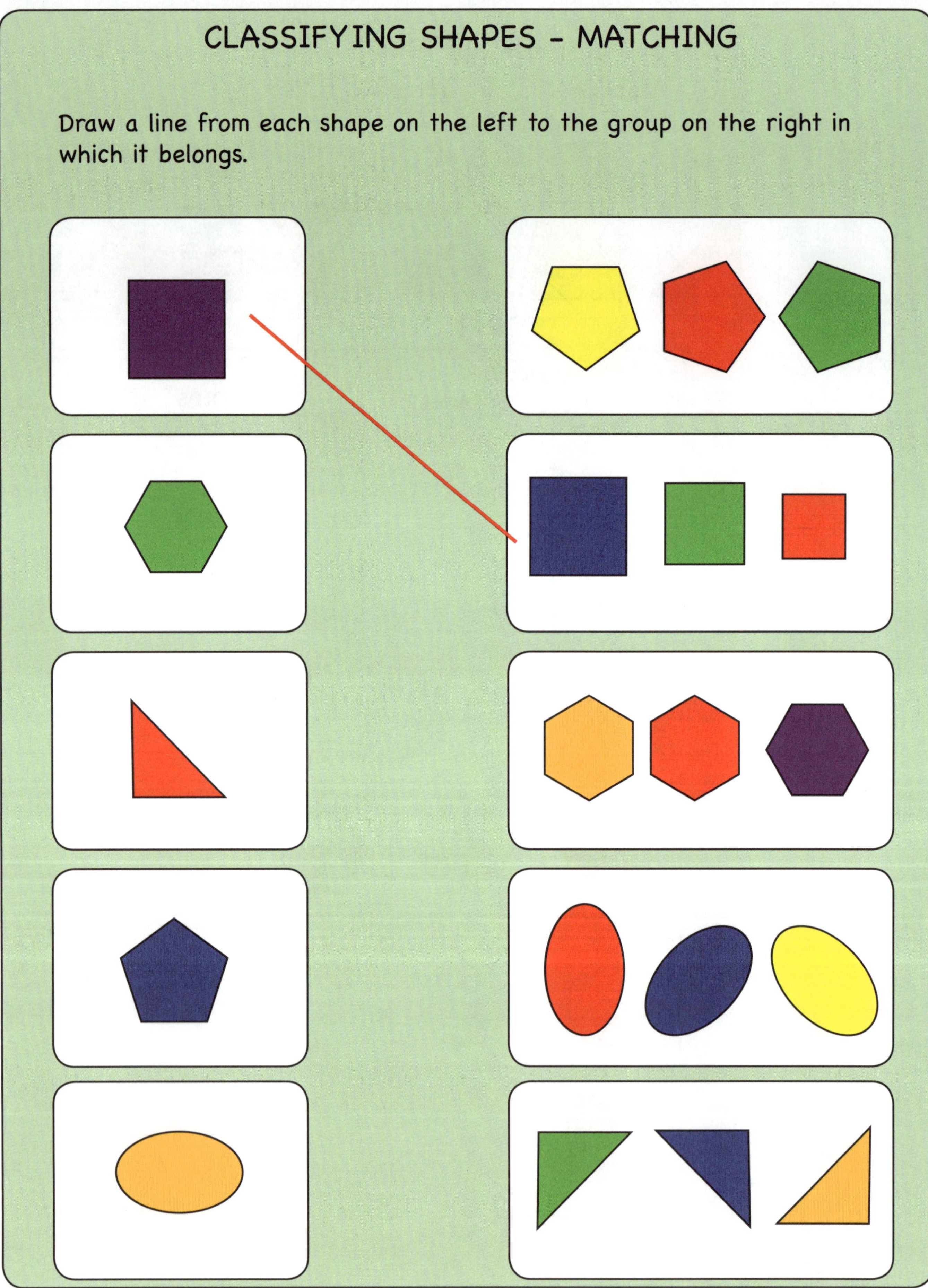

CLASSIFYING SHAPES – FIND THE EXCEPTION

In each row, cross out the shape that does not belong to the class.

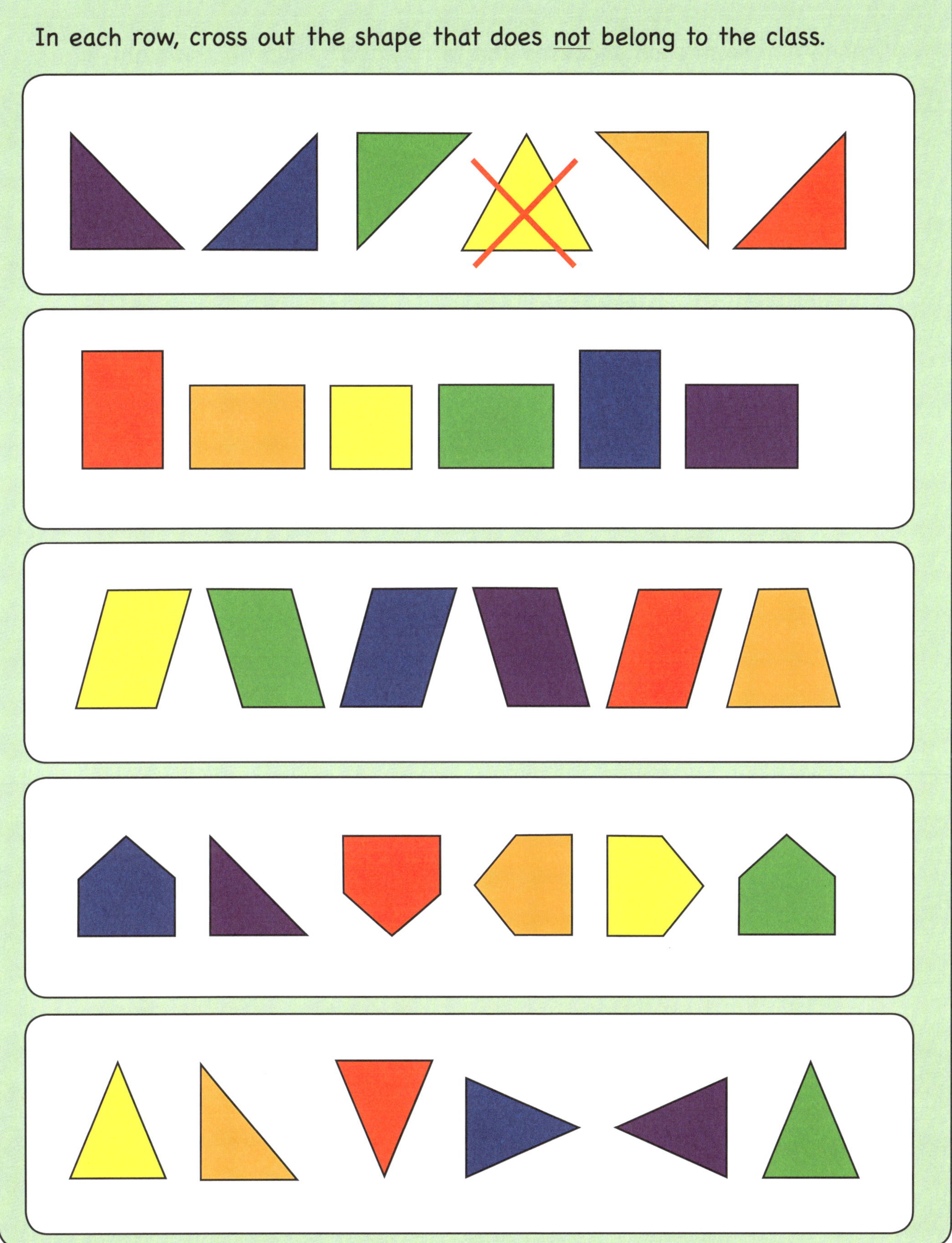

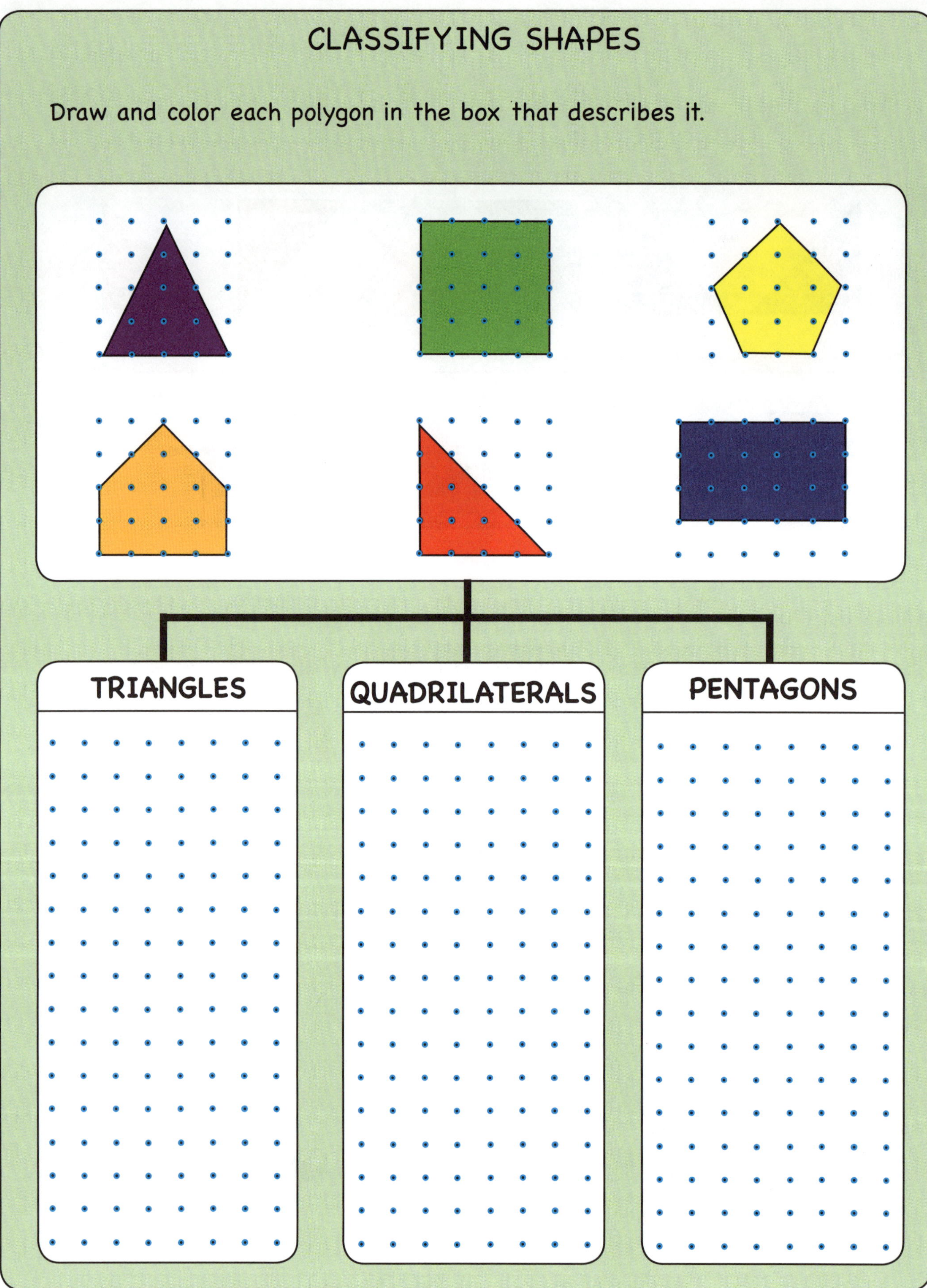
CLASSIFYING SHAPES
Draw and color each polygon in the box that describes it.
TRIANGLES
QUADRILATERALS
PENTAGONS

CLASSIFYING QUADRILATERALS

Draw and color each quadrilateral in the box that describes it. Some may belong in more than one box.

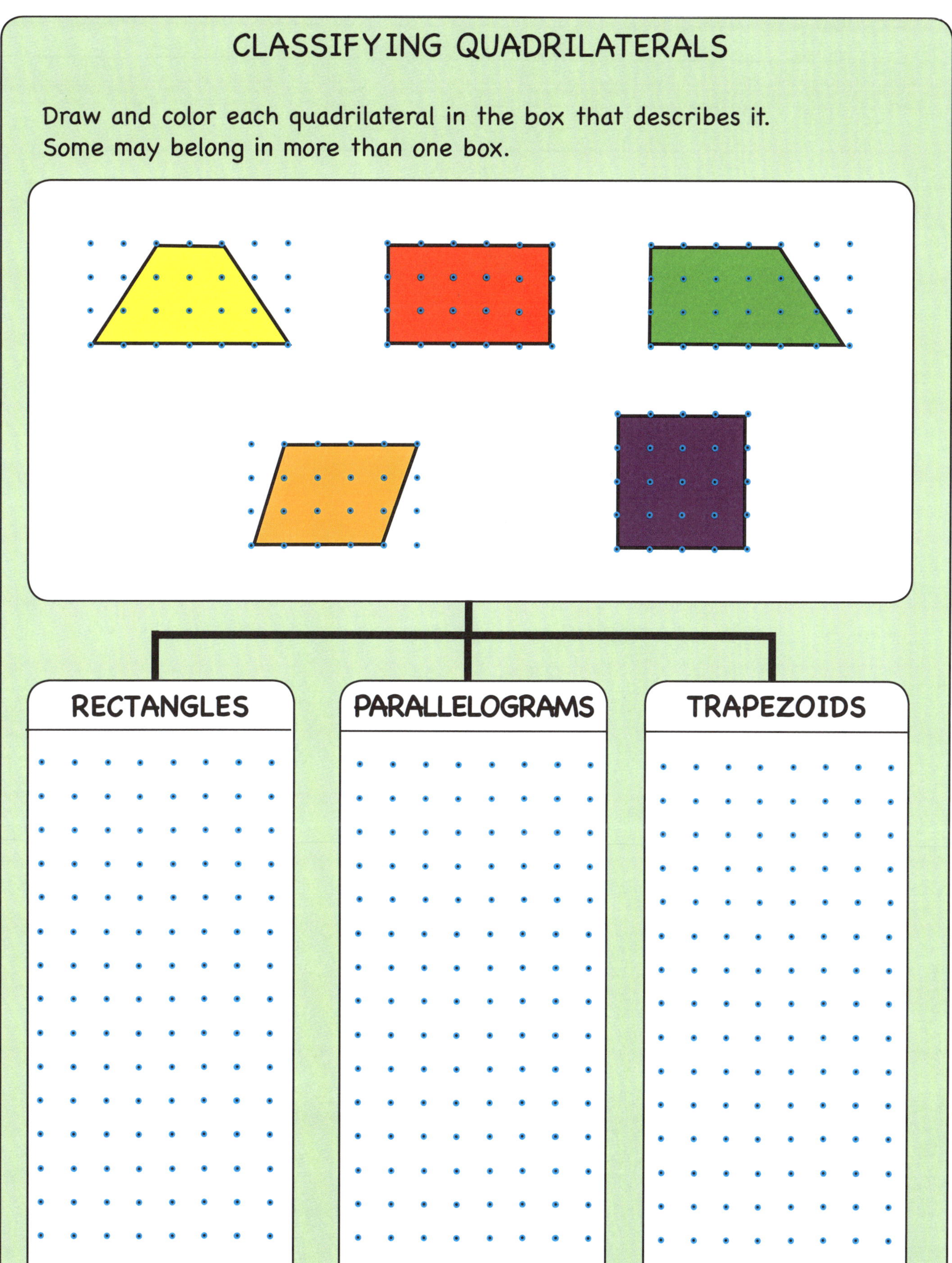

CLASSIFYING SHAPES

Draw and color other polygons that belong in each group.

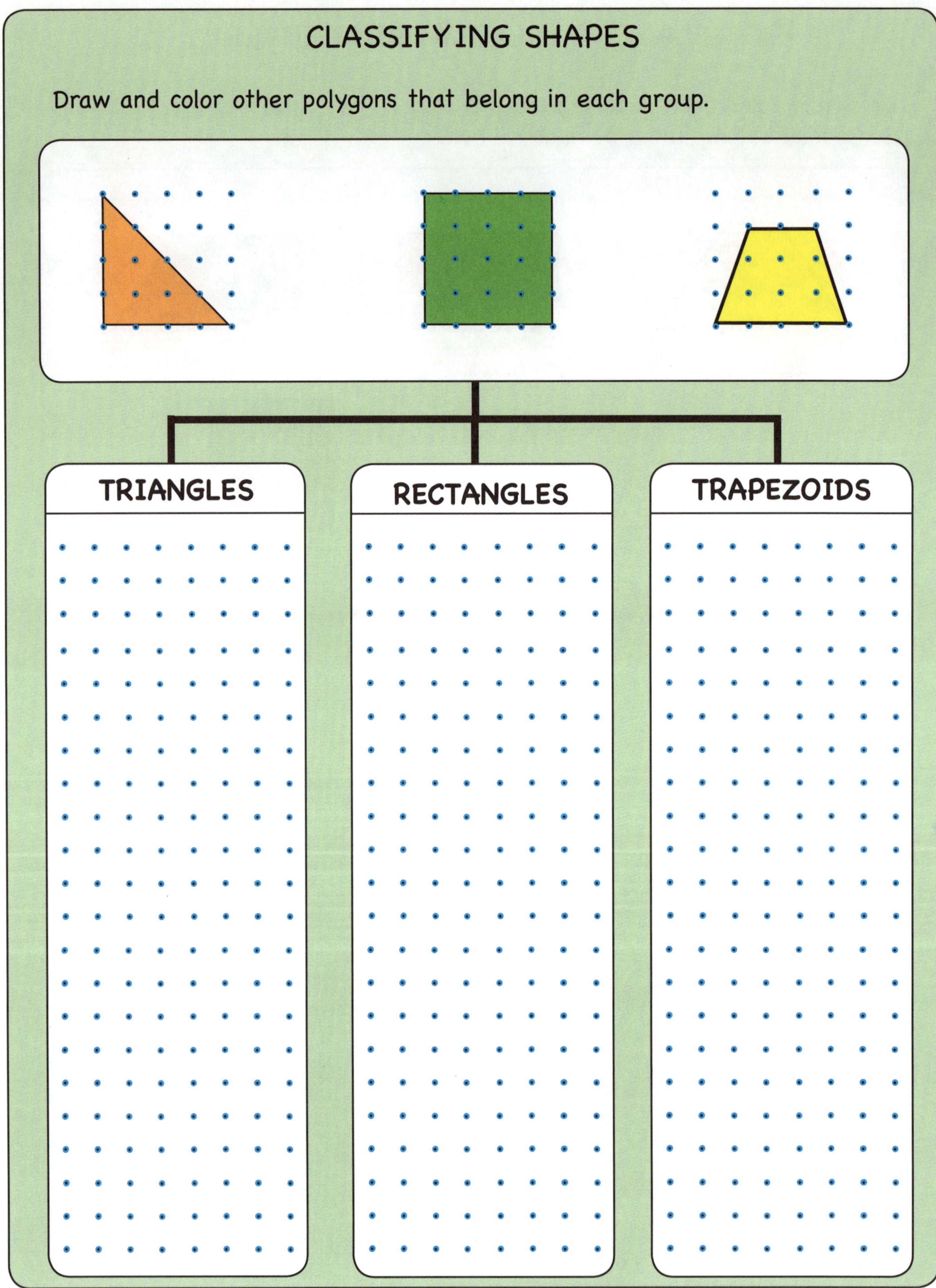

CLASSIFYING SHAPES - FORMING GROUPS

Draw and color each shape in the group where each belongs.

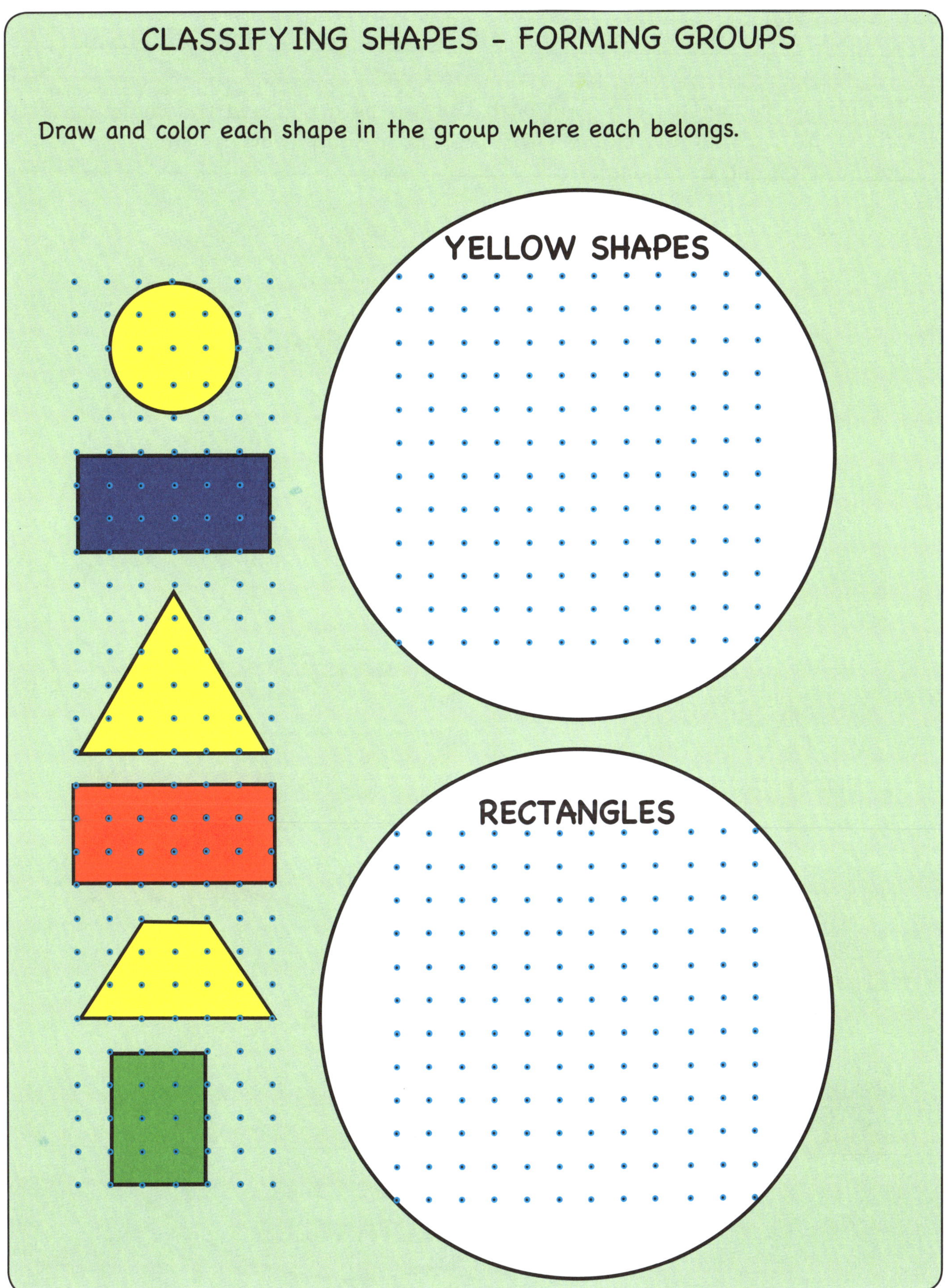

CLASSIFYING SHAPES IN MORE THAN ONE CLASS

The orange rectangle belongs in both the orange group and the rectangle group. Notice that the circles must overlap to show that the shape is both orange and a rectangle.

Draw and color the shapes in the group where each belongs.

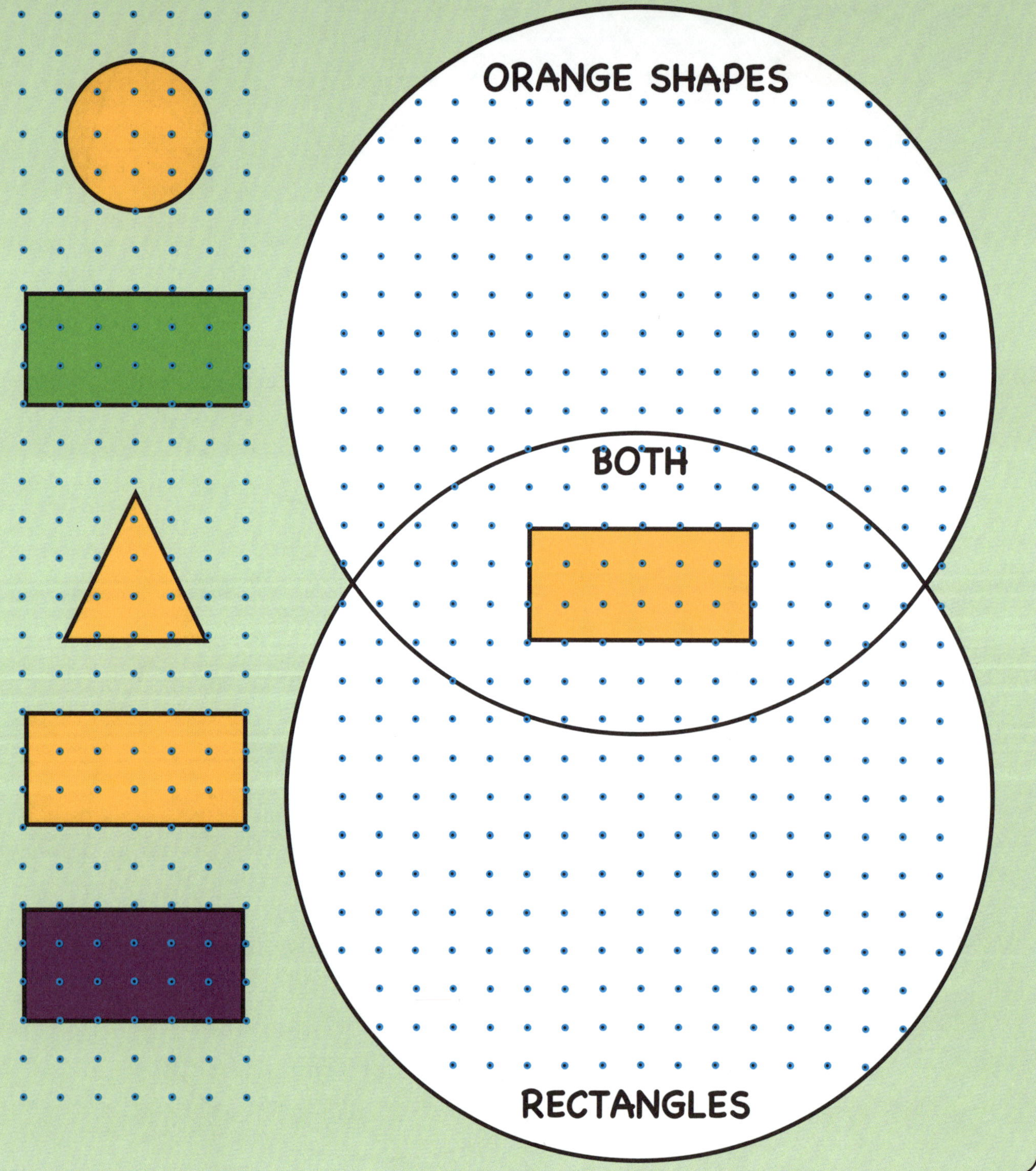

CLASSIFYING SHAPES IN MORE THAN ONE CLASS

Draw and color the shapes in the group where each belongs.

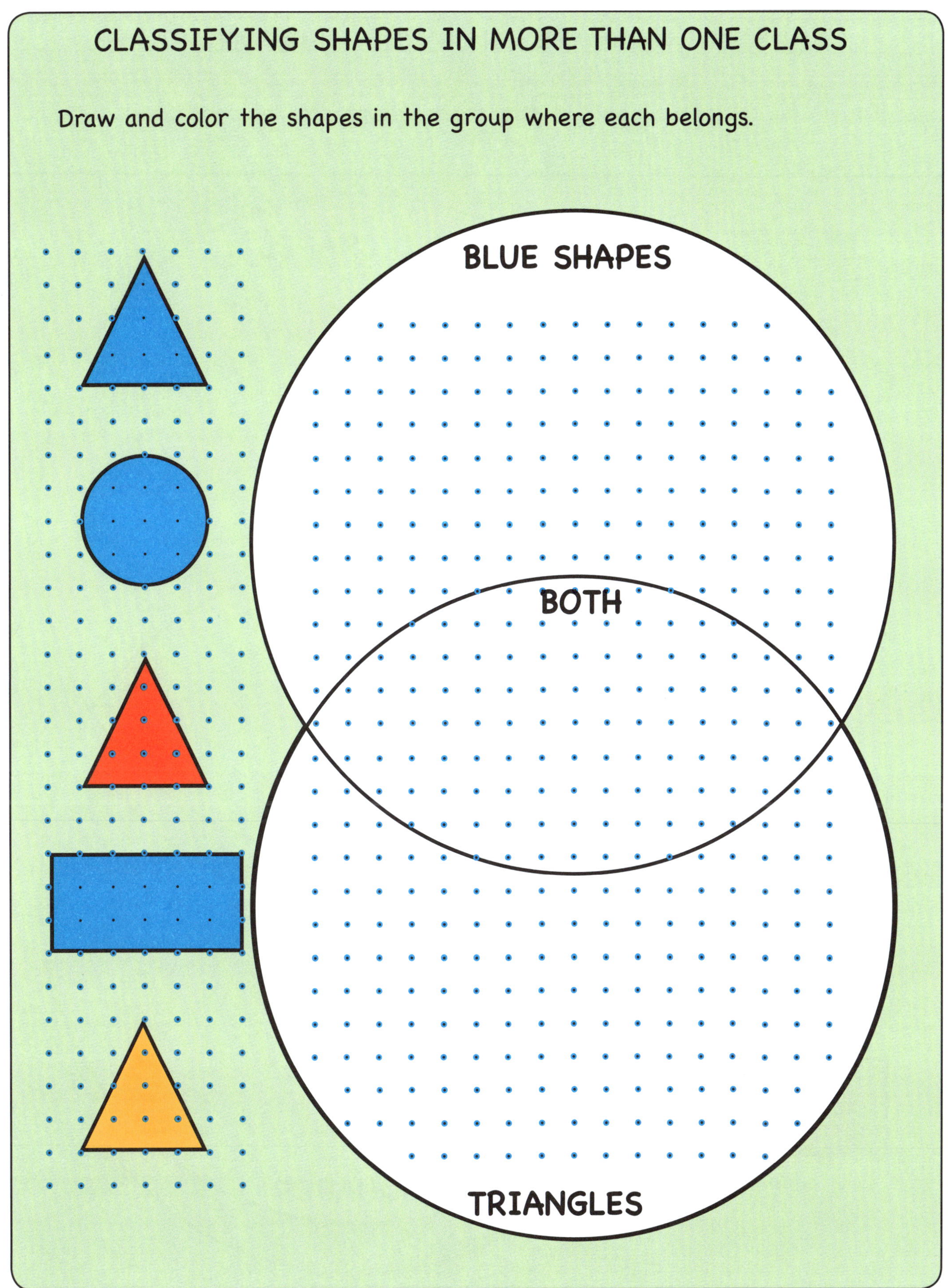

CLASSIFYING SHAPES IN MORE THAN ONE CLASS

Draw and color the shapes in the group where each belongs.

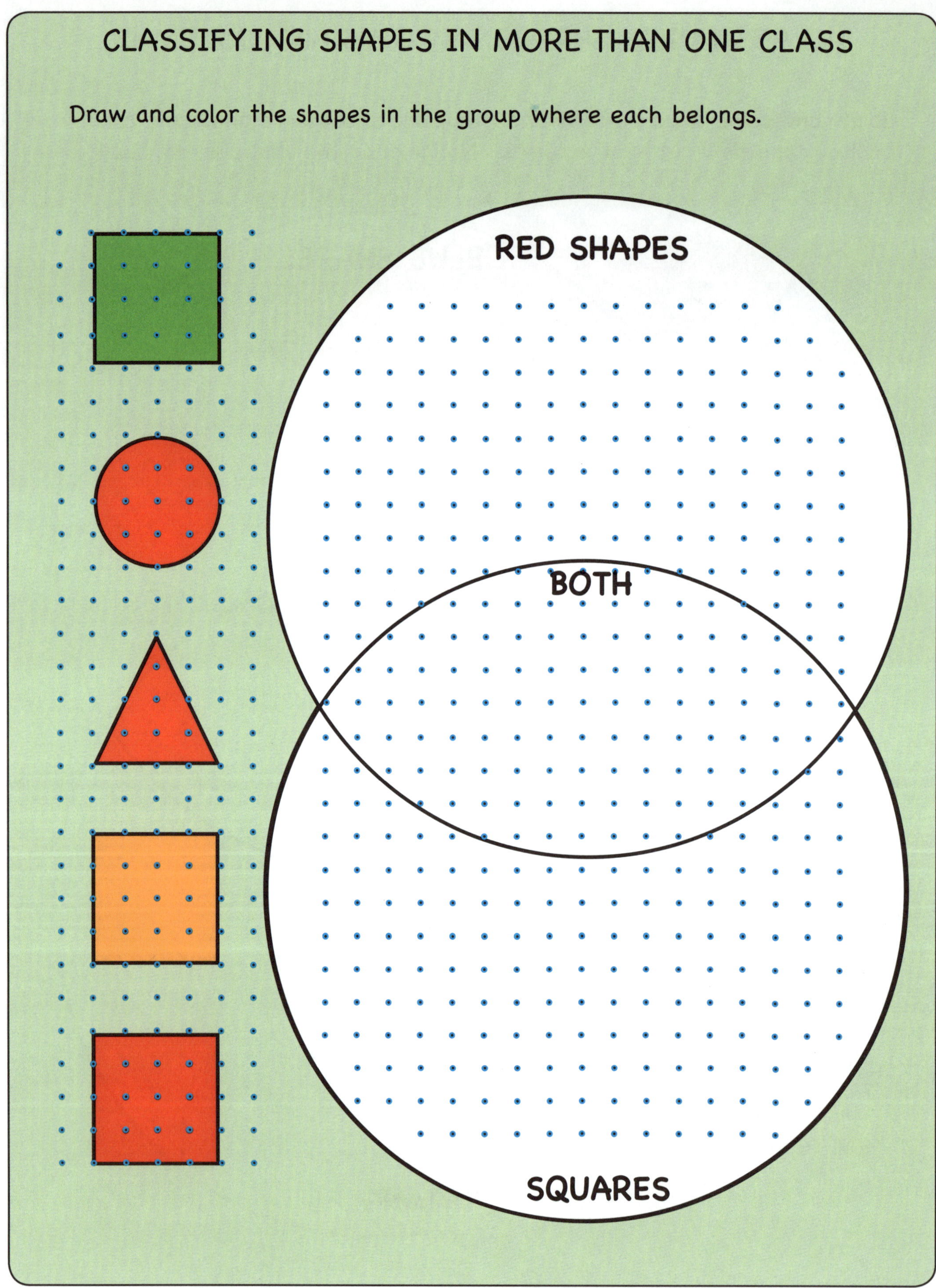

CLASSIFYING SHAPES IN ROWS AND COLUMNS

Look across the rows (⟶). Notice that the shapes are the same color. Look up and down (↕) the columns. Notice that the shape is the same.

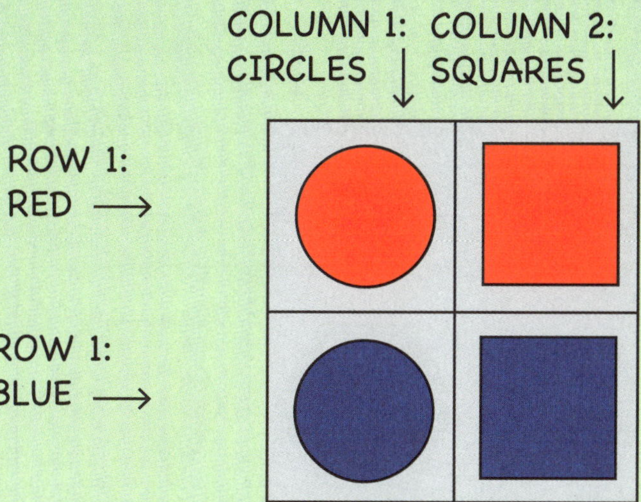

Look across each row and write its characteristic beside each row. Look down each column and write its characteristic. Draw and color the shape that belongs in the empty box.

WORD BOX
red, squares, triangles, yellow

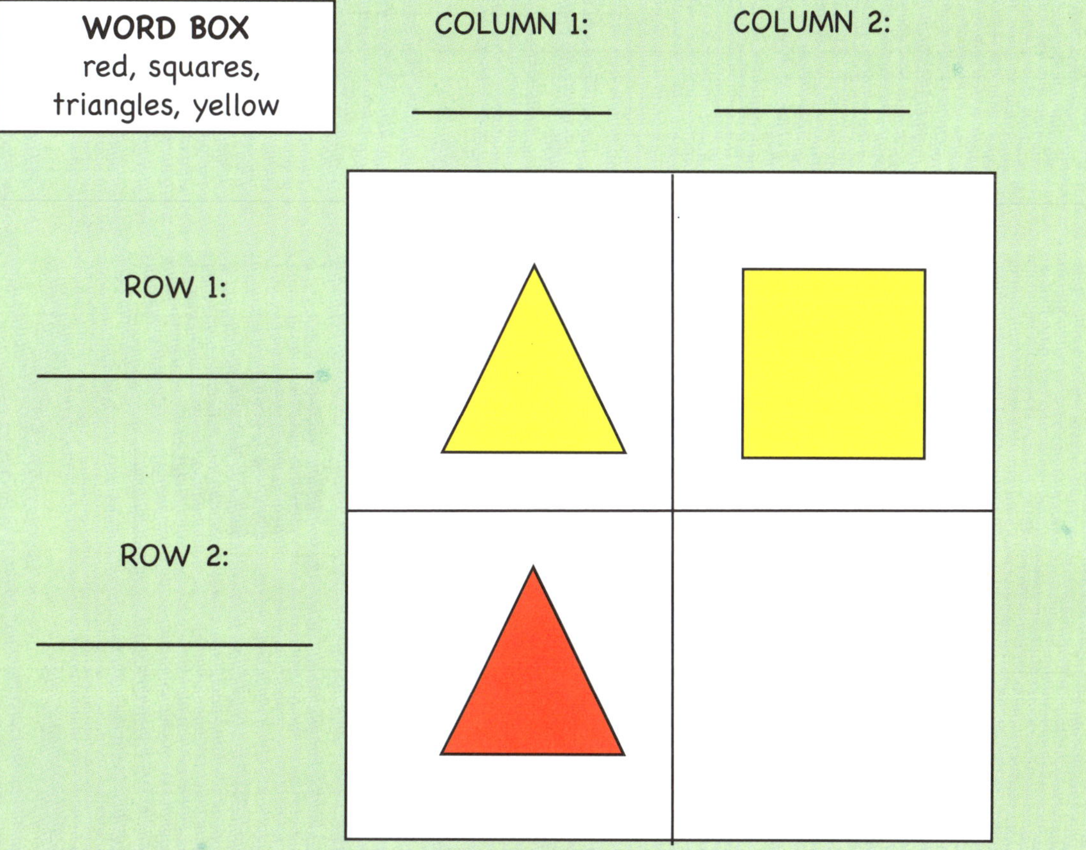

CLASSIFYING SHAPES IN ROWS AND COLUMNS

Look across each row and write its characteristic beside each row. Look down each column and write its characteristic. Draw the shape that belongs in the empty box.

WORD BOX
orange, hexagons, green, squares

COLUMN 1: ____________ COLUMN 2: ____________

ROW 1: ____________

ROW 2: ____________

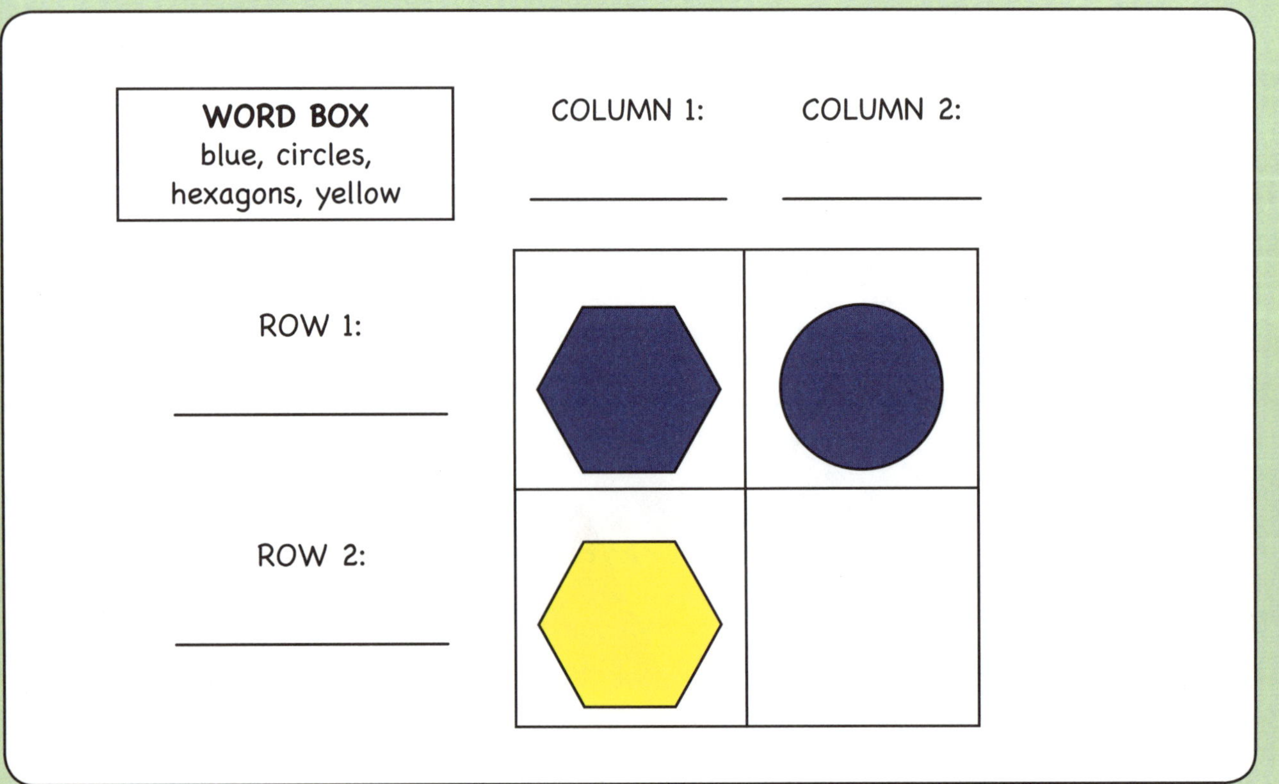

CLASSIFYING SHAPES IN ROWS AND COLUMNS

Look across each row and write its characteristic beside each row. Look down each column and write its characteristic. In each empty box, draw and color the shape that belongs there.

WORD BOX
blue, circles, green
hexagons, red, squares

COLUMN 1: ____ COLUMN 2: ____ COLUMN 3: ____

ROW 1: ____

ROW 2: ____

ROW 3: ____

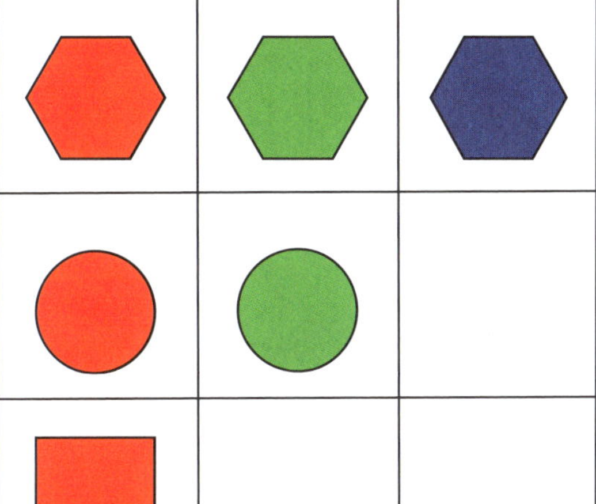

WORD BOX
orange, circles, green
hexagons, yellow, squares

COLUMN 1: ____ COLUMN 2: ____ COLUMN 3: ____

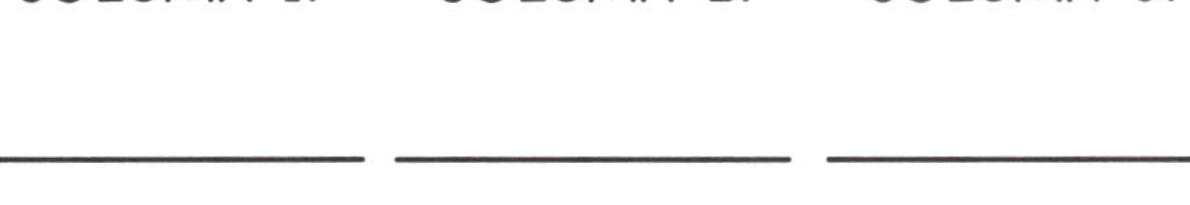

ROW 1: ____

ROW 2: ____

ROW 3: ____

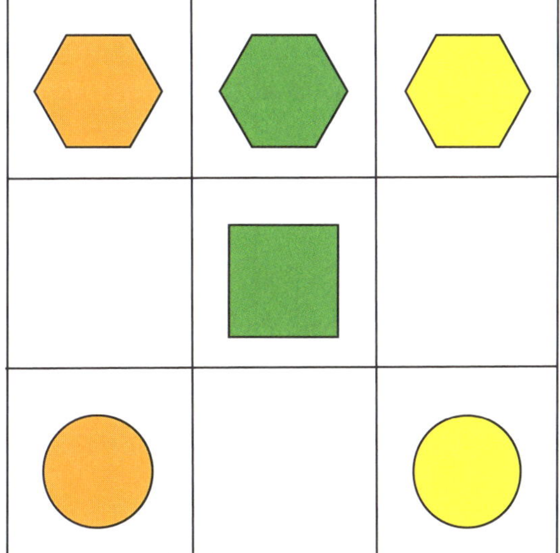

WRITING DESCRIPTIONS OF CLASSES

Look at each group (class) of figures. Decide what characteristic all the figures have in common. Write a description of each class of figures in the DESCRIPTION BOX.

EXAMPLE

DESCRIPTION

All the shapes are circles.

DESCRIPTION

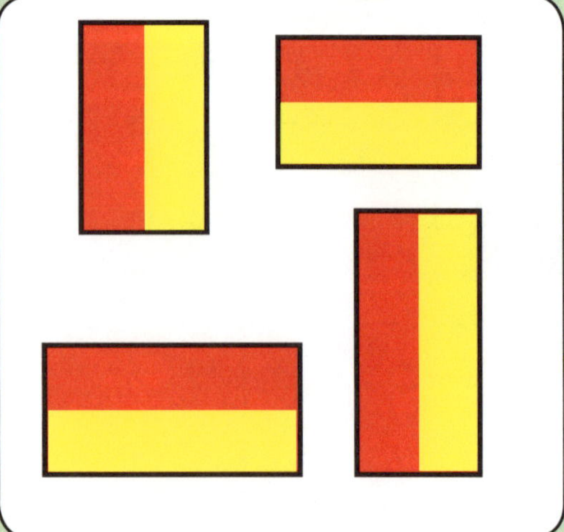

DESCRIPTION

CHAPTER SIX

THINKING ABOUT MATTER, WATER, AND WEATHER

DESCRIBING MATTER

Matter is anything that takes up space and has weight. It can be a solid, a liquid, or a gas. If a liquid is heated, it becomes so light that you do not see it. It has become a gas. Circle the picture of matter that your teacher describes.*

blocks

orange juice

steam

smoke

bricks

paint

waterfall

fog

rocks

*Descriptions are available on page 19 of the free answer guide.

CHANGING FORMS OF MATTER

Matter can change from a solid to a liquid by heating. A liquid can change to a solid by cooling. Draw a line from each picture to the word that describes its form.

ice cream

popsicles

liquid

ice cubes

milk

solid

orange juice

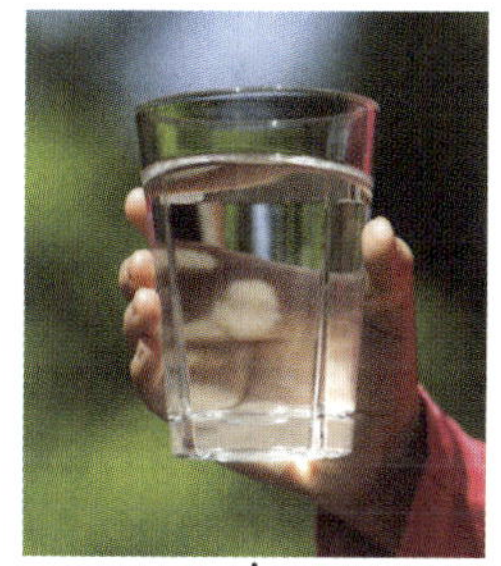
water

Write whether each change in matter is caused by heating or cooling.

milk ⟶ ice cream ______________________ (heating or cooling)

ice cube ⟶ water ______________________ (heating or cooling)

orange drink ⟶ popsicle ______________________ (heating or cooling)

SOLIDS, LIQUIDS, AND GASES

Water can be a solid, a liquid, or a gas.

When water freezes into ice, it becomes a solid. Ice will keep its shape as long as it is kept very cold. You know it has weight because you can feel it press on your hand.

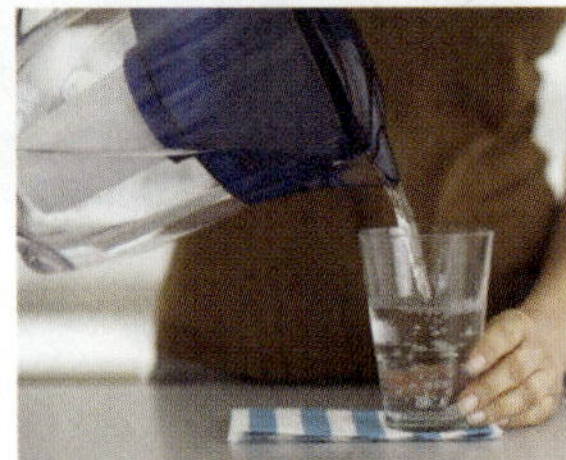

When ice melts, it becomes liquid. When water is a liquid, it takes the shape of its container. You can pour a liquid from one container to another. You can feel its weight when you pick up a container of water.

When water is heated, the liquid becomes hot steam, and then disappears into the air as a gas called water vapor. Since water vapor is an invisible gas, it has no shape. When a liquid becomes a gas, we say it evaporates.

When the water vapor cools or hits a cool surface, it becomes liquid water. When a gas cools to become a liquid, we say that it condenses. When it condenses, water vapor forms drops of water and takes the shape of the container that it falls into.

Check the correct boxes to describe a solid, liquid, or gas.

	SOLID	LIQUID	GAS
CAN BE POURED			
HAS A DEFINITE SHAPE			
MANY ARE INVISIBLE			

HEATING AND COOLING WATER

When water is heated enough, it boils away. The water evaporates and changes to steam. When steam hits a cool surface, it forms small drops of water. When the steam loses heat, it condenses to form water again. If you place water in the freezer, the water will lose heat and change to ice. When you use ice cubes to cool a drink, the ice gains heat and melts back to water.

Use the words in the WORD BOX to describe the changes of water.

WORD BOX
condenses, evaporates, freezes, melts

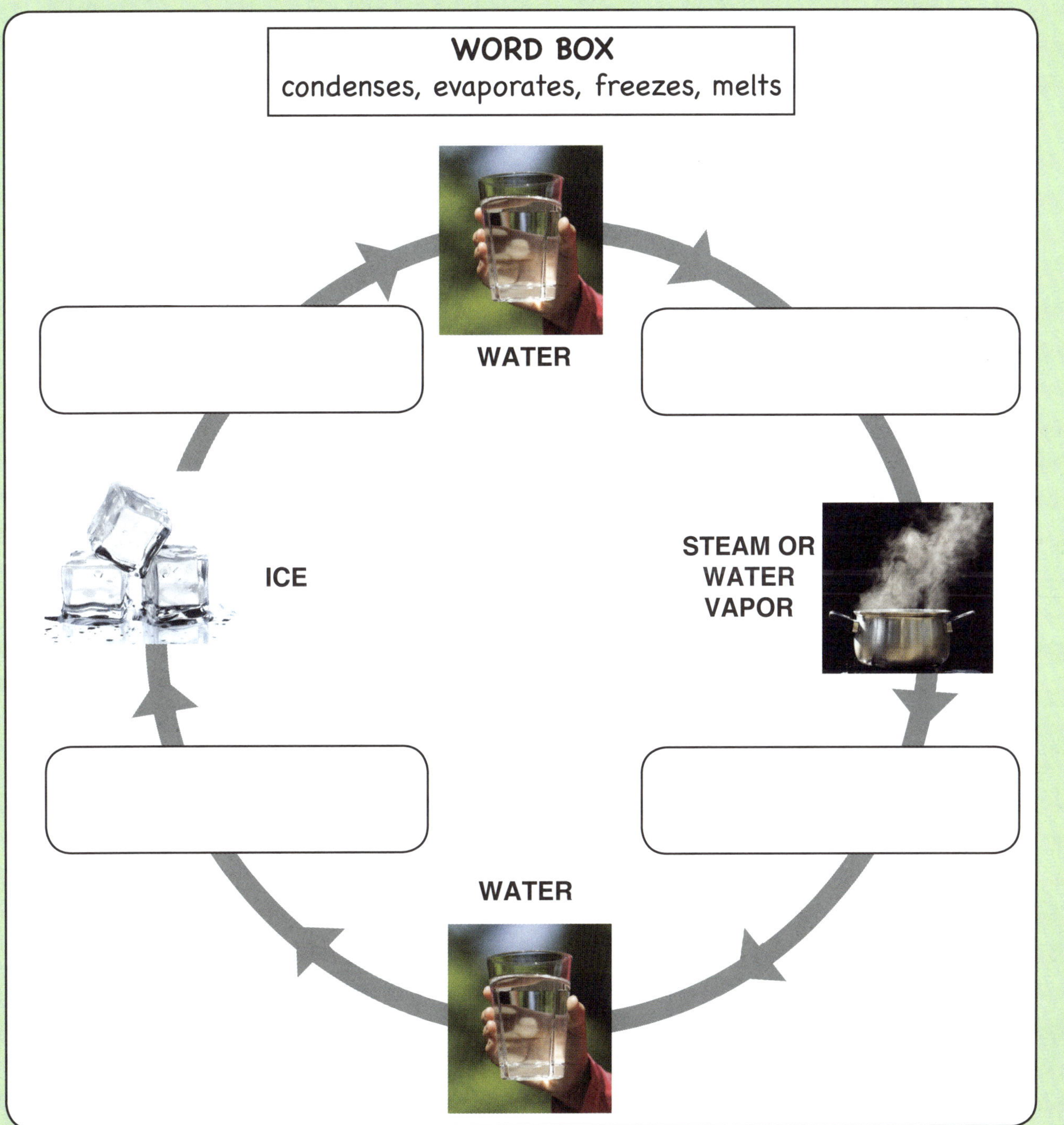

THE WATER CYCLE

Heat from the sun causes water to evaporate from rivers, lakes, and oceans. The warm, invisible water vapor rises higher and higher. As it rises, it cools. When moist air is cooled, tiny water droplets condense into clouds. When the water droplets grow large enough, they fall as rain. The rain runs off the land into rivers. The rivers flow into the ocean.

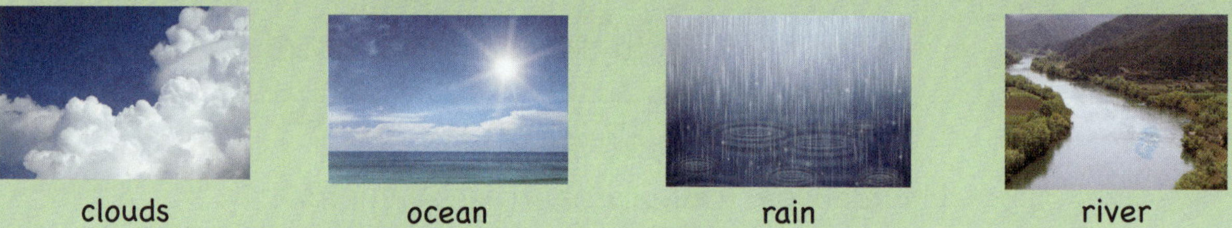

clouds ocean rain river

Use the words in the WORD BOX to complete the water cycle diagram.

WORD BOX

condenses, evaporates, falls, flows

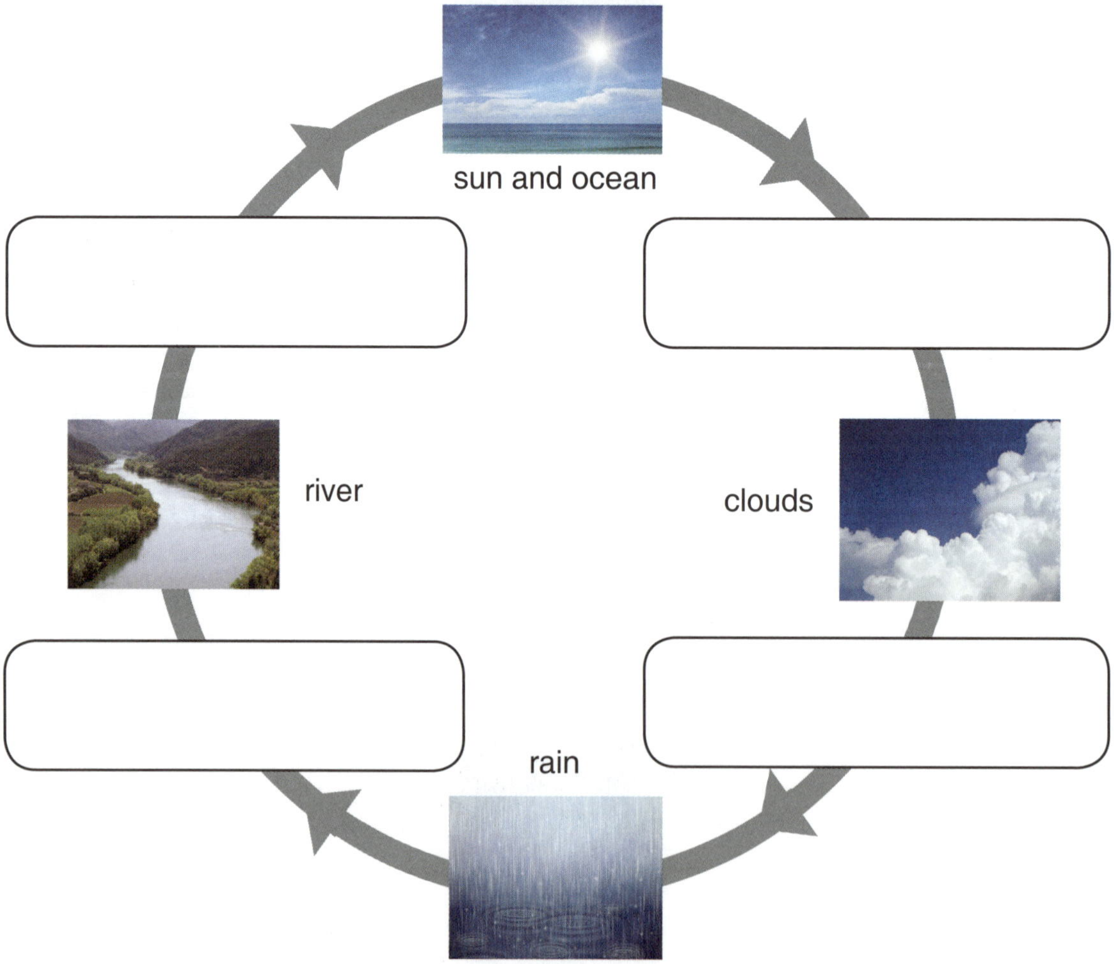

sun and ocean

river

clouds

rain

PRECIPITATION

When water vapor in clouds condenses back into water it falls to the ground in different forms called precipitation. It can fall as solid snow flakes, solid hail, liquid rain, or as fog—a cloud on the ground. Use the words in the WORD BOX to complete the description of each form of precipitation.

WORD BOX
Fog, Hail, Rain, Snow

__________________ is large water drops that fall from clouds above Earth.

__________________ is made when the water vapor in the clouds is frozen into soft, white flakes.

__________________ is small, hard, white balls of ice that fall from thunderclouds.

__________________ is a cloud on the ground. In the picture it makes the Golden Gate Bridge almost invisible.

WEATHER INSTRUMENTS

Weather instruments are used to measure what we need to know about weather. Draw a line from each explanation of what the instrument does to the words that describe what it measures.

INSTRUMENT	WHAT IT DOES	WHAT IT MEASURES
	An anemometer spins to measure how fast the wind blows.	AMOUNT OF RAIN
	A rain gauge collects rain to measure how much rain has fallen.	WIND DIRECTION
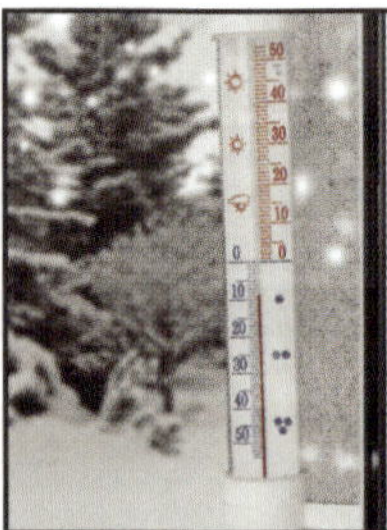	A thermometer shows if the air is hot, warm, or cold.	WIND SPEED
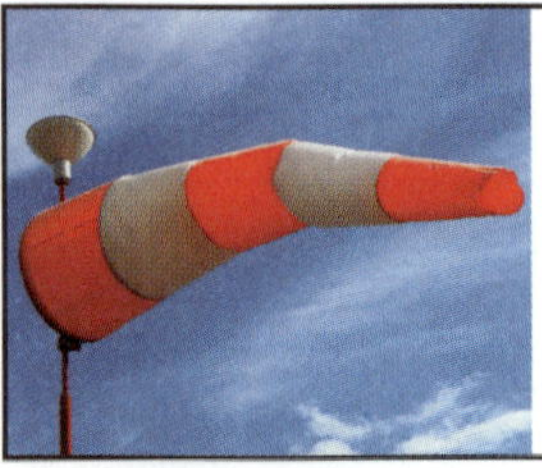	A windsock shows which way the wind is blowing.	AIR TEMPERATURE

CHAPTER SEVEN
THINKING ABOUT LAND FORMS AND BODIES OF WATER

A view of the UNITED STATES from space shows our country's land forms and bodies of water.

DESCRIBING LAND FORMS AND BODIES OF WATER

Circle the picture of the land or water your teacher describes.*

mountain

plateau

valley

pond

canal

stream

wetlands

river

plain

lake

ocean

reservoir

*Descriptions are available on page 19 of the free answer guide.

DESCRIBING LAND FORMS AND BODIES OF WATER

Draw a line from each photograph to the word that describes it.

desert

hill

island

lake

ocean

plain

pond

stream

valley

woodlands

DESCRIBING LAND FORMS

Draw a line from each description to the picture of that land form.

A body of land completely surrounded by water.

Dry, sandy land where few plants and animals can live.

A huge, tall hill that rises high above the surrounding land.

A large area that may be flat or with hills where many trees, plants, and animals can grow.

Large, flat, level land higher than the land around it.

Large, flat, level land that has grass but few trees.

mountain

plateau

island

plain

woodlands

desert

DESCRIBING BODIES OF WATER

Water that falls as rain, comes from melting snow, or bubbles up from springs does not taste salty. This "fresh" water collects in lakes, rivers, streams, and ponds. People and animals drink fresh water. Ocean water tastes salty. People and animals do not drink salt water.

Draw a line from each description to the picture of that body of water.

A lake that people build by blocking a river to collect water for their use.

A body of still, fresh water smaller than a lake.

A large body of salt water that is surrounded on three sides by land.

A large body of fresh water that is surrounded by land.

A thin, shallow flow of fresh water, smaller than a river. It may dry up if there is not enough rain.

A great body of salt water that covers most of Earth.

gulf

lake

stream

ocean

pond

reservoir

HOW PEOPLE CHANGE THE LAND AND WATER

To get what they need, people change the land and bodies of water. Write whether the picture shows changing the land or changing a body of water.

mining

highways

factories

canal

farming

reservoir

HUMAN CHANGES

CHANGING THE LAND	CHANGING WATER

DESCRIBING LAND FORMS

Use the words in the WORD BOX to describe land forms.

mountain

plain

plateau

WORD BOX

farming, grass, land, mountain, plain, plateau, snow

A ______________ is a large, flat land form that stretches many miles. It has __________, but few trees and is used for ______________.

A ________________ is large, flat land form higher than the ______________ around it.

A ________________ is the highest land form. Its top is often covered with ____________.

DESCRIBING BODIES OF WATER

Use the words in the WORD BOX to describe bodies of water.

gulf

lake

river

WORD BOX
gulf, lake, land, long, ocean, river, water

A ________________ is ____________, flowing fresh water that empties into a lake or ____________.

A ____________ is a large body of salt ____________ that is surrounded on three sides by ____________.

A ____________ is a body of fresh ____________ that is surrounded on all sides by ____________.

KINDS OF LAND AND WATER

Using the WORD BOX write the words that describe the kinds of land forms or bodies of water. Write the names of the examples on the lines below it.

WORD BOX
bodies of fresh water, high land forms, reservoir, river, lake, plateau, mountains, hills

CLASS

____

EXAMPLES

____

____

____

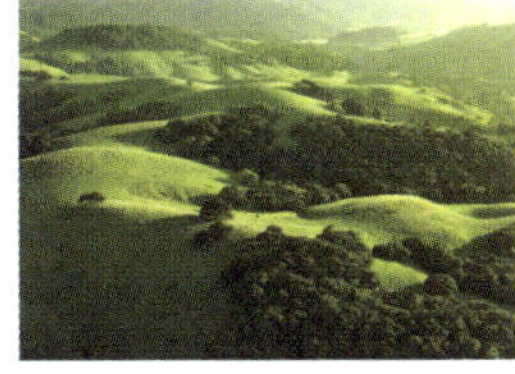

CLASS

____

EXAMPLES

____

____

____

SIMILAR LAND OR WATER

Use the words in the WORD BOX to write sentences telling how the two land forms or bodies are alike.

WORD BOX
flowing, fresh, river, stream, water

____

____

WORD BOX
flat, land, large, plain, plateau, forms

____

____

WORD BOX
fresh, hold, lake, pond, water

____

____

WORD BOX
canal, man-made, reservoir

____

____

COMPARING LAND FORMS OR BODIES OF WATER

List these bodies of water from smallest to largest.

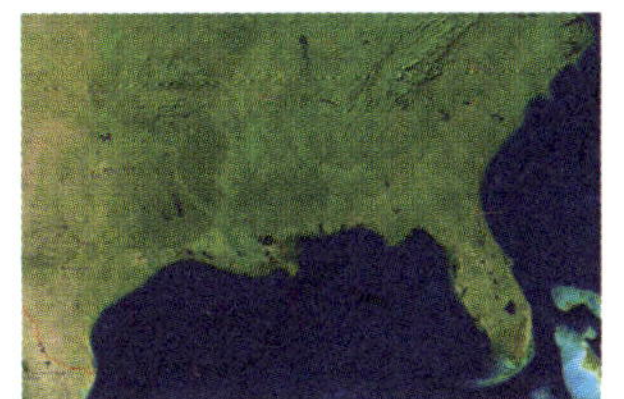
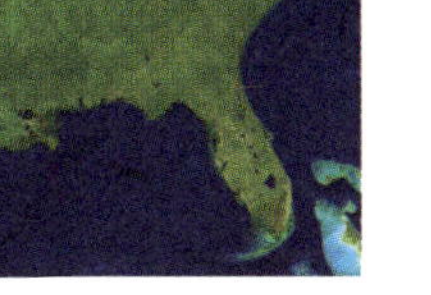

gulf

lake

ocean

SMALLEST

LARGEST

____

____

____

List these land forms from highest to lowest.

mountain

plain

plateau

HIGHEST

LOWEST

____

____

____

CANAL & RESERVOIR – HOW ALIKE AND HOW DIFFERENT

A canal is built to move ships between two bodies of water.

A reservoir is made by blocking a river to make a large lake to hold water until it is used.

Read the descriptions and use the diagram to explain how a canal and a reservoir are alike and different.

CANAL

RESERVOIR

HOW ALIKE?

____

____

HOW DIFFERENT?

Canal		Reservoir
_______________		_______________
_______________	WHY BUILT?	_______________
_______________		_______________
_______________		_______________

PLAIN & DESERT – HOW ALIKE AND HOW DIFFERENT

A plain is a very large, flat land form that is often planted to provide food. There is enough water that large fields of grass grow there. Small animals and buffalo can live there.

A desert is a very large, flat, dry, sandy land form. Only a few plants and small animals live there.

Use the diagram to explain how a plain and a desert are alike and different.

PLAIN

DESERT

HOW ALIKE?

____

____

HOW DIFFERENT?

PLAIN		DESERT
__________	WATER	__________
__________	PLANTS	__________
__________	ANIMALS	__________

DESCRIBING A LAND FORM

To describe a land form, we must tell these important things about it. Write this land form in the center box and the details about it in the boxes.

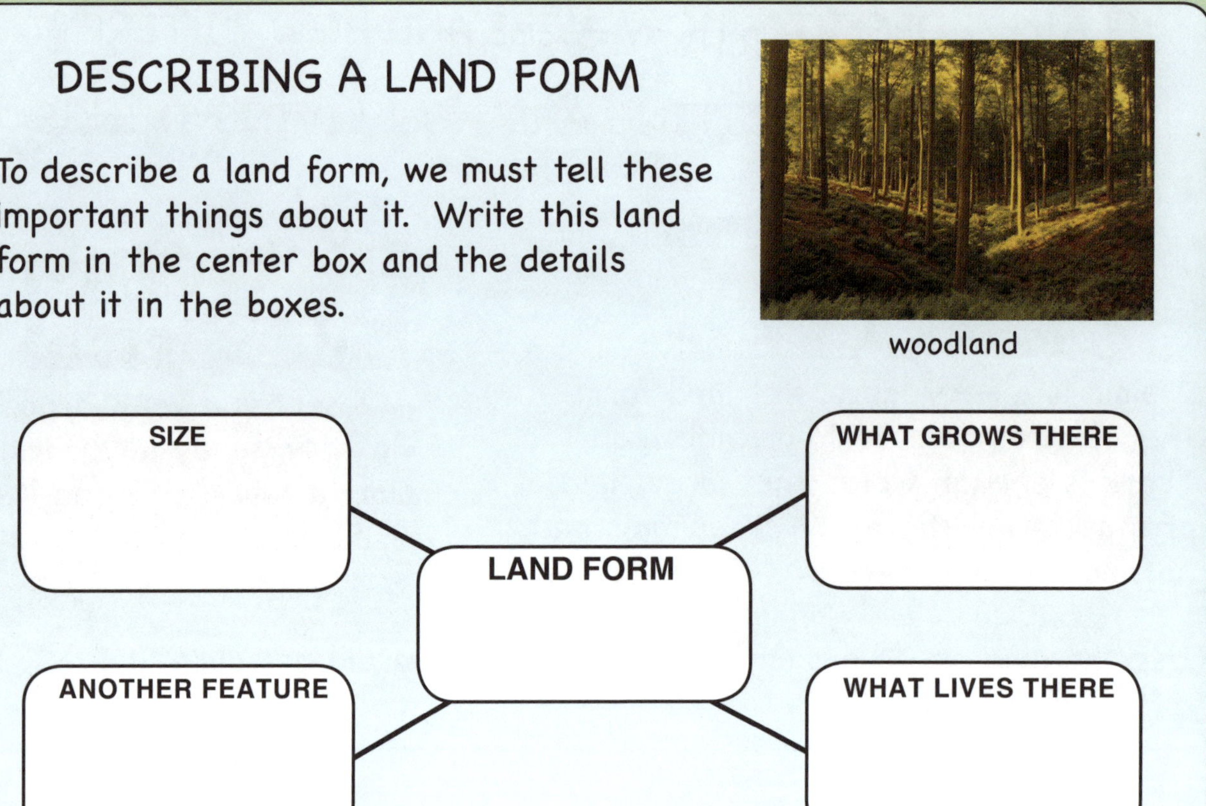

woodland

stream

DESCRIBING A BODY OF WATER

To describe a body of water, we must tell these important things about it. Write this body of water in the center box and the details about it in the boxes.

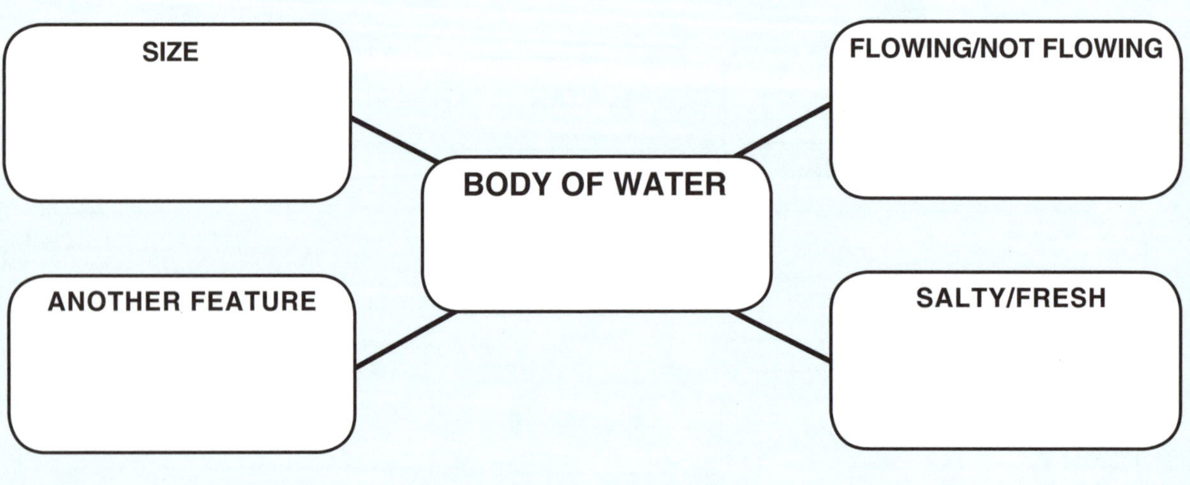

CHAPTER EIGHT

THINKING ABOUT LIVING AND NON-LIVING THINGS

Living Things

A Maple Tree

A Grasshopper

Non-Living Things

The Planet Saturn

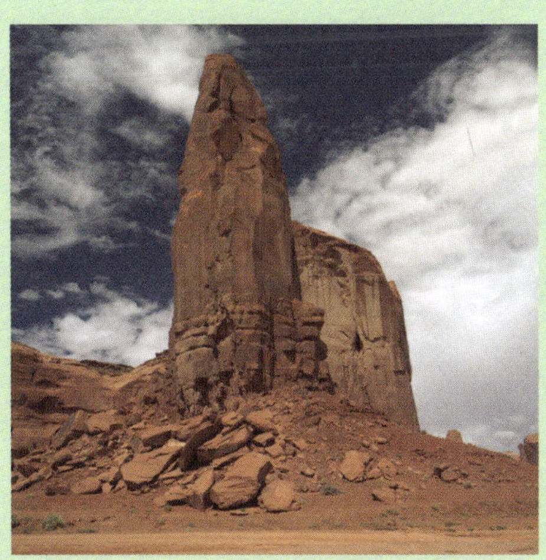

A Rock in Monument Valley

DESCRIBING LIVING AND NON-LIVING THINGS

Living things grow, need food, air and water, and can reproduce. Write "YES" or "NO" to show whether each thing grows, needs food, needs air and water, or reproduces itself. In the last box write "L" to show it is living, or write "N" to show that it is non-living.

LIVING OR NON-LIVING?	Grows	Needs Food	Needs Air & Water	Reproduces	Living or Non-Living
cactus	YES	YES	YES	YES	L
cell phone					
fire					
cloud					
lemons					
potatoes					
sun					
turtle					

COMPARING PLANTS AND ANIMALS

Plants grow in one place and make their food from sunlight and water. Some plants make new ones from seeds. Animals move by themselves and eat plants or other animals. They make baby animals from eggs or from inside their bodies.

In each box write "YES" or "NO." Decide whether each living thing is a plant or an animal. In the last box write "P" for plant or "A" for animal.

LIVING THINGS	Makes its food from air, water, and light?	Must stay where it is planted?	Gets its food from plants and animals	Moves itself?	Plant or Animal?
alligator	NO	NO	YES	YES	A
butterfly					
palm trees					
peaches					
roses					
rabbit					
whale					

DESCRIBING ANIMALS

Circle the picture of the animal that your teacher describes.*

beaver

prairie dog

rabbit

salmon

shark

tuna

duck

blue jay

bat

lizard

snake

alligator

butterfly

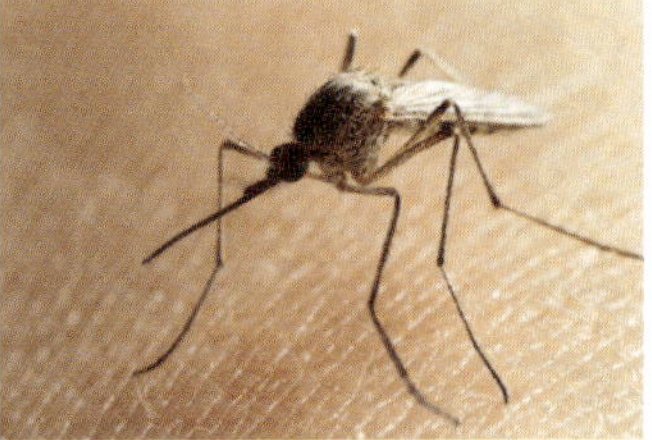
mosquito

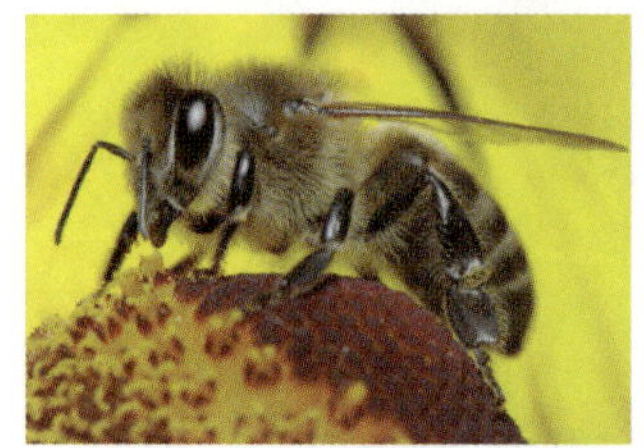
bee

*Descriptions are available on page 19 of the free answer guide.

DESCRIBING ANIMALS

When the mother animal lays an egg, the new animal is not fully formed yet. Its body parts develop inside the egg.

When the baby animal grows inside its mother's body, its body parts are already developed when it is born. When the baby animal is a "live birth," it looks similar to the adult animal.

To understand what animals need to survive, we need to know whether it is warm- or cold-blooded. Warm-blooded animals make heat inside their bodies, can huddle together to stay warm, and have a better chance to survive in cold weather. Cold-blooded animals must get heat from their surroundings.

Draw a line from the picture of each animal to the words that describe it.

cold-blooded

warm-blooded

lays eggs

gives live birth

DESCRIBING ANIMALS

For each kind of animal, write whether it reproduces by eggs or by live birth; and whether it lives on land, in water, or in the air. Large animals have a backbone that supports the weight of the animal. Instead of a backbone, some small animals have stiff skin to support their weight. Complete the diagram to tell the characteristics of each of these kinds of animals.

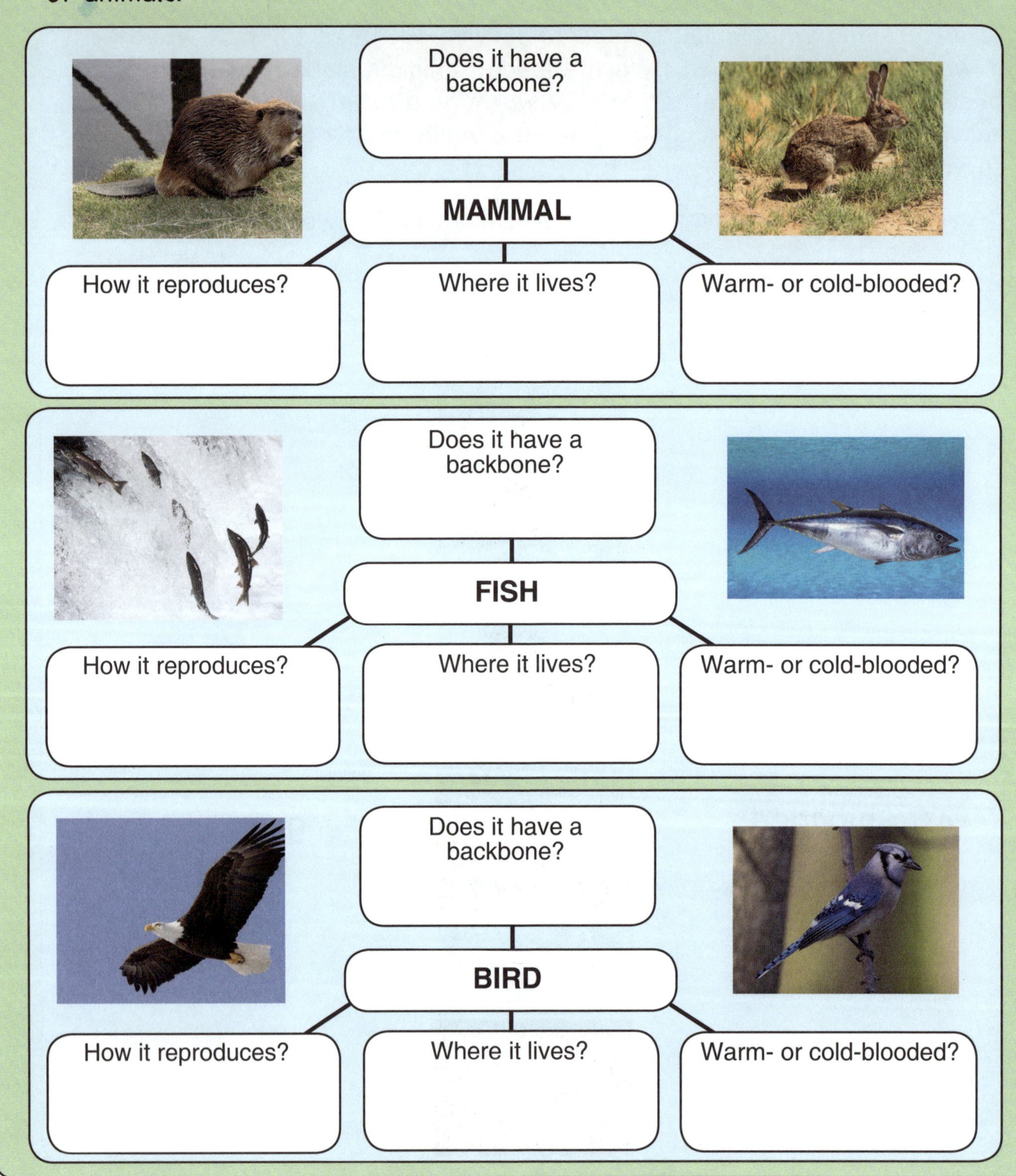

DESCRIBING ANIMALS

For each kind of animal, write whether it reproduces by eggs or by live birth. Write whether it lives on land, in water, or in the air. Write whether it is warm- or cold-blooded. Write whether it has a backbone. Complete the diagram to tell the characteristics of each of these kinds of animals.

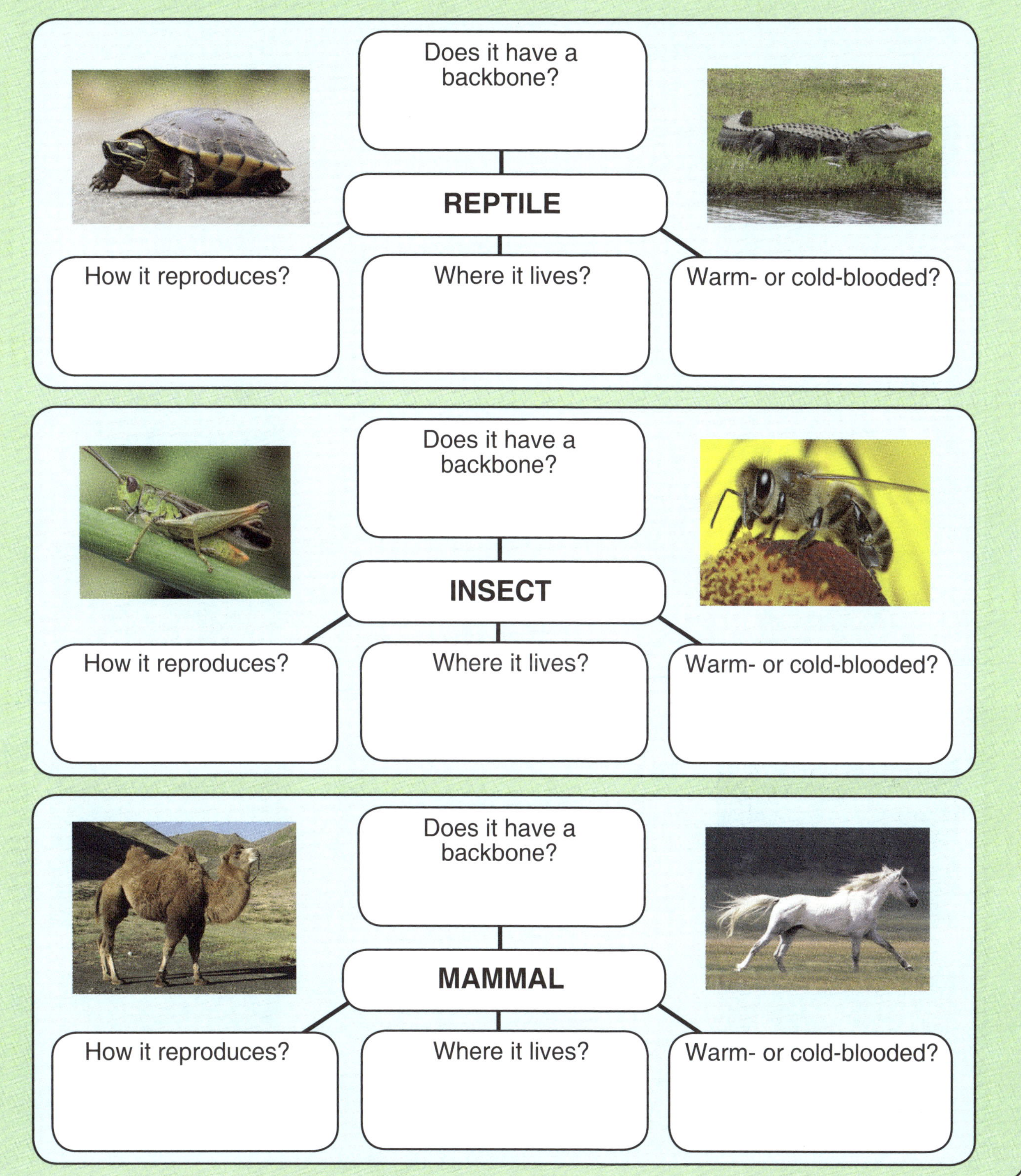

KINDS OF ANIMALS

Birds lay eggs and have feathers and wings. Fish are animals that lay eggs and live in water. Insects are tiny animals that lay eggs and have at least six legs and antennae. Mammals have hair. Mammal mothers carry their babies inside their bodies and make milk to feed them are and are warm blooded. Reptiles are animals that lay eggs, have scaly skin, and move by crawling and are cold blooded.

Draw a line from each animal to the word that describes its kind.

lizard

Bird

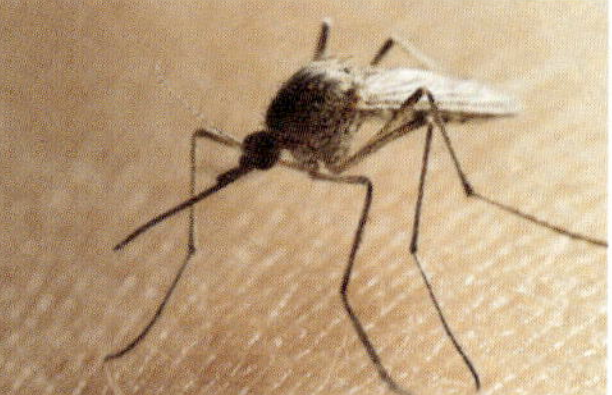
mosquito

salmon

Fish

blue jay

giraffe

Insect

bear

snake

Mammal

grasshopper

duck

Reptile

tuna

UNUSUAL ANIMALS

Some animals are different from others of their kind. Draw a line from the description to the animal.

This animal lives in the ocean and is the largest mammal on Earth.

This insect works with others to carry objects that are heavier than its own weight.

This mammal flies like a bird and only comes out at night.

This bird can run fast, but cannot fly.

This mammal builds its home in a river.

This insect makes food that people eat.

ant

bat

bee

beaver

ostrich

Blue whale

ANIMAL HABITATS

Some animals live on the land – dry deserts, grassy plains, or shady woodlands. Some animals live in large, salty oceans or freshwater rivers. The land form or body of water where they live is their "HABITAT."

Draw a line from each animal to its HABITAT.

beaver

camel

catfish

lizard

giraffe

HABITAT

desert

river

ocean

plain

woodlands

deer

buffalo

shark

squirrel

tuna

DESCRIBING PARTS OF AN ANT

An ant is an insect, a tiny animal that has six legs. The outside of the ant's body is a hard shell for protection. On its head it has two long feelers called antennae that it uses to find food. Its mouth has a strong jaw that it uses to carry food, construct its nest, and to defend itself.

Look at the picture of the ant. Complete each sentence to describe the parts of an ant.

The outside of the ant's body is a hard shell for

__________________________.

An ant has six

__________________________.

On the ant's head are two long feelers called antennae that it uses to find

__________________________.

An ant carries food in its strong

__________________________.

Tell your teacher or partner why each part of an ant's body is important. What would happen if that part was missing or damaged?

Each ant lives and works in a large colony. Tell your partner what may happen to an ant if it is separated from the colony.

THE LIFE CYCLE OF A FROG

Use the words in the WORD BOX to describe the life cycle of a frog.

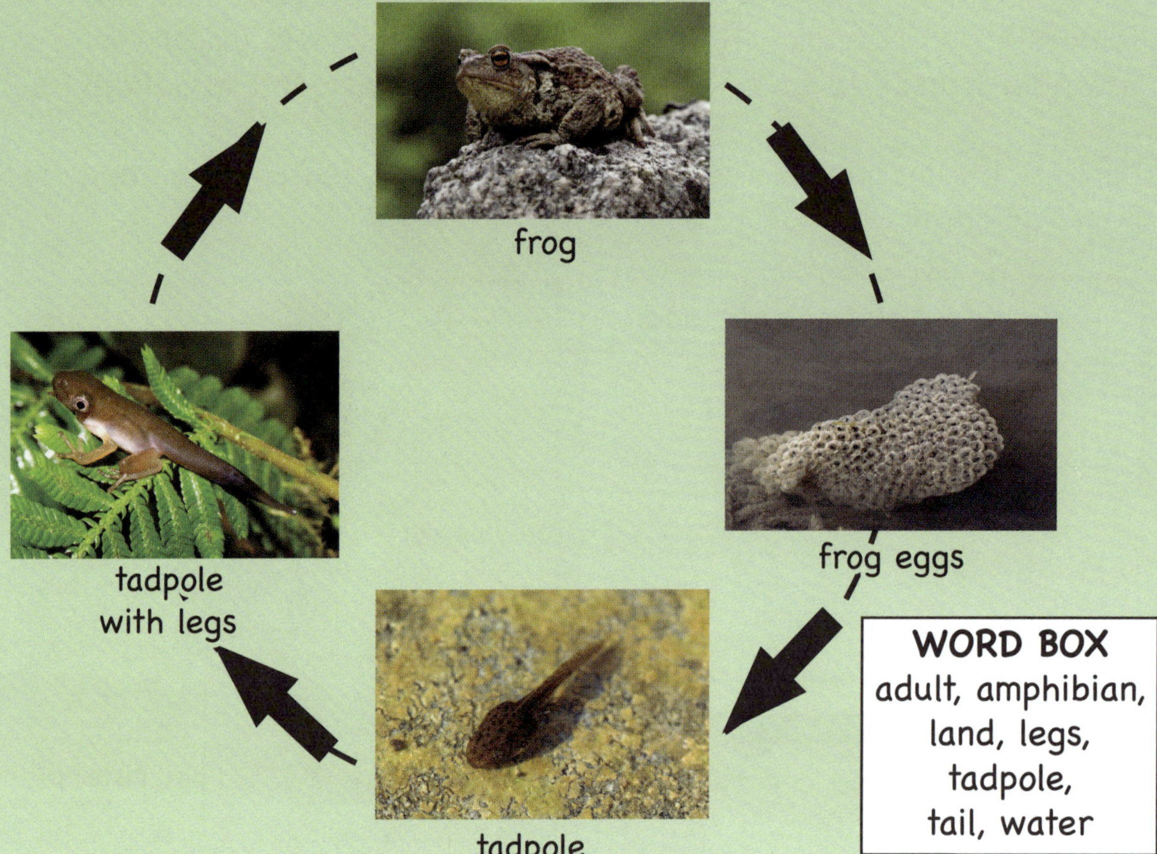

WORD BOX
adult, amphibian, land, legs, tadpole, tail, water

A frog is an ______________________, an animal whose body changes to live first in ____________ and then on ____________. A frog's egg hatches into a ______________ that can breathe in water and swims with a long ____________. As it grows up, it loses its ____________ and grows __________. The way it breathes changes as it become an _____________ frog.

THE LIFE CYCLE OF A BUTTERFLY

Use the words in the WORD BOX to describe the life cycle of a butterfly.

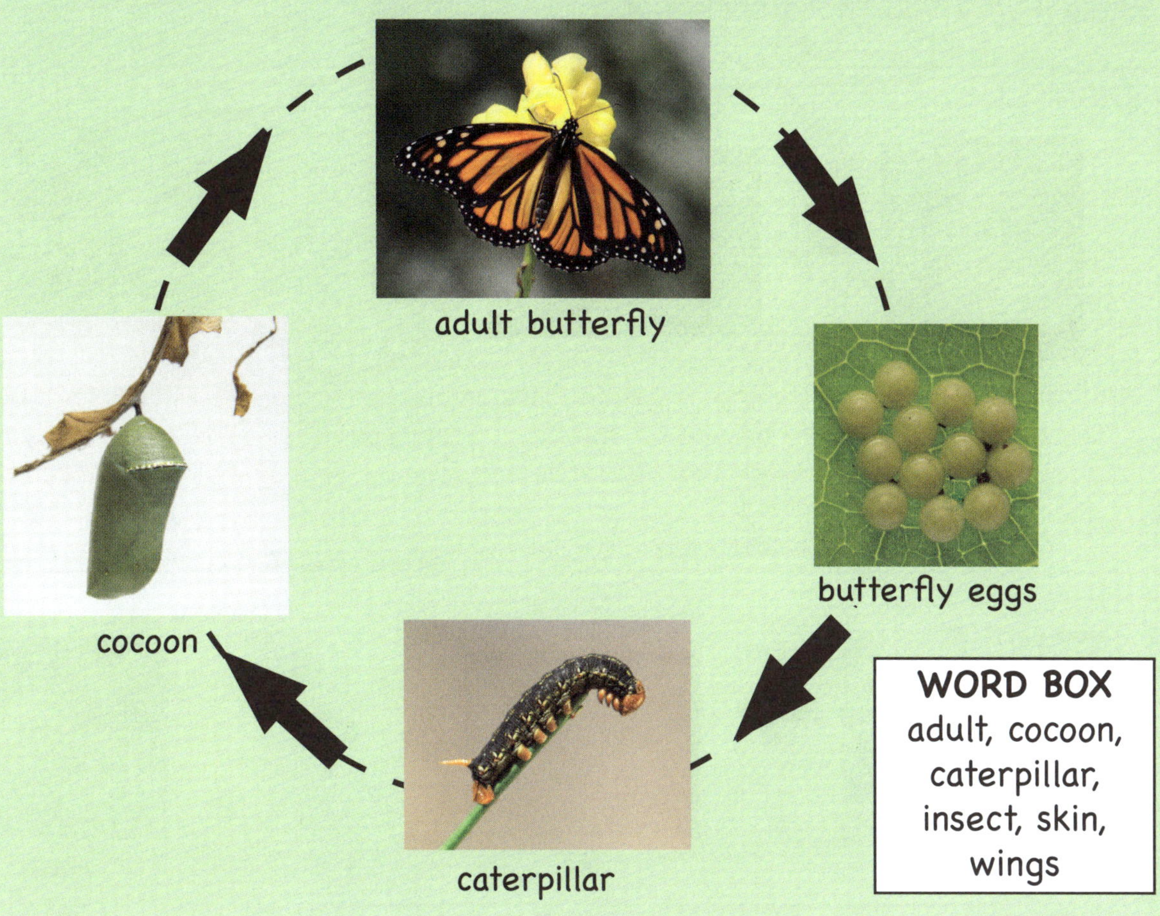

WORD BOX
adult, cocoon, caterpillar, insect, skin, wings

A butterfly is an ________________. Its egg hatches into a _____________________ that looks like a worm that moves slowly on tiny legs. It sheds its fuzzy ______________ that becomes harder each time it sheds. It sticks itself to a branch and its thick skin becomes a ________________. Inside the cocoon it develops _____________. The cocoon breaks open and an _______________ butterfly comes out.

SIMILAR ANIMALS

Circle the picture of the animal most like the one on the left. Then explain why you chose each picture.

EXAMPLE

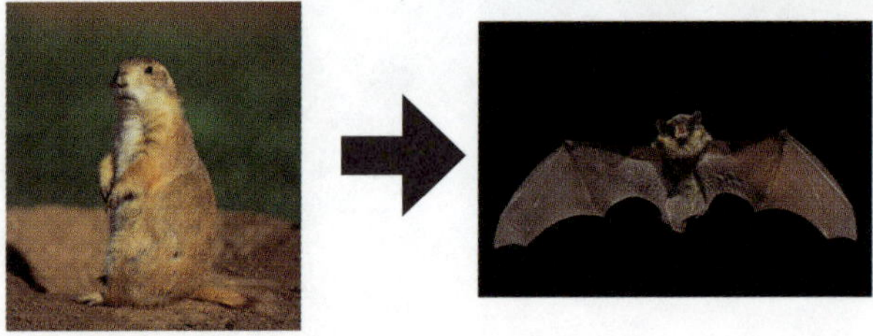

Reason: Both the prairie dog and rabbit are small, furry mammals with four legs. They make homes in the ground on the prairie and eat grass. The bat is a flying mammal that lives in trees. The beaver is a medium-size mammal that makes its home in water.

buffalo

deer

ostrich

sheep

alligator

snake

spider

lizard

tuna

catfish

whale

shark

HOW ARE THESE ANIMALS ALIKE?

Use words from the WORD BOX to explain how these animals are alike.

WORD BOX
birds, colonies, hooves, insects, large,
legs, mammals, milk, plains, small

elephants

giraffe

Both are __________ ______________ that live on the ______________ in Africa.

They both have ____________ on their feet.

owl

eagle

Both are large _________________ that eat ________________ animals.

cow

goat

Both are ______________ with four ______ and ____________ on their feet. Both make ___________ that is made into cheese.

ant

bee

Both are _________________ that live in _________________.

HOW ARE THESE ANIMALS DIFFERENT?

Use words from the WORD BOX to explain how these animals are different.

WORD BOX
eagle, fly, goat, insect, mammal, mosquito, milk, ostrich, sheep, six, spider, tuna, whale

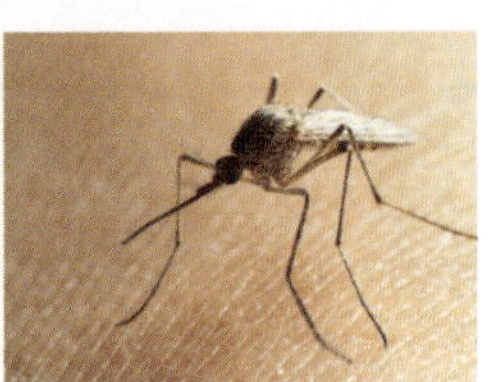
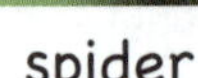
spider mosquito

The ____________ has eight legs, but the ________________ is an ___________ that has _______ legs.

sheep goat

People get wool from the ____________ but they get _____________ from the _____________.

tuna whale

The ____________ is a large fish.

The __________ is a large ____________ that lives in the ocean.

eagle ostrich

The ____________ can ________ high for long distances, but the ____________ cannot.

DESCRIBING SIMILARITIES & DIFFERENCES

Use words from the WORD BOX to explain how these animals are alike and how they are different.

WORD BOX
bat, buffalo, elephant, insects, mammal, night, mammals, owl, plains, prairie dog, squirrel, woods

owl
bat

Both the ____________ and the ____________ are active at ________________ and eat ________________. The __________ is a bird, but the ________ is a ________________.

prairie dog
squirrel

Both the ______________________ and the ______________ are small, fast ______________. The ________________ lives in large groups on the ______________, but squirrels live in small groups in the ____________.

elephant
buffalo

Both the ________________ and the ________________ are large ______________ that live on large ___________. The ________________ has tusks for protection, but the ______________ has horns. The ____________ is found in North America, but the ________________ is found in Africa and Asia.

DESCRIBING SIMILARITIES AND DIFFERENCES

Write a few words on each line to describe how an ant and a bee are ALIKE and how they are DIFFERENT.

Both ants and bees are small insects that live in large colonies. Both sting or bite for protection. Ant colonies live below ground in tunnels that they dig. Bee colonies live above ground in a hive that they build.

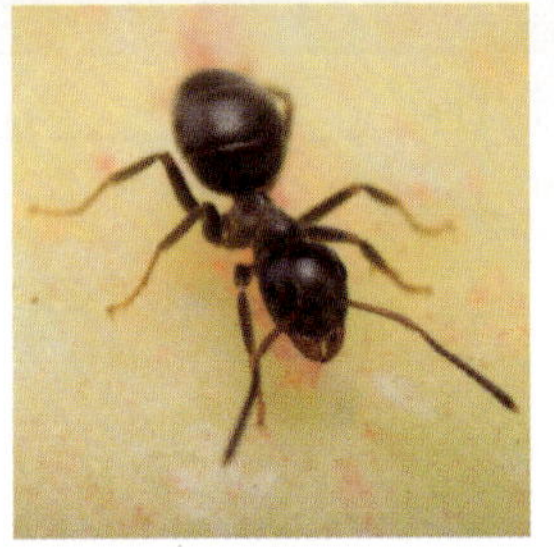
ant

bee

HOW ALIKE?

____

____

____

____

HOW DIFFERENT?

ANT		BEE
______________	HOW IT MOVES ⟷	______________
______________		______________
______________	WHERE ITS HOME IS BUILT ⟷	______________
______________		______________

A DIFFERENT KIND OF ANIMAL

Three of these animals are the same kind. Circle the animal that is different. Explain your answer to your partner or teacher.

EXAMPLE

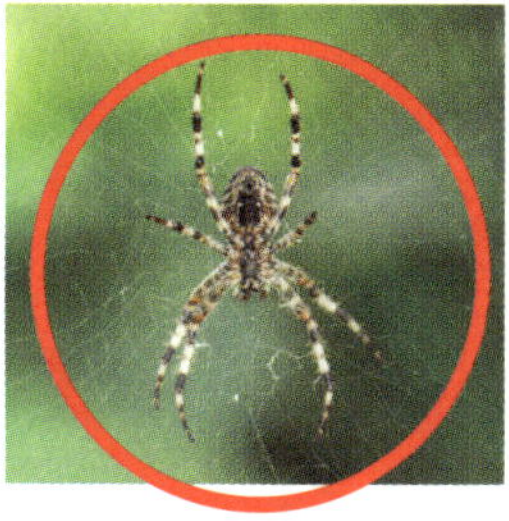

REASON: The butterfly, the grasshopper, and the bee are insects. The spider is not.

bat

eagle

owl

ostrich

buffalo

giraffe

alligator

deer

squirrel

duck

prairie dog

beaver

CLASSIFYING ANIMALS

Use the words in the WORD BOX to describe the class of animals and examples of animals in that class.

WORD BOX
lizard, camel, snake, goat, mammals, reptiles, cow, turtle

CLASS

____

EXAMPLES

____

____

____

CLASS

____

EXAMPLES

____

____

____

CLASSIFYING ANIMALS - PROTECTION

Some animals have stingers, horns, or tusks to protect themselves. Some animals can hide because their colors blend into their environment. Some animals can move very fast to stay safe.

List each animal by how it protects itself.

WORD BOX
ant, bee, buffalo, eagle, elephant, grasshopper, ostrich, owl

STINGER	HORNS OR TUSKS
____________	____________
____________	____________

COLOR	SPEED
____________	____________
____________	____________

ANIMAL ANALOGIES

Circle the picture that completes each analogy. Say the analogy to your teacher or partner.

A 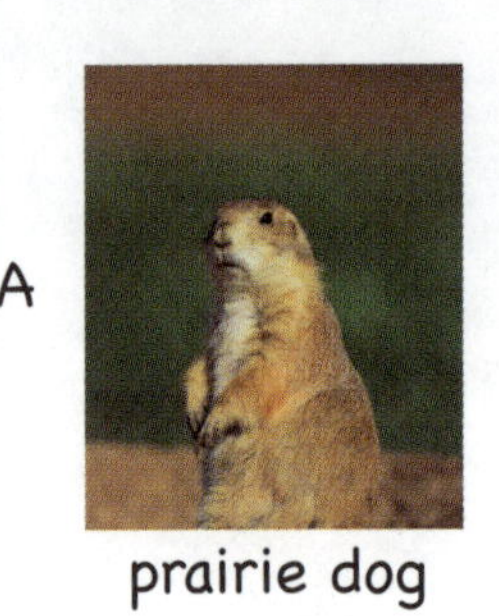 prairie dog lives on a  plain like a  beaver lives in a

plateau.

stream.

woodland.

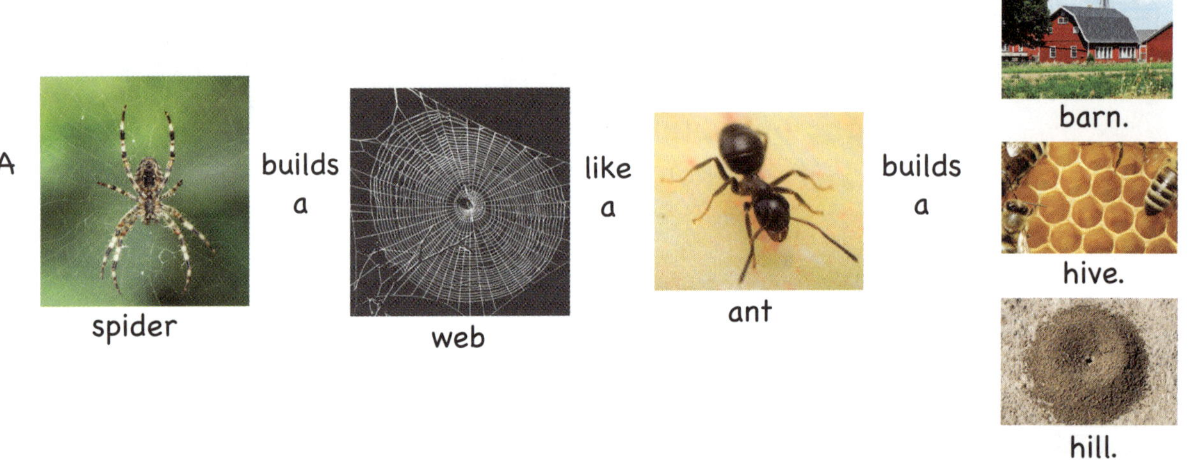

A spider builds a web like a ant builds a

barn.

hive.

hill.

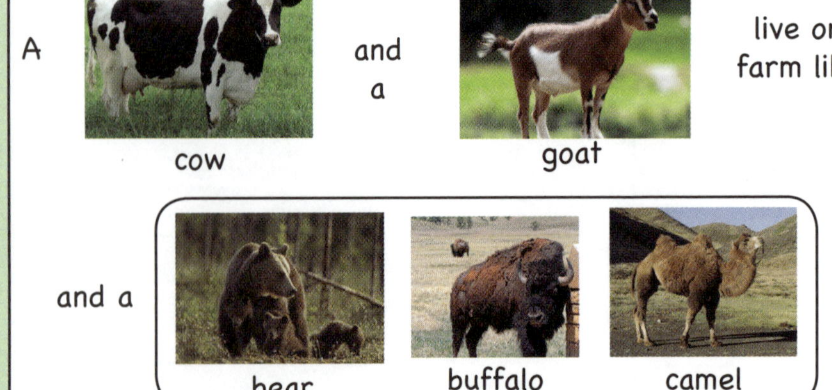

A cow and a goat live on a farm like a squirrel

and a bear buffalo camel live in the woodlands.

WRITING A DESCRIPTION OF AN ANIMAL

To describe a mosquito, we must tell these important things about it.

- **SIZE**: tiny
- **KIND**: insect
- **FOOD**: blood
- **MOSQUITO**
- **UNUSUAL FACT**: carries diseases
- **WHERE IT LIVES**: where it is warm
- **PROTECTION**: stinger

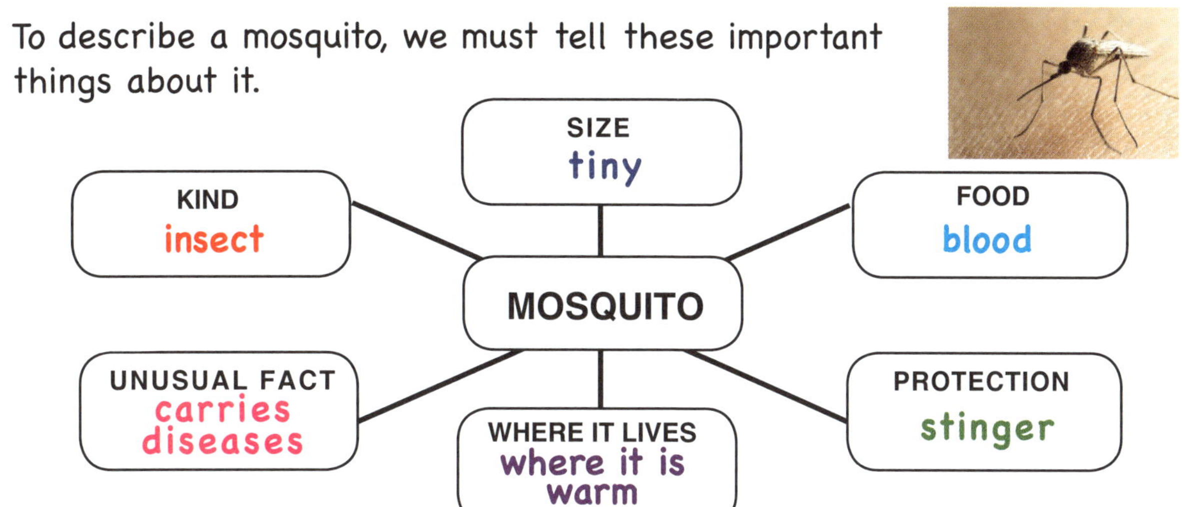

A mosquito is a tiny insect that sucks blood for food. It protects itself with a stinger. It lives anywhere that is warm and carries diseases to humans and animals.

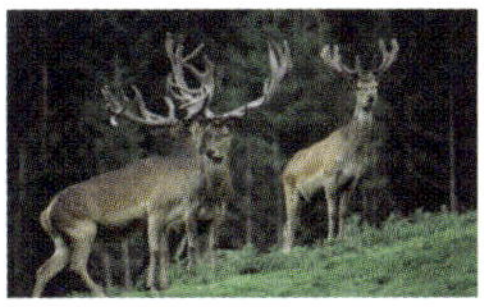

Write the details in each box that you would need to say to describe a deer.

- **SIZE**:
- **KIND**:
- **FOOD**:
- **DEER**
- **UNUSUAL FACT**:
- **WHERE IT LIVES**:
- **PROTECTION**:

Put these details together to describe a deer.

____

____

____

CHAPTER NINE

THINKING ABOUT COMMUNITIES

JOBS THAT PRODUCE GOODS

FAMILIES

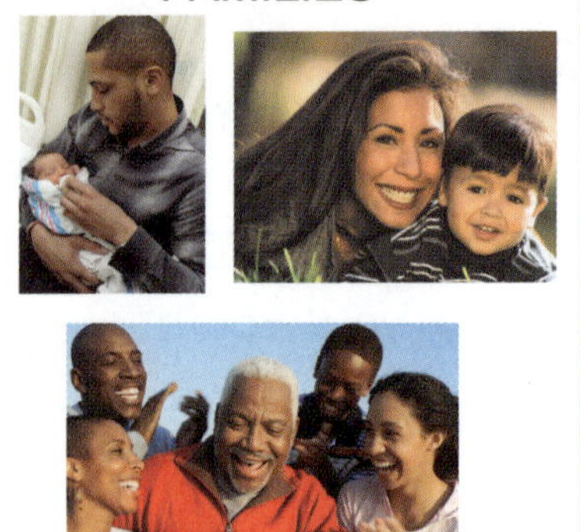

JOBS THAT PROVIDE A SERVICE

OUR COMMUNITY

GOVERNMENT

BUILDINGS

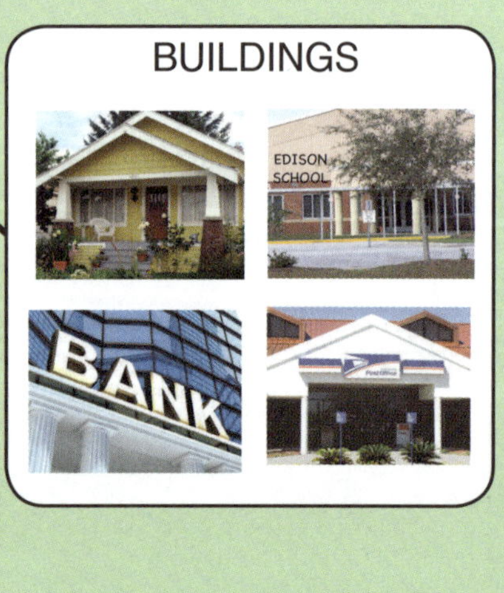

VEHICLES

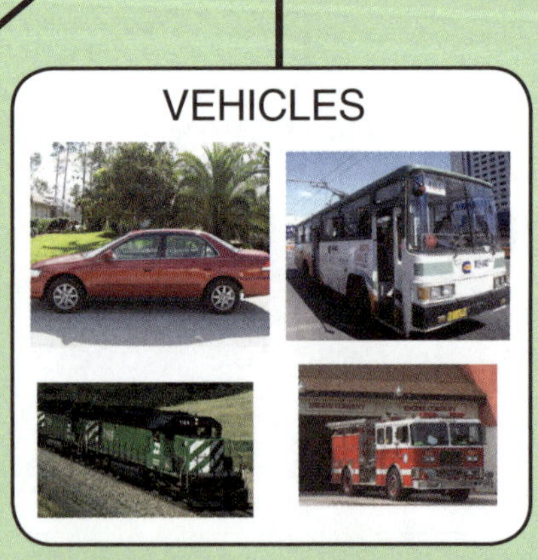

WHAT A FAMILY NEEDS

Use the words in the WORD BOX to write the family need shown in each picture.

WORD BOX
education, food, health care, safety, shelter, transportation

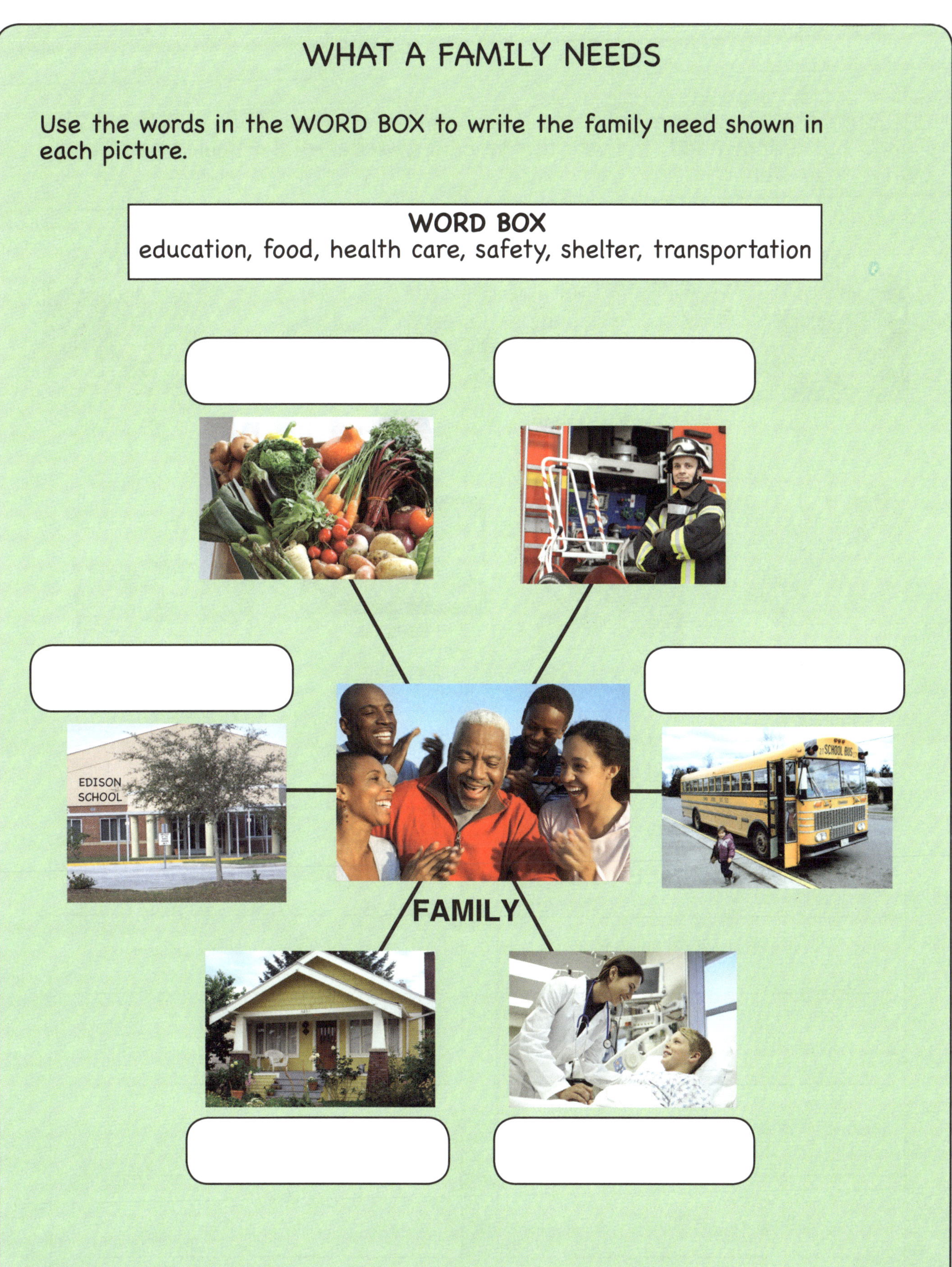

NEEDS AND WANTS

People must have some things to live. Families also buy things that they want, but do not need, to live. In the boxes, write what families need and what they want.

shelter basketball bicycle food

teddy bear shoes television water

NEEDS AND WANTS

THINGS FAMILIES NEED	THINGS FAMILIES WANT

DESCRIBING JOBS

Circle the picture of the job that your teacher describes.*

architect

artist

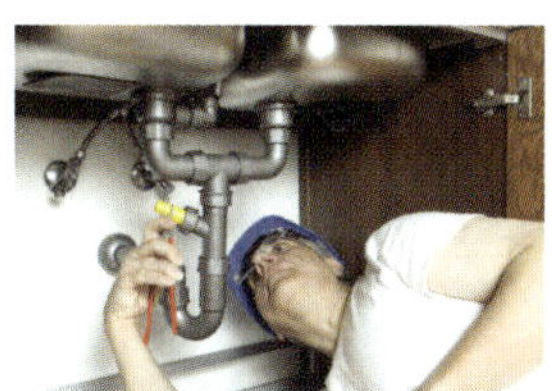
plumber

lawyer

librarian

firefighter

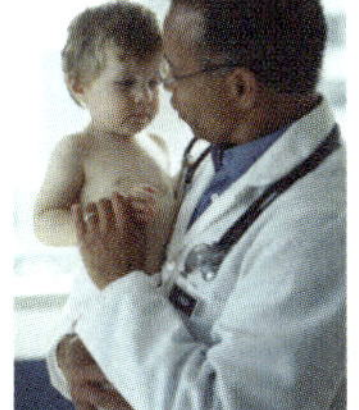
doctor

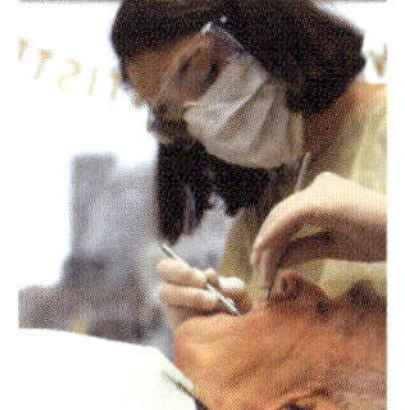
dentist

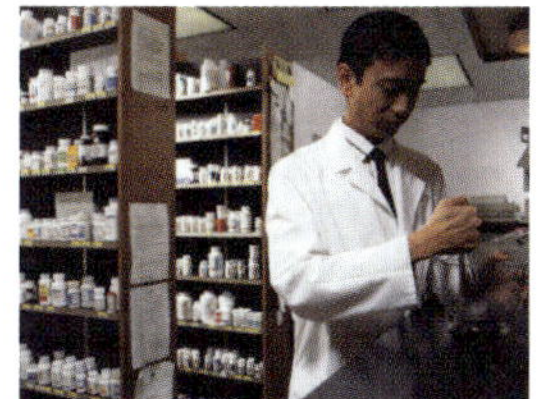
pharmacist

bank teller

barber

teacher

construction worker

carpenter

sanitation worker

* Descriptions are available on page 20 of the free answer guide.

DESCRIBING JOBS

Some workers enforce the law. Some people sell goods. Some people help others learn. Some people prepare food. Some people repair parts of a home. Draw a line from each picture to the word or phrase that describes what the worker does.

lawyer

enforces the law

grocer

sales clerk

sells

cook

baker

helps people learn

police officer

teacher

prepares food

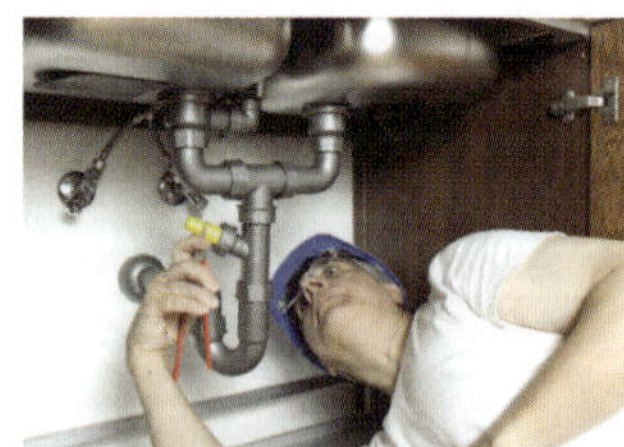
plumber

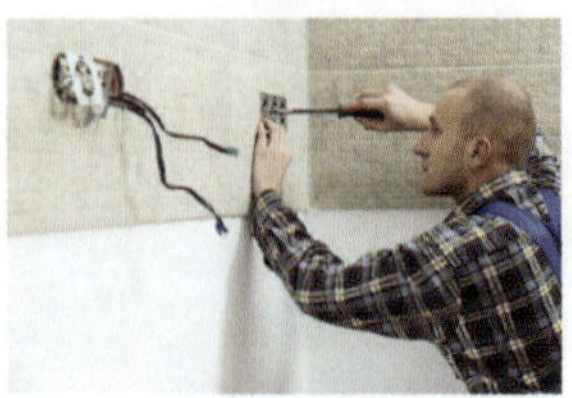
electrician

repairs

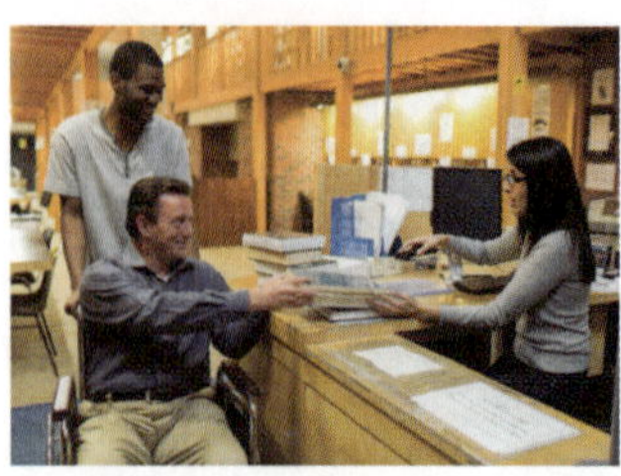
librarian

MATCHING WORKERS TO THEIR VEHICLES

Families need vehicles to go to their jobs, to buy what they need, and to go to school. Some workers need vehicles to carry out their jobs. Businesses need vehicles to deliver what they sell. Draw a line from each worker to the vehicle he or she uses.

construction worker

fire truck

farmer

trash truck

firefighter

bus

sanitation worker

dump truck

bus driver

tractor

DESCRIBING BUILDINGS

A community is made up of buildings where people work and go to get what they need. Draw a line from each description to the picture of that building and to the picture of the person who works there.

airport

bank

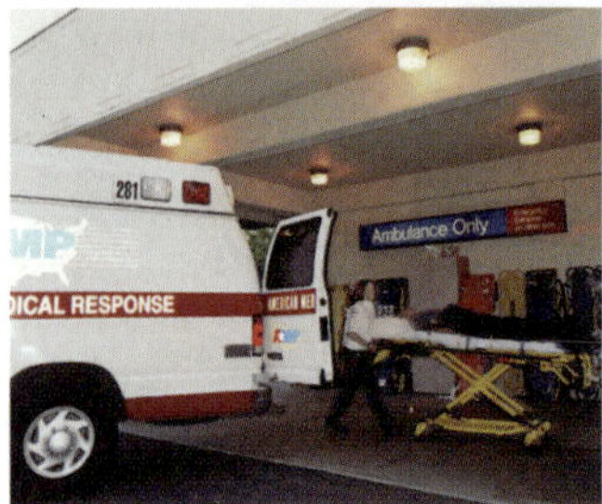

hospital

library

post office

DESCRIPTION

A government building where people borrow books and movies.

A business where people deposit or borrow money.

A government building where people buy stamps and mail letters and packages.

A building where doctors and nurses treat sick or injured people.

A building and a large area where airplanes take off and land.

mail carrier

librarian

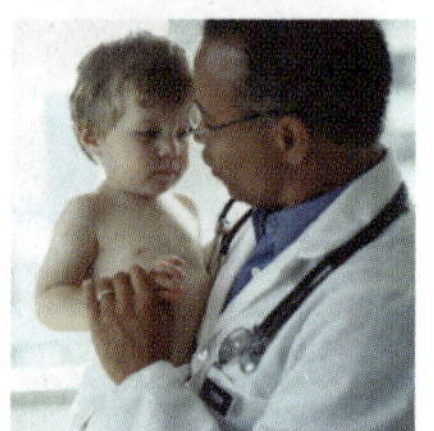
doctor

pilot

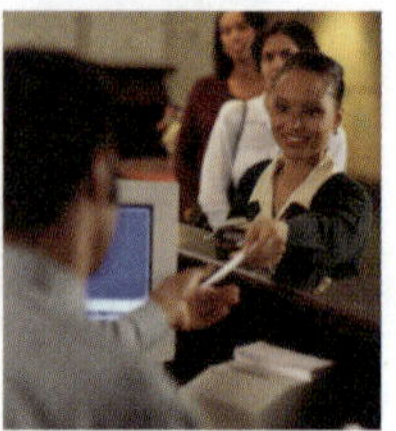
bank teller

KINDS OF JOBS - PRODUCERS OR SERVICE PROVIDERS

Some workers make or grow things that families need. The things that they produce are called "goods." Other workers do a job that people need. They provide a service. Write whether these workers are producers or service providers.

artist

baker

bank teller

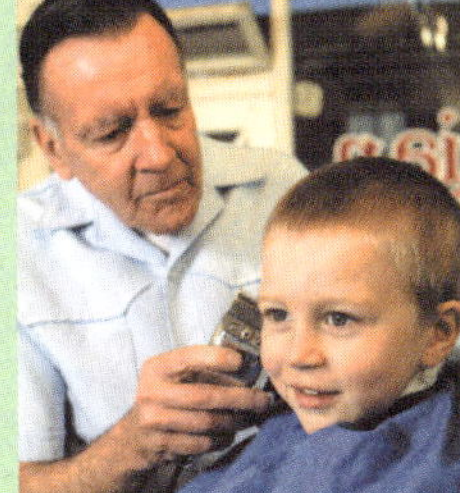
barber

farmer

librarian

PRODUCERS OR SERVICE PROVIDERS

PRODUCERS	SERVICE PROVIDERS

WORKERS WHO PROVIDE SERVICES

Some workers provide services that the community needs. Some workers help people stay healthy or treat them when they are sick. Some workers are paid by the government to provide a service that people need. Some workers sell a product. Write whether each worker gives health care, provides a service for the government, or sells a product.

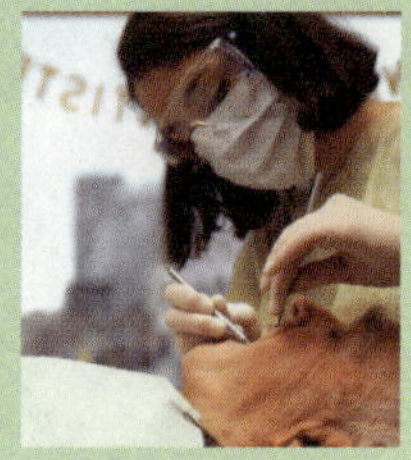
dentist

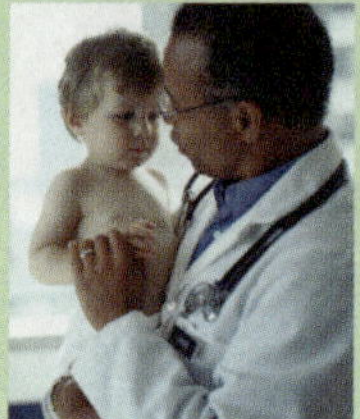
doctor

firefighter

grocer

mail carrier

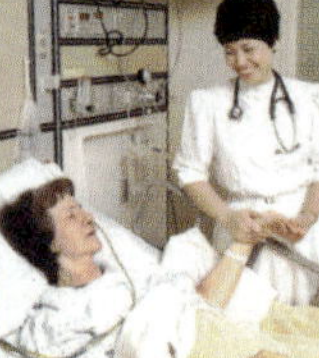
nurse

police officer

pharmacist

sales clerk

SERVICE WORKERS

GIVE HEALTH CARE

____

____

____

SELL A PRODUCT

____

____

____

PROVIDE GOVERNMENT SERVICES

____

____

____

SIMILAR JOBS

Circle the picture of the job most like the one on the left. Then explain why they are similar.

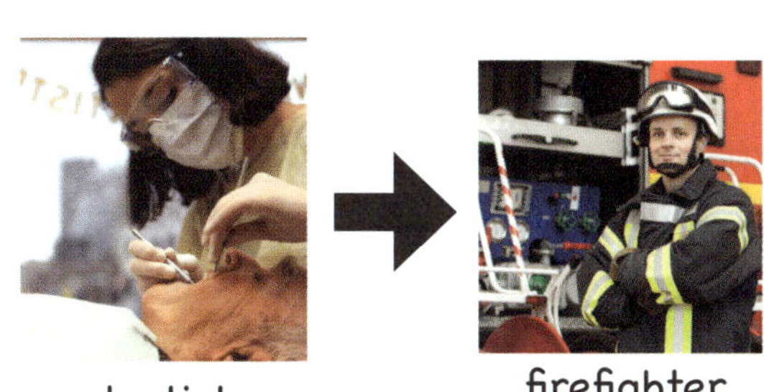
dentist → firefighter

lawyer

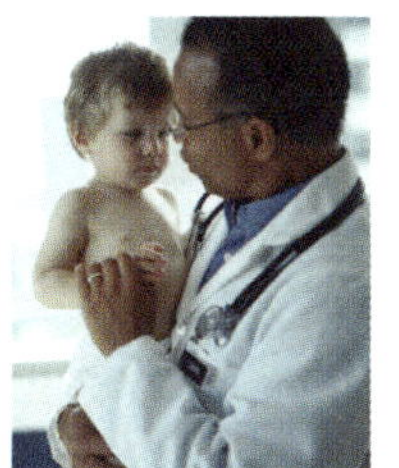
doctor

police officer

librarian

pharmacist

mail carrier

construction worker

teacher

cook

farmer

grocer

baker

server

electrician

sanitation worker

pilot

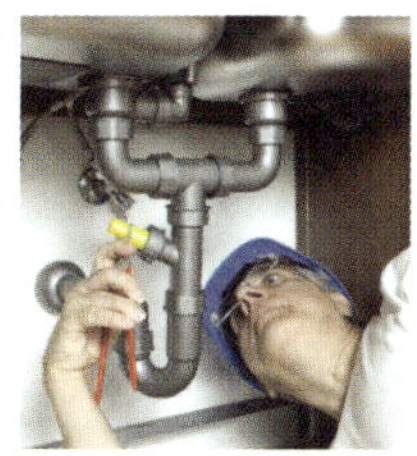
plumber

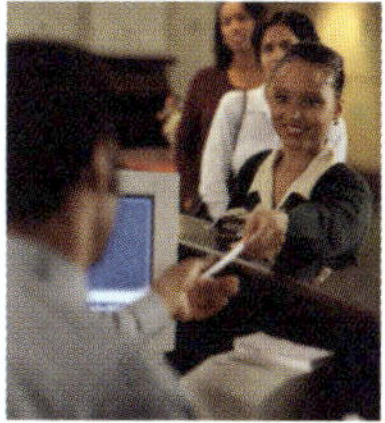
bank teller

DESCRIBING SIMILARITIES AND DIFFERENCES – JOBS

Write a few words on each line to describe how an architect and an artist are ALIKE and how they are DIFFERENT.

Both an architect and an artist produce something new. They both make drawings from their ideas. People pay them for their drawings. An architect draws with a computer or with ink, but the artist draws with paint. An architect's drawings are directions for construction workers or carpenters to build a building.

architect

An architect must study a long time to learn what materials are strong enough to build a building. Artists may study art or teach themselves.

artist

HOW ALIKE?

____

____

____

HOW DIFFERENT?

ARCHITECT		ARTIST
________________ ________________	HOW THEY DRAW ⟷	________________ ________________
________________ ________________	HOW DRAWINGS ARE USED ⟷	________________ ________________
________________ ________________	EDUCATION ⟷	________________ ________________

A DIFFERENT KIND OF JOB

Three of these jobs are the same kind. Circle the job that is different. Explain your answer to your partner or teacher.

baker

server

cook

carpenter

sales clerk

teacher

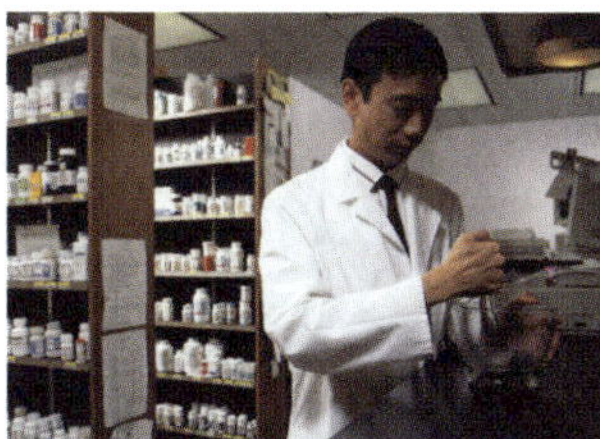
pharmacist

grocer

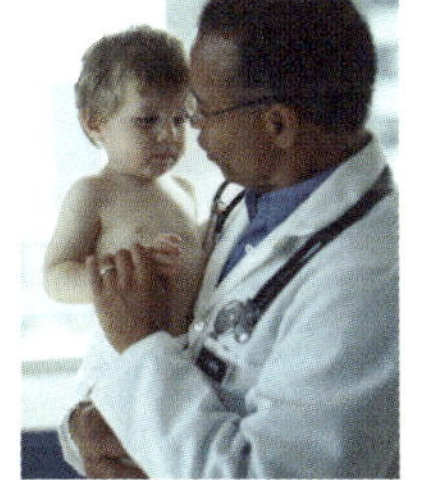
doctor

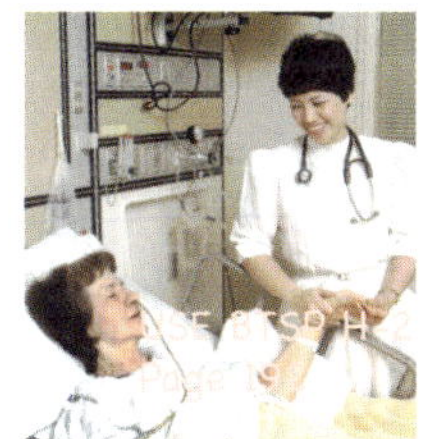
nurse

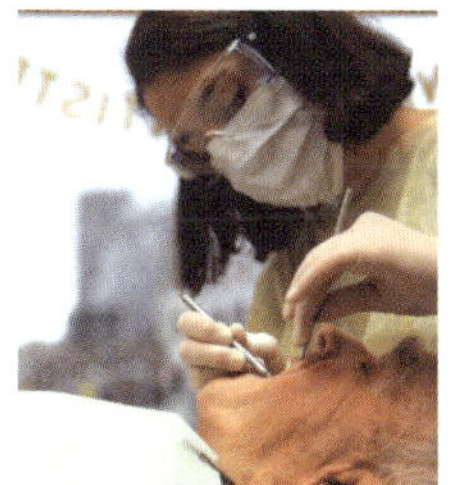
dentist

barber

architect

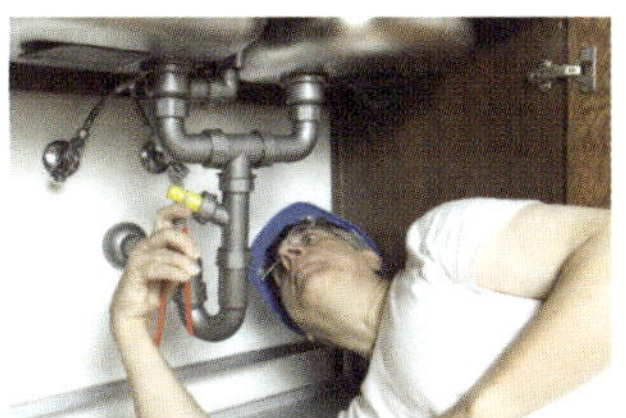
plumber

firefighter

electrician

A SEQUENCE OF JOBS

List these workers in the order that they get food to families.

cook

farmer

grocer

server

FIRST

____

____

____

____

LAST

HOW WORKERS MAKE THEIR MONEY

The grocer sells food to the plumber. The plumber fixes the sales clerk's sink. The sales clerk sells paint to the barber. The barber cuts the grocer's son's hair. Write how each worker earns money.

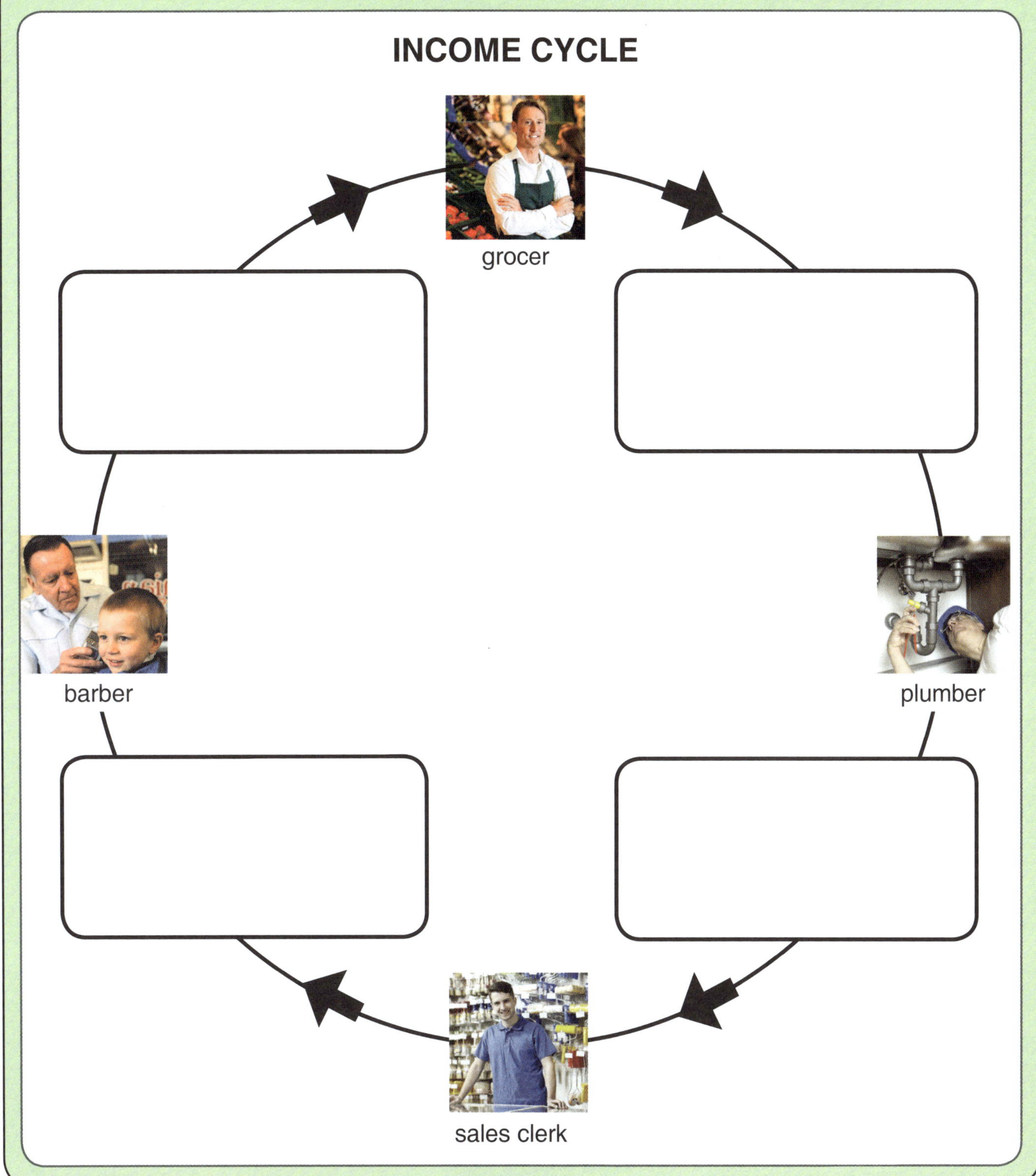

HOW WORKERS SPEND THEIR MONEY

A grocer pays the barber for his son's haircut. The barber buys paint from the sales clerk. The sales clerk pays the plumber for fixing his sink. The plumber buys food from the grocer. Write how each worker spends his money.

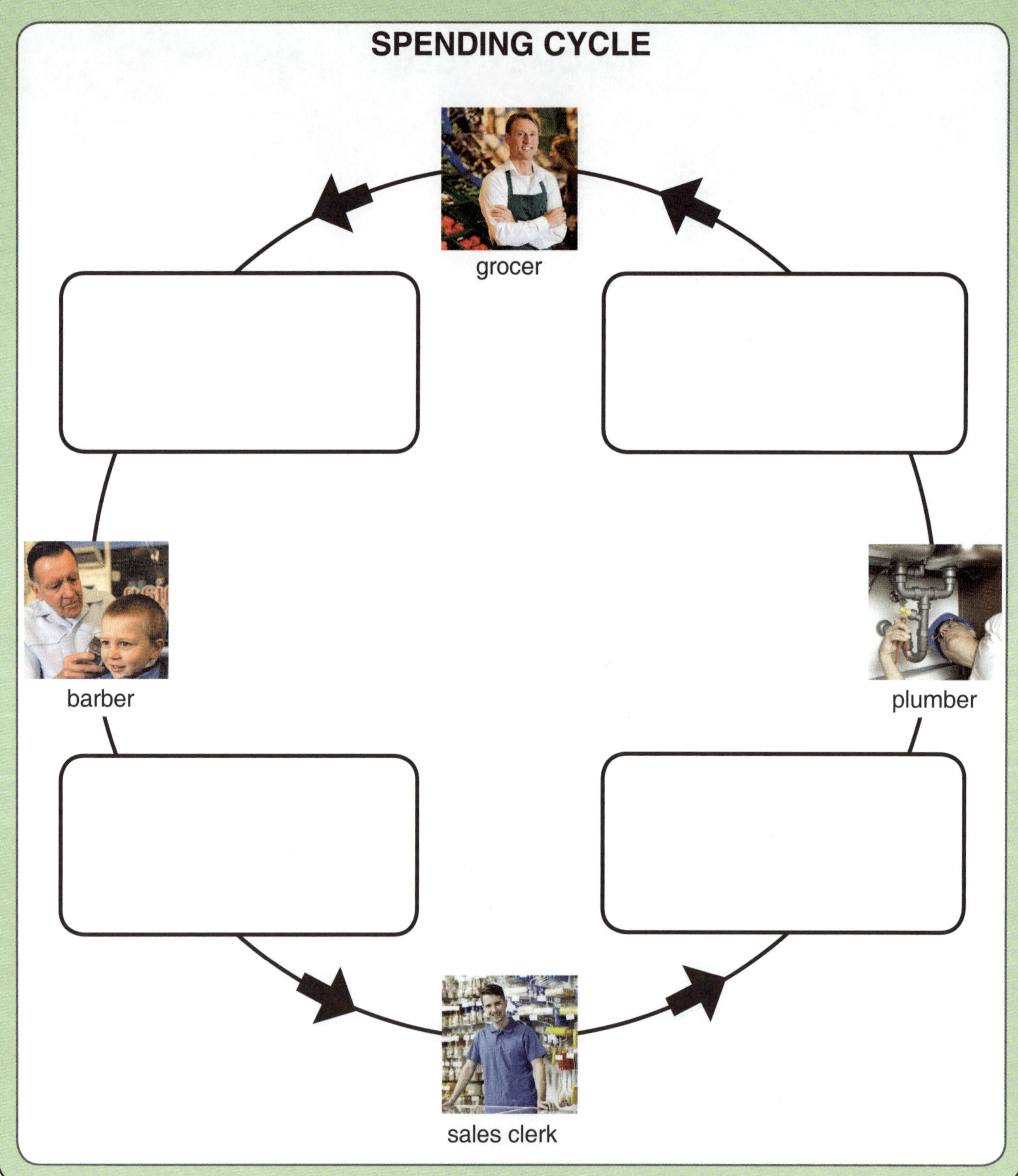

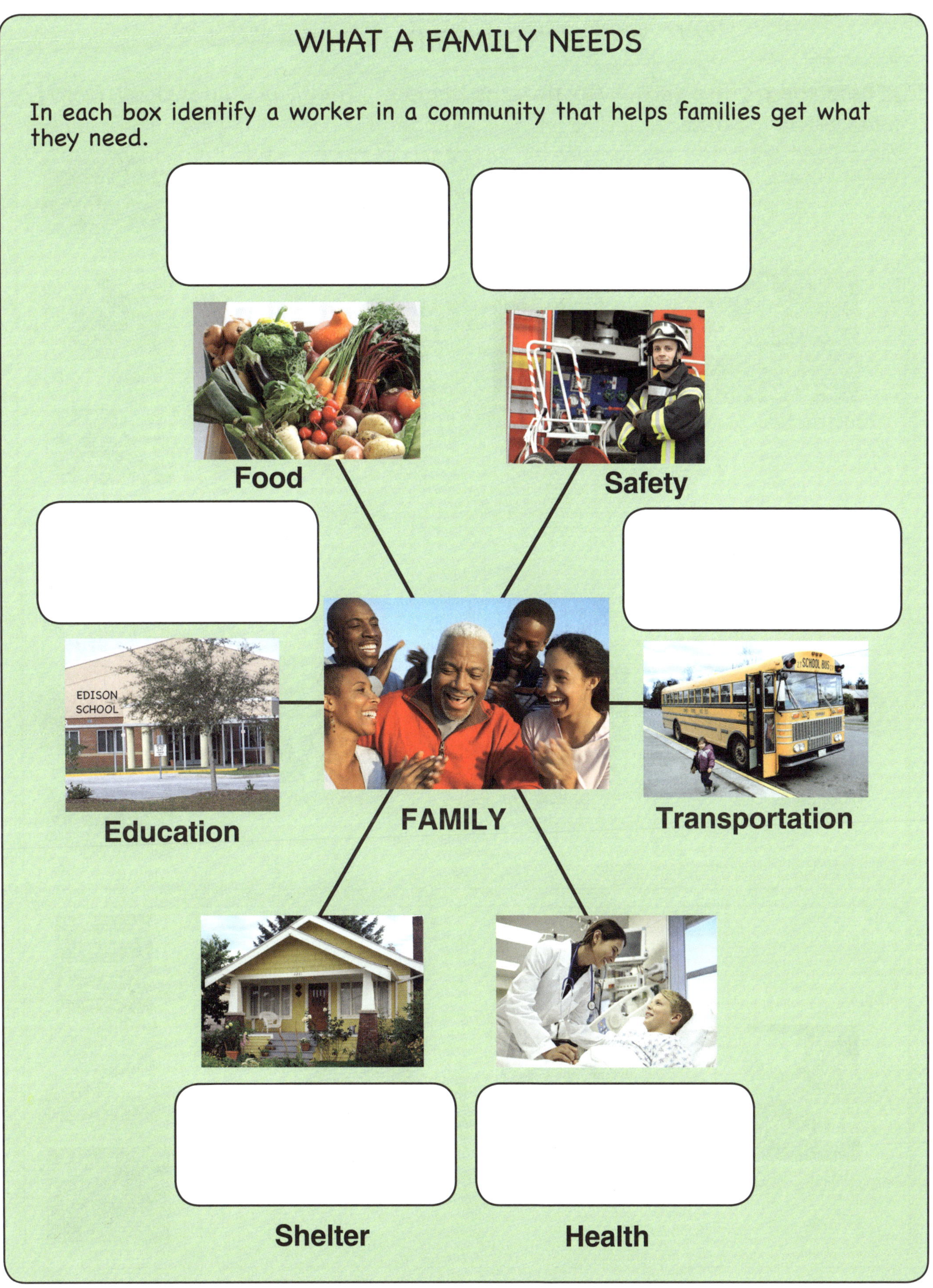
WHAT A FAMILY NEEDS
In each box identify a worker in a community that helps families get what they need.
Food
Safety
EDISON SCHOOL
Education
FAMILY
SCHOOL BUS
Transportation
Shelter
Health

ANALOGIES ABOUT JOBS

Circle the picture that completes the analogy. Then say the analogy to your teacher or partner.

A  construction worker uses a  dump truck like a  farmer uses a

car.

motorcycle.

tractor.

A  police officer drives a 

police car like a  firefighter drives a

dump truck.

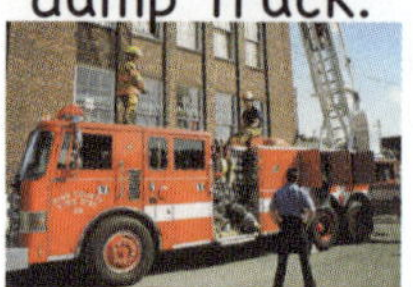
fire truck.

pickup truck.

A  bus driver drives a  bus like a  pilot drives a/an

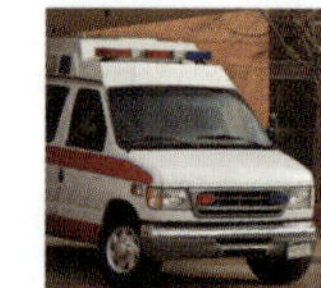
ambulance.

airplane.

train.

ANALOGIES ABOUT JOBS

Circle the picture that completes the analogy. Then say the analogy to your teacher or partner.

A 
food server

works in a

restaurant

like a

grocer

works in a

farm.

gas station.

supermarket.

A 
librarian

works in a

library

like a

teller

works in a

bank.

post office.

school.

A 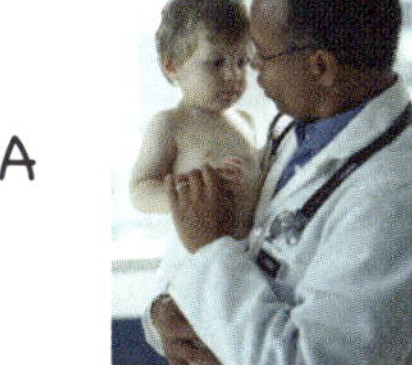
doctor

works in a

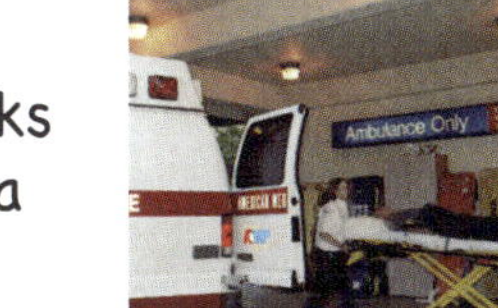

hospital

like a

firefighter

works in a/an

airport.

fire station.

police station.

WRITING A DESCRIPTION OF A JOB

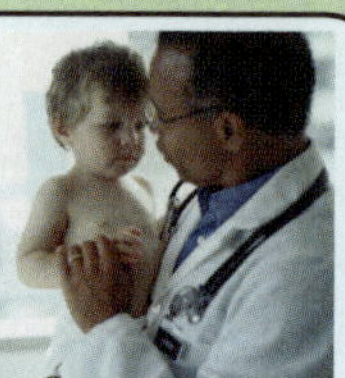

To describe a doctor, we must tell these important things about that job.

DOCTOR

KIND OF JOB
health care worker

WHAT THE WORKER DOES
decides what sick or injured people need to heal

EQUIPMENT
listens to a person's heart or checks fever with special tools

LOCATION
works in a hospital or office

A doctor is a health care worker who decides what sick or injured people need to heal. He works in a hospital or office. He uses special equipment to listen to a person's heart or check whether they have a fever.

Write the details in each box that you would need to say to describe a firefighter.

FIREFIGHTER

KIND OF JOB

WHAT THE WORKER DOES

EQUIPMENT

LOCATION

Put these details together to describe a firefighter.

____

____

____

DESCRIBING LOCATIONS

Use the map to answer the questions.

CENTERVILLE

farm

NORTH PARK

airport

D STREET

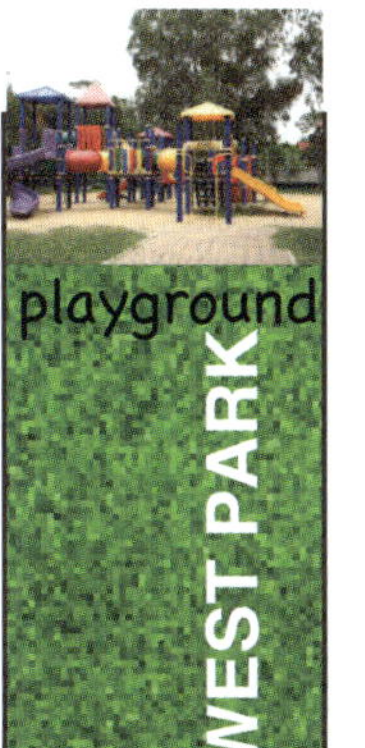
playground

WEST PARK

FIRST AVENUE

home

library

gas station

SECOND AVENUE

C STREET

C STREET

school

City Hall

THIRD AVENUE

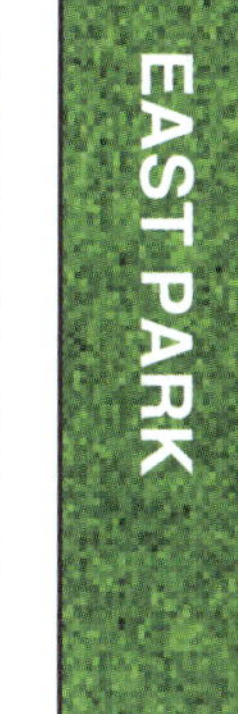
EAST PARK

B STREET

B STREET

post office

restaurant

supermarket

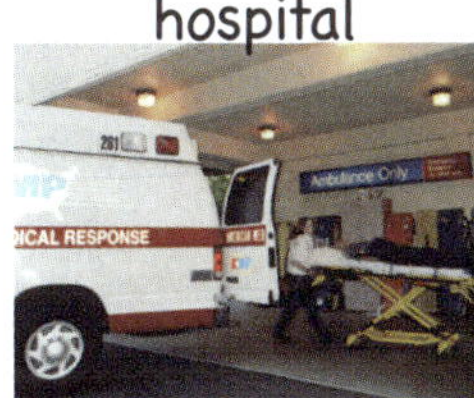
hospital

A STREET

SOUTH PARK

fire station

The home is on the corner of _____ Street and ___________ Avenue.

The bank is on the corner of ______ Street and _____________ Avenue.

The supermarket is on the corner of _____ Street and ___________ Avenue.

The library is on the corner of ______ Street and _____________ Avenue.

The school is on the corner of ______ Street and _____________ Avenue.

DESCRIBING DIRECTIONS

Use the map to answer the questions.

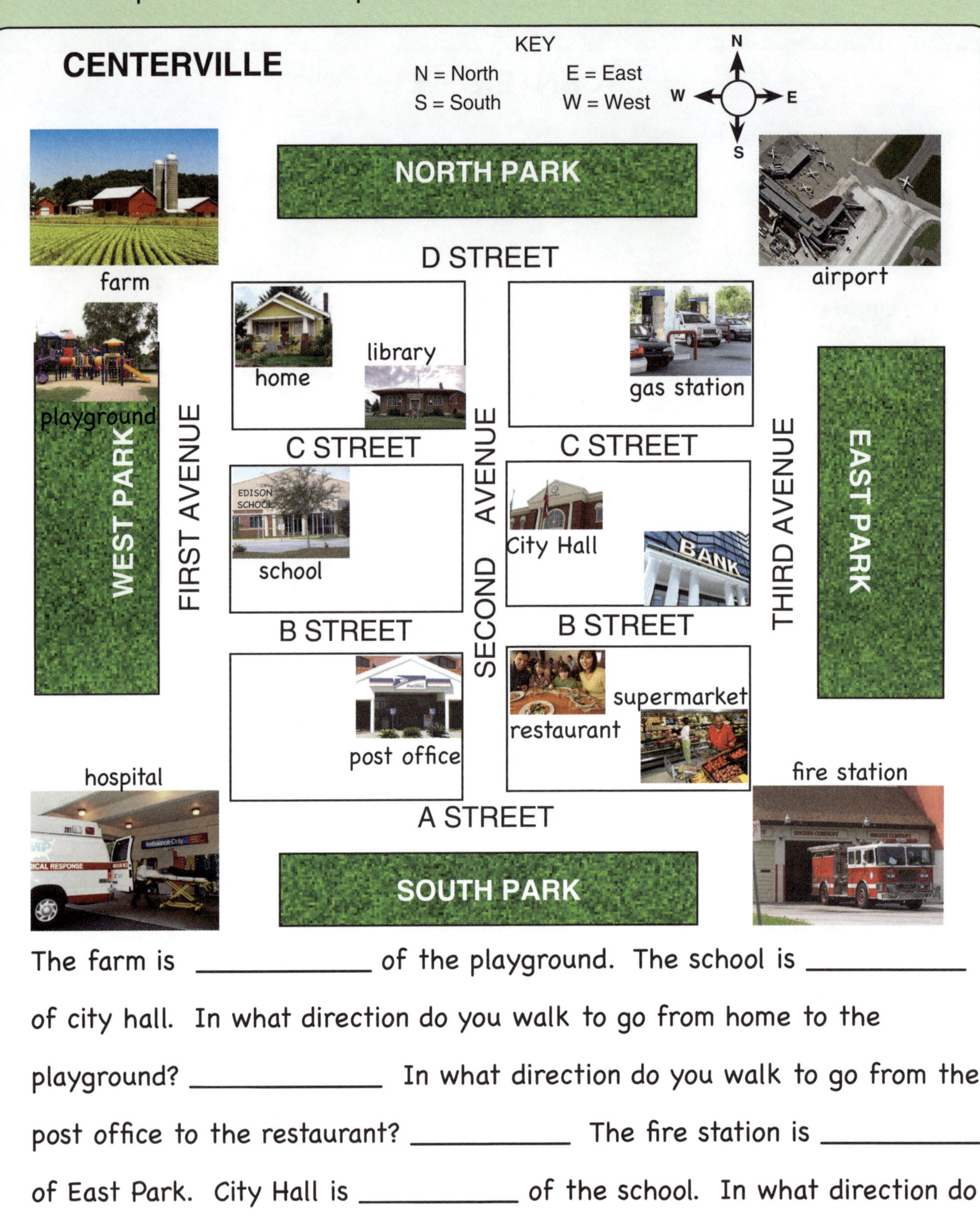

The farm is ____________ of the playground. The school is ___________ of city hall. In what direction do you walk to go from home to the playground? _____________ In what direction do you walk to go from the post office to the restaurant? ___________ The fire station is ___________ of East Park. City Hall is ___________ of the school. In what direction do you walk to get from the bank to the supermarket? ___________

DESCRIBING DIRECTIONS

Use the map to answer the questions.

CENTERVILLE

KEY
NW = Northwest
NE = Northeast
SW = Southwest
SE = Southeast

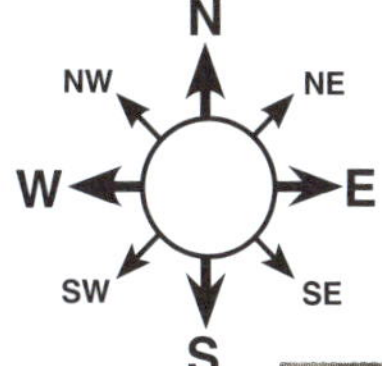

farm

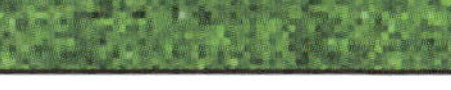
NORTH PARK

airport

D STREET

playground

WEST PARK

FIRST AVENUE

home
library

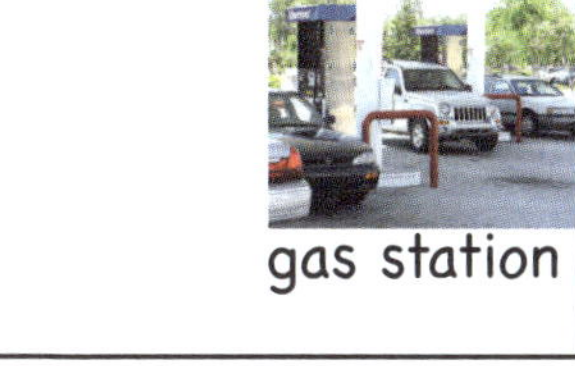
gas station

C STREET

C STREET

SECOND AVENUE

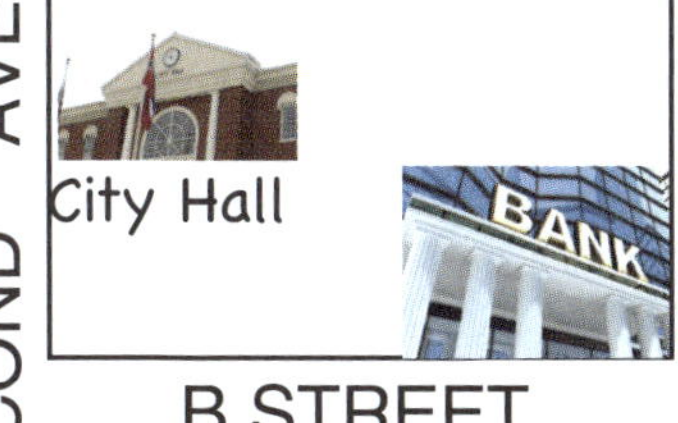
City Hall

THIRD AVENUE

EAST PARK

school

B STREET

B STREET

post office

supermarket
restaurant

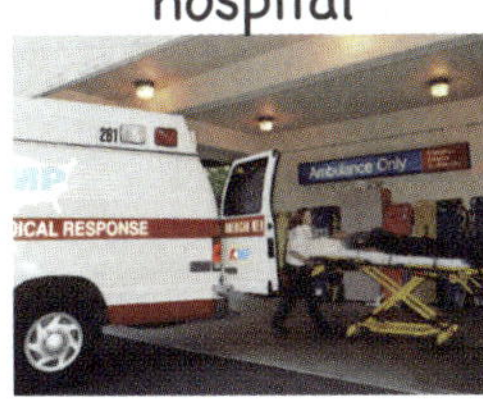
hospital

A STREET

SOUTH PARK

fire station

The airport is in the ____________________ corner of Centerville.

The hospital is in the ____________________ corner of Centerville.

What place is in the northwest corner of Centerville? _______________

What place is in the southeast corner of Centerville? _______________

CHAPTER TEN
THINKING ABOUT OUR COUNTRY

DESCRIBING OUR CONTINENT

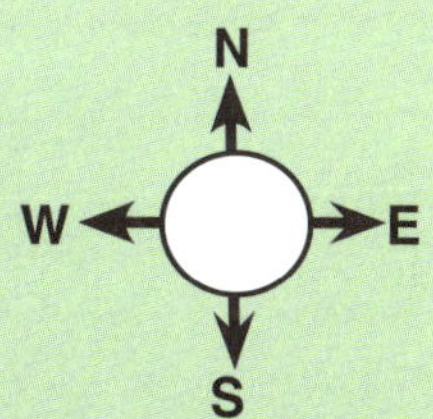

The largest land forms are continents. Continents are surrounded by oceans. The United States is on the continent of North America.

A picture of our continent.

A picture of our country.

The first photograph shows the continent of North America on Earth; the second is a photograph of the United States that shows its dry, brown deserts, its mountains and its green plains and woodlands. Use the picture of the United States to describe our country.

What body of water is south of the United States?

____

What ocean is east of the United States?

____

What ocean is west of the United States?

____

What large bodies of water are in the northern part of the United States? ______________________________

What large land forms does the picture show in the western part of the United States?

____________________ and ____________________

DESCRIBING GLOBES

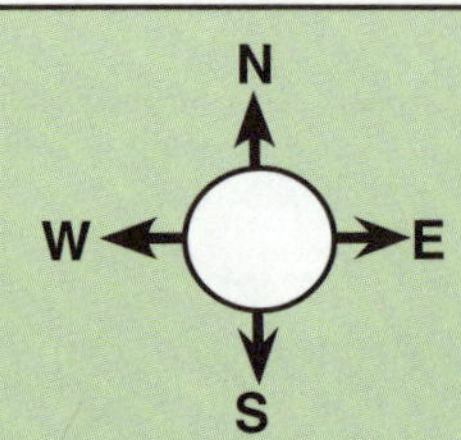

Globe: A spherical map of Earth.

Use the picture of the globe to describe our continent.

What country is north of the United States? ____________________

What country is south of the United States? ____________________

Complete the sentence using the WORD BOX.

WORD BOX
Earth, sphere, map, globe

This ________________ is a ____________________ of

____________________ on a __________________.

DESCRIBING GLOBES

The imaginary line around the middle of Earth is called the Equator. Because places close to the Equator get more heat from sunlight, they have a hot climate. →

The lines on the globe that circle the world east to west are called lines of latitude. These circles look smaller toward the North Pole and the South Pole. These lines show where a place is located north or south of the Equator.

←

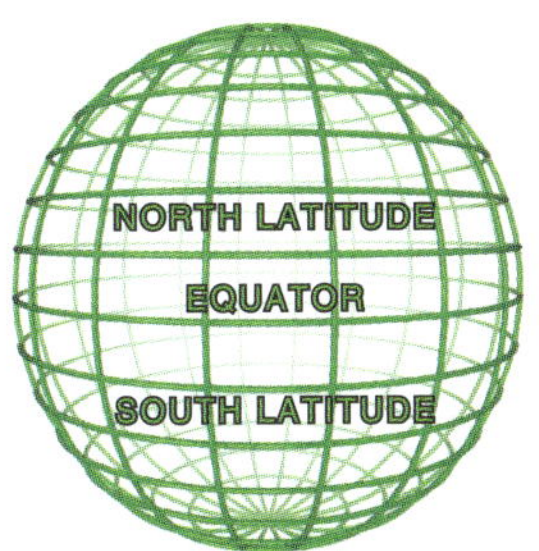

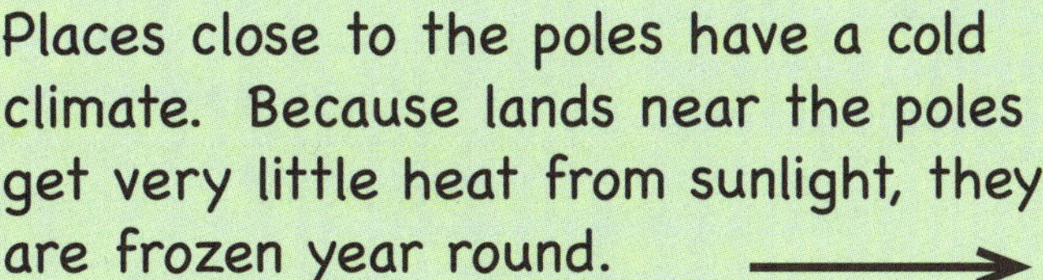

Places close to the poles have a cold climate. Because lands near the poles get very little heat from sunlight, they are frozen year round. →

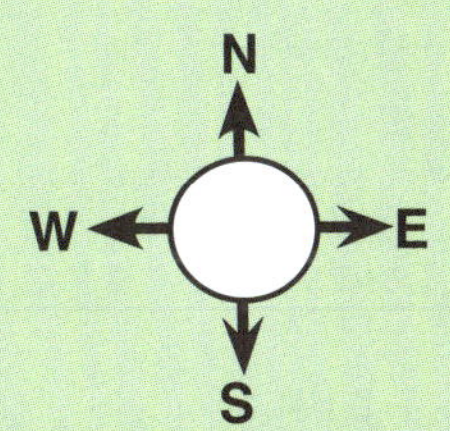

The imaginary circles that come together at the North Pole and at the South Pole are called lines of longitude. These lines show where a place is located east or west on Earth. →

Write north, south, east, or west in the blanks below.

Lines of latitude circle the globe from ____________ to ____________.

They tell where a place is located, ____________ or ____________ of the Equator. Lines of longitude come together at the ____________ and ____________ Poles. They tell where a place is located ____________ or ____________ on Earth.

DESCRIBING OUR COUNTRY

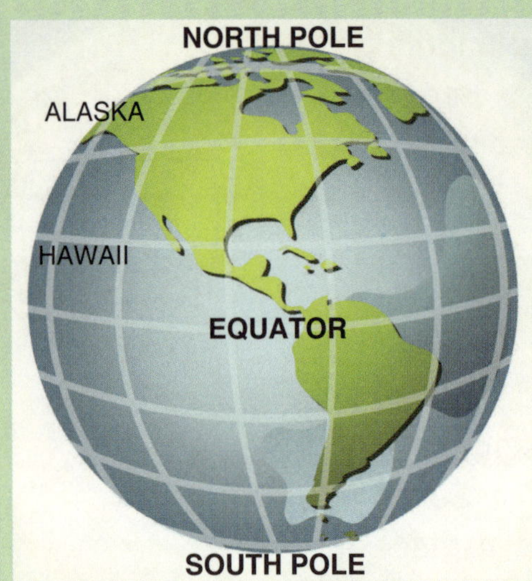

Our country is between the North Pole and the Equator. Land that is close to the North Pole has a cold climate. Alaska has very long, cold winters and short, cool summers.

Land that is close to the Equator has a warm climate. Hawaii is warm all the time.

The northern states have long, cold winters. The southern states have long, hot summers.

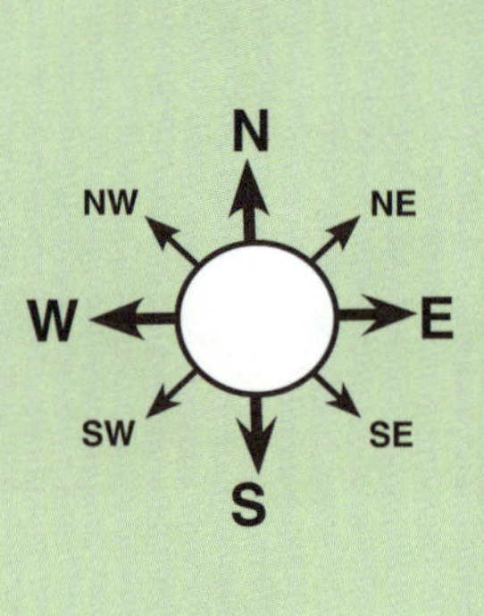

KEY
NW = Northwest
NE = Northeast
SW = Southwest
SE = Southeast

Boston is in the ____________________ part of the USA.

Which city is in the southeast corner of the United States of America? ____________________

Seattle is in the ____________________ part of the USA.

Which city is in the southwest corner of the United States of America? ____________________

DESCRIBING OUR COUNTRY

In each box name a plant or animal that can grow in this area. Pick one that people can use for food, clothing, or houses.

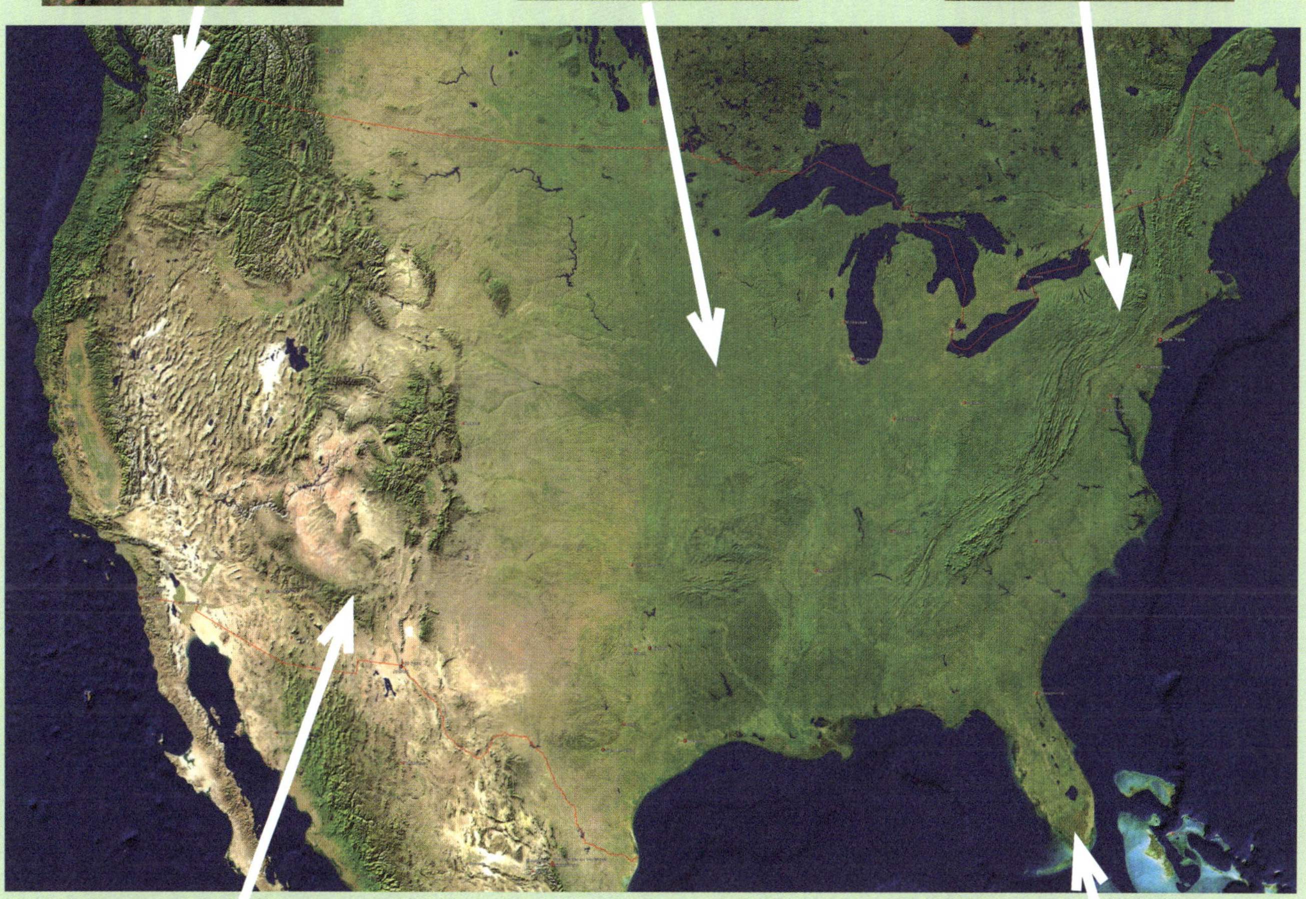

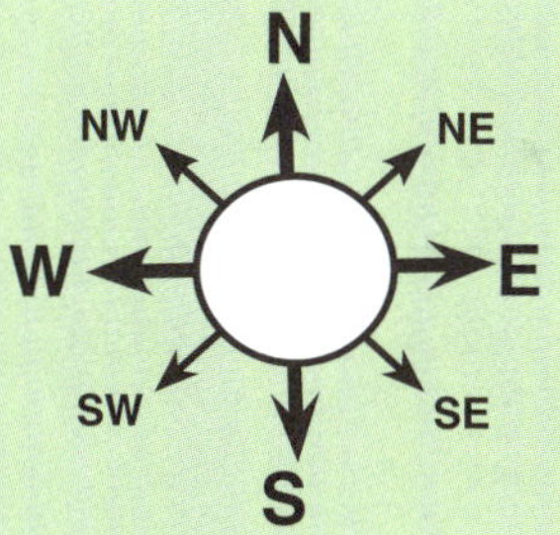

N
NW NE
W E
SW SE
S

DESCRIBING NATIVE AMERICANS

Native Americans used the plants and animals where they lived for food, clothing, and houses. Plants and animals that live in the north where the winters are long and cold are different from those that live in the south where the summers are long and hot. The plants and animals that live in the desert or on the plains are different from the ones that live along rivers, in the woodlands, or in the wetlands.

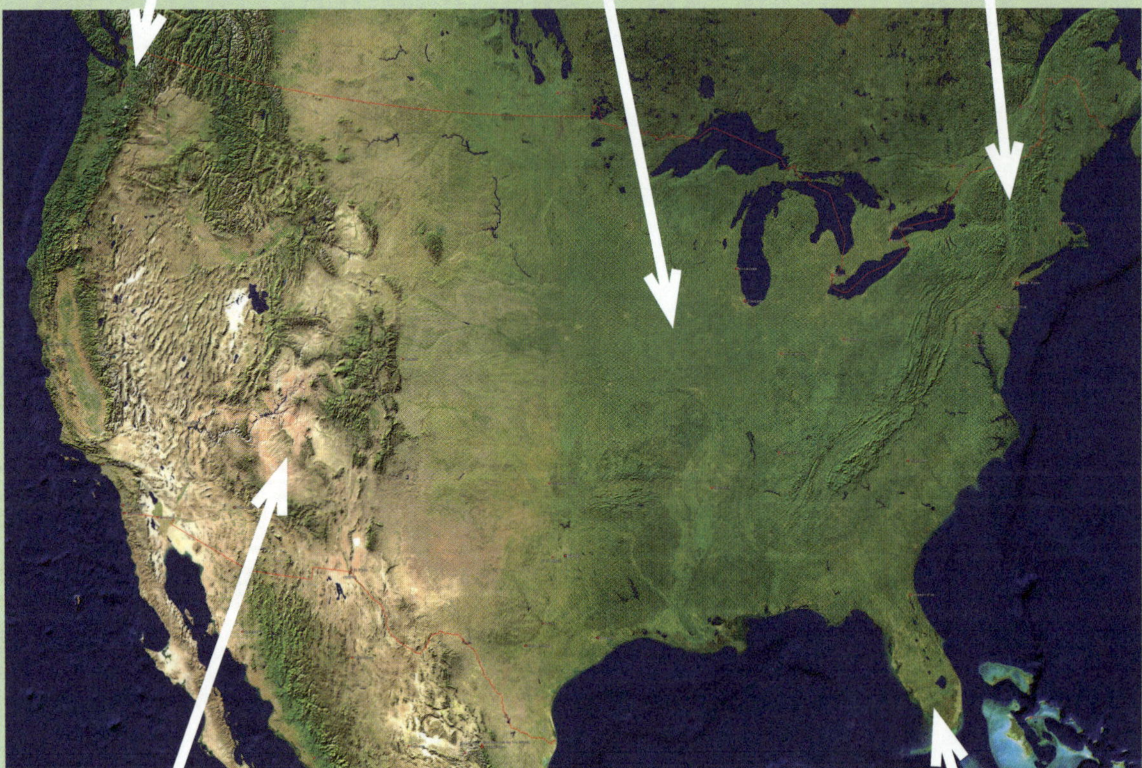

Tell your teacher or partner what you know about the weather and the land where each of these Native Americans live.

NEEDS OF THE NORTHWEST TRIBES

totem

Native Americans in the Northwest used wood from the thick forests to build their houses. They hunted bear and deer for food and skins to make clothes. They fished in the Pacific Ocean and in large rivers. Some tribes hunted whales. They carved trees to make large sculptures. Some tribes made cloth from the hair of wild goats.

catching whales

dancing

salmon

longhouse

What were the needs of the Northwest tribes?

NEEDS OF NORTHWEST TRIBES

CLOTHING

____

____

FOOD

____

____

SHELTER

____

____

NEEDS OF THE SOUTHWEST TRIBES

Native Americans in the Southwest made bricks by drying a mixture of dirt, water, and straw. Some groups grew corn. They raised sheep for food and wool. They used wool to make blankets, rugs, and clothing.

hogan

ovens and brick house

corn

rug

herder

What were the needs of the Southwest tribes?

NEEDS OF SOUTHWEST TRIBES

CLOTHING

____

____

FOOD

____

____

SHELTER

____

____

NEEDS OF THE PLAINS TRIBES

Native Americans who lived on the Plains hunted buffalo and deer for food and clothing. They lived in tepees made of deer skins. Tepees can be easily taken down and moved to follow the buffalo herd. In summer, some tribes grew corn.

hunting buffalo

tepee

buffalo herd

moving a tepee

What were the needs of the Plains tribes?

NEEDS OF PLAINS TRIBES

CLOTHING

____

____

FOOD

____

____

SHELTER

____

____

NEEDS OF THE NORTHEAST TRIBES

Native Americans in the Northeast used wood and bark from the thick forests to build their houses. They grew corn and fished in the many rivers and streams. They hunted bear and deer for food. They made clothing from deer skin.

cornfield

wooden house

What were the needs of the Northeast tribes?

NEEDS OF NORTHEAST TRIBES

CLOTHING

____

____

FOOD

____

____

SHELTER

____

____

NEEDS OF THE SOUTHEAST TRIBES

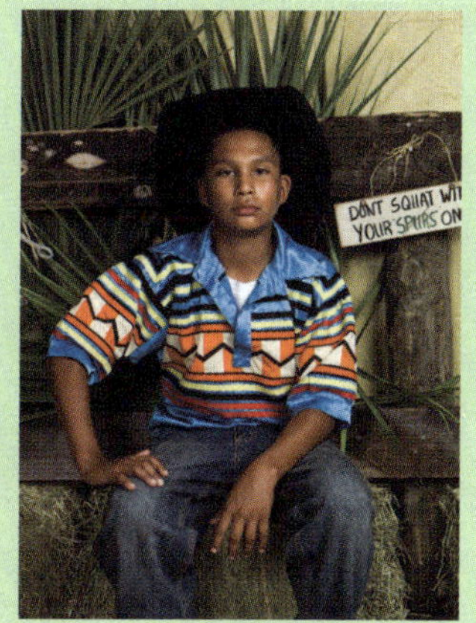

Native Americans in the Southeast built open shelters called "chickees." They fished and hunted alligators for food. They traded alligator hides for bright cotton cloth. They grew corn and ate "swamp cabbage" which is the inside stem of a palm tree.

chickee

hunting an alligator

swamp cabbage

What were the needs of the Southeast tribes?

NEEDS OF SOUTHEAST TRIBES

CLOTHING

____

____

FOOD

____

____

SHELTER

____

____

NEEDS OF THE COLONISTS

colonial house

When colonists came to America, they built houses close together with fences and streets like their villages at home. They planted corn like Native Americans did. Their houses were made of wood from the surrounding forests. They had some farm animals. They hunted deer for food and fished in the ocean and rivers. Clothing was made of wool or linen and hand sewn.

colonial village

tending crops

farm animal

What were the needs of the colonists?

NEEDS OF THE COLONISTS

CLOTHING

____

____

FOOD

____

____

SHELTER

____

____

WHAT AMERICANS NEED – THEN AND NOW

Since colonial times Americans have changed the ways that they get what they need. Use the WORD BOX to write the need shown in the pairs of pictures.

COLONIAL TIMES	WORD BOX clothing, cooking, food, light, shelter	TODAY
	**NEED** ________________	
	**NEED** ________________	
	**NEED** ________________	
	**NEED** ________________	
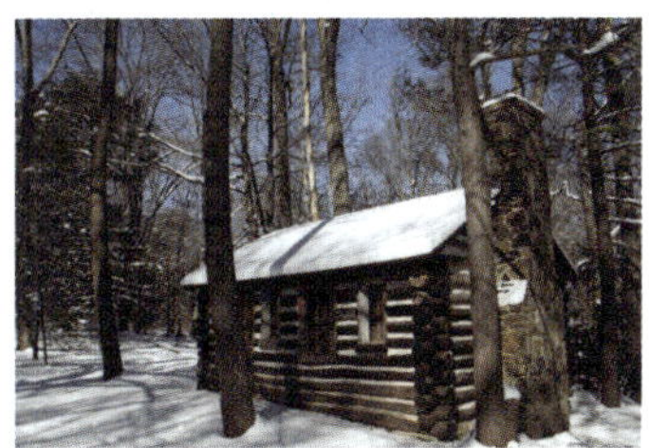	**NEED** ________________	

ANALOGIES ABOUT OUR COUNTRY

Circle the picture that completes the analogy. Say the analogy to your teacher or partner.

The  Northwest tribes hunted  deer like the  Southeast tribes hunted

alligator.

sheep.

buffalo.

The 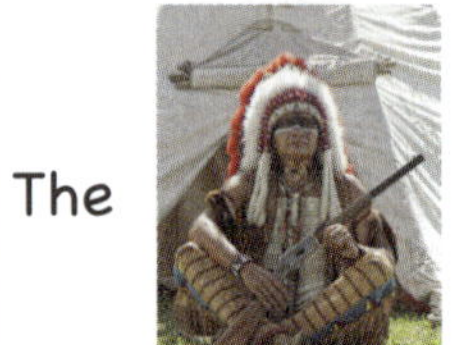 Plains tribes lived on the  plains like the  Northeast tribes lived in the

plateau.

desert.

woodlands.

The  Southwest tribes raised   sheep like the  colonists raised

farm animals.

deer.

bear.